RECOLLECTIONS
The French Revolution of 1848

RECOLLECTIONS
The French Revolution of 1848

Alexis de Tocqueville

Edited by J.P. Mayer and A.P. Kerr
Introduction by J.P. Mayer

With a New Introduction by Fernand Braudel

Translation of the de Tocqueville Manuscript
by George Lawrence
Translation of the Braudel Essay by Danielle Salti

Transaction Publishers
New Brunswick (U.S.A.) and London (U.K.)

Eleventh printing 2009
Published by Transaction Publishers.
New material this edition copyright © 1987 by Transaction Publishers, New
Brunswick, New Jersey. Original edition copyright © 1970 by J. P. Mayer.

This book is printed on acid-free paper that meets the American National
Standard for Permanence of Paper for Printed Library Materials.

Library of Congress Catalog Number: 86-1485
ISBN: 978-0-88738-658-9
Printed in the United States of America

Library of Congress Cataloging-in-Publication Data

Tocqueville, Alexis de, 1805-1859
    Recollections: The French Revolution of 1848.

    (Social science classics theory)
    Translation of : Souvenirs.
    Reprint. Originally published: Recollections. Garden City, N. Y.:
Doubleday, 1970
    Bibliography: p.
    1. France—History—February Revolution, 1848. 2. Tocqueville, Alexis
de, 1805-1859. 3. Historians—France—Biography. I. Title. II. Series.

[DC270.T652   1986]   944.07   86-1485
ISBN 0-88738-658-X

CONTENTS

PART THREE

APPENDICES

No other book on the French Revolution of 1848 has stood the test of time so well as Tocqueville's *Recollections*. In this classic, Tocqueville has woven together an historical and sociological approach, and it is this synthesis that gives these pages their unique power and contemporary significance—a significance that found its unmistakable echo in France as recently as 1968. Such eminent French analysts as Raymond Aron and Bertrand de Jouvenel have testified to it. Their publications on the events of 1968 are given in our bibliography. The bibliography of my 1959 American edition has been brought up to date to include those books, apart from a few exceptions, that have appeared since then which may help the reader to pursue further the wide ramifications of Tocqueville's text. We have not aimed at completeness—the subject is too large—but have tried to mention those works that seem to us essential for a deeper understanding of the problems raised by the Revolution of 1848. The present English edition, translated by George Lawrence, is published here for the first time. The help of my colleague, Miss A. P. Kerr, in preparing the text for print, was as painstaking as it was invaluable. For the notes marked (Ed.) we both share responsibility. We also wish to record our gratitude to our editor at Doubleday, Anne Freedgood, who went over the text and indicated where further footnotes might be added.

J. P. Mayer

University of Reading
April 1969.

FOREWORD (1986)

I am profoundly grateful to Irving Louis Horowitz for having suggested to me the reprinting of my edition of Alexis de Tocqueville's *Recollections* which I published with Doubleday in 1970.

In the meantime, I published in 1978, a new French edition of this work, for which my friend and colleague, Fernand Braudel, has contributed an important preface in which he discusses the significance of Tocqueville's work. He has kindly given permission for a translation of this preface to be incorporated into this volume. No one is better qualified to put Tocqueville's *Souvenirs* into the European context of 1848 and after. My own preface to this French edition is a slightly condensed version of my introduction to the 1970 volume.

For the present edition I have also added a short additional bibliography taken from the 1978 French edition and listing those works which were not mentioned in the 1970 edition.

J.P. Mayer

INTRODUCTION TO THE TRANSACTION EDITION

Fernand Braudel

To enhance your enjoyment in reading or rereading Alexis de Tocqueville's *Recollections: The French Revolution of 1848*, I propose a relatively easy game: Imagine that this prestigious author is unknown to you, that you are about to discover him from this reading alone. Imagine that you are not acquainted with either *Democracy in America* or *The Old Régime and the French Revolution*; that you are unaware of the stages and details of his biography and that, while perusing this book, you will not reach into your bookshelf for the admirable edition of Tocqueville's complete works which we owe to the perseverance and erudition of J.P. Mayer.

You will thus approach, as if it were a first reading, this vivid work written by a man suddenly at leisure in the wake of a revolutionary storm that rocked the whole nation. This is a man who is attempting to organize his impressions to understand his own itinerary and to try to disengage himself from an obsessive past. You will follow him through a brief period: from January-February 1848, on the eve of the Revolution which would dethrone Louis-Philippe, until the resignation of the Odilon Barrot regime (31 October 1849) which ended his brief governmental career.

Hopefully, this all too quick itinerary will enable us to judge objectively Tocqueville's exceptional talent, his rare human qualities, and the worth of his testimony. This is our first problem. Yet we are dealing with a whole period no less than with a man, a writer, and a thinker. Even with its speed, this social storm uncovers, both contemporaneously and historically, unforeseen horizons on the face of France. Can we compare this ambiguously drawn France, from which we are not removed by more than a century, to the France of today? Is it possible to read this book through our experiences, knowledge, apprehensions, and language? That is our second problem. We must read or reread Tocqueville in present-day terms, without fearing anachronism. Classics are only classics at that price: the capacity to speak to us about ourselves, to force us to think about ourselves, regardless of the distance in time and events.

After four or five pages of reading, our doubts—if any—vanish. The writing is perfect and it is a pleasure to lose oneself in the text. The sentence follows its course, then often sharply turns on itself at the end. The rhythm might risk monotony in the long run, but the movement is expertly broken: verbs, nouns, and epithets joust in a learned war. This art of stating and counter-stating is not only a style. It is also a perspective, where the pleasures of hearing and understanding blend into each other, particularly in the course of the frequent character sketches that enliven the narrative.

Are these portraits cruel? I do not think so. Besides, Tocqueville also makes fun of himself. He is more likely to judge himself critically than be critical of others. His gaze is that of a historian who wants to place his characters in proper perspective: he is critical even when he loves them and may praise them even when he does not like them. His purpose is not to affect them: this text was not to be—and indeed was not—published in Tocqueville's lifetime nor in that of his contemporaries. Let us also say that the politicians he deals with are no giants, even those who attempt, unsuccessfully, to repeat the gestures of the Revolution of 1789. Tocqueville wrote: "I have sometimes come to believe that while social mores vary, politicians' morals are everywhere the same. All the party leaders I met in France seemed equally unworthy of leadership. Some, due to character flaws or lack of intelligence; most, due to a lack of commonplace virtues." Reread these lines: has France changed that much?

Our research will be limited, for now, to a way of writing, a way of being. Tocqueville reveals himself in the very act of describing others. Let us watch him, then, beginning with Louis-Philippe. Two lines will suffice to reveal Tocqueville in his blending of benevolent light and harsh shadows. Here is the king: "His wordy conversation, loose, original, trivial, anecodotal, full of little facts, of salt and sense, provided all the amenities one can find in the pleasures of the mind when refinement and loftiness are absent." The future Napoleon III, President of the Republic since the election of December 1848, received the same treatment: "A benevolent and easy disposition, a humane personality, a sweet and even tender soul, without being delicate." Then Tocqueville adds: "His dissimulation, deep as that of a man who has spent his life plotting, was singularly complemented by the immobility of his features and the insignificance of his gaze: his eyes were dull and opaque, like thick glass designed to allow light to enter a room but through which one cannot see." Time and again, malice and smiles coexist: "*This* Portalis had neither the rare intelligence, the exemplary behavior, nor the pitiful platitude of his uncle." This time, two birds with one stone. Rémusat, his friend and colleague at the Académie Française, "sees always so clearly what one might do and so obscurely what one should do." Duchâtel, secretary of the interior, was, in 1848, "a man one could neither love nor hate." Odilon Barrot, "who adds some foolishness to both his weaknesses and his virtues . . . had all it takes to act upon [crowds]: a loud voice, a swollen eloquence, and an intrepid heart." About Lamartine, whose courage and eloquence he admires, Tocqueville has this harsh judgment: "I do not recall ever having encountered, in this world of selfish ambition in whose midst I have lived, a spirit more devoid of concern for public welfare than his." And so it goes. What is surprising is that despite the ferocity of his words, the prevailing impression is one of serene judgment without personal bias. This may be because, for Tocqueville, all these actors do not determine events as much as they are determined by them— victims rather than responsible for their roles. We shall return to this.

We must not demand of Tocqueville a complete explanation of

the Revolution of February 1848 nor of the ensuring counter-Revolution—if only because today we are more exacting at the economic and sociological levels of analysis. Tocqueville's account and thought become more meaningful if, following the works of Ernest Labrousse, we study the economic crisis unleashed in 1846, becoming violent in 1847, which shook the country to its foundations. Economic factors had, under similar circumstances, prepared if not caused the explosions of 1789 and 1830. The grain harvest of 1846 was poor; food prices rose 100 to 150 percent, and the crisis soon expanded to the textile, mining, and metallurgic sectors. Workers' salaries fell by 30 percent and unemployment spread. "The wave of inflation rushed over the country like a flood, and, like receding waters, left in its wake a wrecked and economically annihilated population. Very often, as pawnshops bear witness, furniture itself had to be pledged." The crisis unhinged credit, and the railroad construction program was suspended. "Close to a million francs of public works were thus postponed, equivalent to about 500 million labor days at a rate of two francs per day."

This multiple crisis was both old and new, and it preceded the Revolution. It was old insofar as it was born in the past, in the agricultural economic sector, and new insofar as it reached into industry, textiles, metallurgy, and credit. But does historical precedence absolve the government from responsibility? Should we place the crisis itself and its universality on the stand? The question may be asked in the same terms in 1977, both in France and elsewhere.

Tocqueville, doubtless comfortable in terms of his own material resources, was rather inattentive to underlying economic realities. He barely formulates a couple of remarks in this regard, on the eve of the violence of June 1848: "For thirty years the industrial revolution [the term was not common at the time, and Tocqueville should be credited for its use] had made Paris the leading manufacturing city in France. It had attracted a whole new population of workers, to which the fortification works [in the capital about 1840] had added another population of unemployed farmers." Or these strong and true words, also on the eve of June: "Money [seemed to] . . . sink under the ground."

Complementing this shortcoming, Tocqueville has a sharp sense of social realities, which he observes and endeavors to explain. His is a sharp sociological perception guided by historical experiences. Sociology and history are, in Tocqueville, but one way of focusing on society. The enjoyment we derive from his works is due to the blending of a mind close to our own and an old language, removed from the clichés of our time. His expression "class war [or combat]" has a curious ring. Note too how a short trip to Germany and the correspondence he receives at the Department of Foreign Affairs allows him to gauge the reflux of revolutionary events in Germany: "From one end of Germany to the other, the perpetuity of land revenues, seigneurial levies, rights of property transfer, hunting, and justice, which constituted a sizable portion of the wealth of nobility, were abolished. The kings were reestablished, but the aristocracy was unable to regroup." These comments summarized a political situation, but Tocqueville is far less interested in politics than in society as a whole, which he perceives as underlying the political structure, like "the seat of political life." When revolutionaries aim at society, they direct their attacks "lower than the government." This tiered organization would have delighted Georges Gurvitch. As would any sociologist, Tocqueville ponders over the existence of "immutable laws of society." He arrives at no conclusions on the matter, but who today would answer such an embarrassing question?

In any event, that underlying social reality determines, for Tocqueville, the phenomena on the surface. Thus, how might one explain the aftermath of the Revolution of 1830 if not through the advent and "victory of the middle class," of "its dynamic, industrious, often dishonest spirit"? "Not only was the middle class the sole leader of society, but it became its manager. It settled itself into all positions, prodigiously increased their number, and increasingly lived off the public treasury almost as much as off its own industry." Whence an abusive exploitation which eventually destroyed society's equilibrium and the middle class's own privilege. "These flaws derived from the natural instincts of the dominant class . . . [to which] King Louis-Philippe had greatly contributed. He was the accident that rendered the disease fatal."

Tocqueville links the responsibility of the king to that of the bourgeoisie. In this profound sense he sketches a theory of the explosion of revolutions (a social, not economic theory, such as Labrousse's). "In France, a government would always be wrong to support itself exclusively on the interests and passions of one class alone." This privileged class exercises criticism too freely, preferring "the pleasure of slandering [the government] along with everyone else, to assure privileges." The abuses, irresponsibility, and moral bankruptcy of the privileged class would pave the way to catastrophe. Such was the behavior of the old French aristocracy, and such would be that of a certain bourgeoisie at the time of the Banquets campaign. Would it be the permanent French malaise? Said Tocqueville: this "thought often crossed my mind." Hurrah for England, "the only [country] in the world where aristrocracy still governs."

We might say that Tocqueville betrays himself in this instance, were it not obvious that his heart and instincts favor the status quo. He feels no need to explain himself on this point (nor do the times favor this kind of exercise), to specify his social and economic parameters. He states just as simply his antipathy toward Thiers and Blanqui, and feels no need to justify these judgments ideologically. Besides, he is far more interested in understanding than in judging.

Tocqueville's rationale for thinking and acting is explanation: to perceive the world as lucidly as his intelligence and passion for observation will allow. This passion leads him, almost in spite of himself, to a definition of history. It is here, beyond the boundaries of his finite experience, that he compels our interest the most. Here he is drawn to the center of gravity of his thoughts, toward a deep history, slow in unfolding, which he distinguishes from the incidental: "I perceived—more clearly, I believe, than others—the general causes that were leading the July monarchy to its downfall. I did not see the precipitant accidents." More characteristic yet is his speech of 27 January 1848 (note the date) to the Chamber of Representatives: "They say that since there are no riots there is no peril; that since there is no conflict on the surface of society, revolution is far away. Gentlemen, permit me to tell you that I believe you are wrong. . . . Observe what is taking place in the bosom of the working classes, which, I admit, are quiet today. It is true that they are not moved by political passions as such, to the same degree that they were in the past. But do you not see that their passions have shifted from the political to the social realm?. . . . I told you earlier that this malaise would eventually bring . . . the gravest revolutions to this country; be assured of it." Tocqueville seeks the "chain of history" and perforce encounters the long run of all deep history and its very dynamics. This dynamics is repetition: "What we call events, are, most of the time, only forgotten events," therefore repeated. "Behold the French Revolution starting over again, since it is always the same one." "One passion alone remains alive in France: hatred for the Ancien Régime and defiance against the old privileged classes that represent it in the eyes of the people. This feeling works its way through revolutions without changing or dissolving, like the water of those marvelous fountains which, according to the ancients, flowed through the sea without merging nor disappearing."

Certainly, Tocqueville sometimes hesitates, introduces nuances, and skips a beat. Events take place; he recounts them. If he is forced in all conscience to limit the role of great personages, they slip to the first row in his observation. He will not get rid of the former nor the latter. "I clearly see that event, that accidental or superficial cause. . . . It is not that I believe that accidents have played no part in the February revolution. Quite the contrary, they have played a very large role, but they have not done it all." He would even say of Guizot's fall that "one must see it as more than an incident, rather as a great event that would change the face of things." This time he does not wonder about process or sum of forces; the incident is carried beyond itself to the dignity of a "great event."

As cautious a historian as any, Tocqueville is wary of easy comparisons: "One period never fits exactly into another." He is aware of revolutionary continuity, but adds: Are we not "busier performing the French Revolution rather than continuing it?" He does see a potential social revolution on the horizon, but does not explicitly connect it to the revolutionary process. "Will we arrive, as we are told by other prophets . . . at a social transformation more complete and profound than our ancestors had anticipated, and than we ourselves are yet able to fathom? . . . . I do not know when this long journey will end." That long journey has not ended yet. As in the past, it proceeds from order to disorder, from freedom to constraint, from the real to the ideal, from equilibrium to revolution, from revolution to equilibrium: the brief, tumultuous revolution that burns in a huge blaze; the lasting equilibrium with the fire carefully burning beneath the ashes. These are not Tocqueville's textual words, but he is so close to us in his questions without answers that one finds oneself speaking in his behalf.

Tocqueville's wavering between the incidental and the profound, event and structure, is worth following, day by day, during the revolutionary times he witnesses as a tireless journalist, alert to the incident, the encounter, the experience—driven by a "piercing curiosity" rather than by intrepidness. His lucidity and passion for observation are matched by a boundless quest untouched by fears or base feelings. Those of us who witnessed, in May and June 1968, the revealing sketch of a revolution, can readily comprehend Tocqueville's insatiable curiosity. On 22 and 23 February, he was in the House of Representatives. On 24 February "I went out, and no sooner had I stepped into the street that I felt for the first time a revolutionary atmopshere: the center of the street was empty, shops were closed, there were neither carriages nor strollers, one did not hear the usual calls of street vendors. . . . All faces were distorted by anxiety or anger." The only carriage appearing in Tocqueville's account is a cabriolet which Mr. Thiers, in his frantic flight, managed to take from the bois de Boulogne to the Porte de Clichy, then taking several side streets to return home.

Despite a carriageless Paris (their return would signify the return of order) Tocqueville takes to the streets—to go to the House, visit a friend, attend a political meeting. More often than not, he probes the city with boundless curiosity: on 25 February, "as soon as it was day, I set out to take a look at the city." That same day, "I spent the afternoon strolling through Paris." on 23 June 1848, at the first sign of the June insurrection: "[It is] the largest and most significant in our (and maybe in any other) history. The largest because, for four days, more than 100,000 men were engaged in it." On that eventful day Tocqueville does not cease to cover Paris: the House, then from the Bourbon palace off to pick up his nephews, whose safety he would ensure. Next he would be at the Royal Palace, as a delegate to the National Assembly, and then at City Hall. In the barricaded streets "men were in shirt sleeves, which for them is the dress for combat as well as work. . . was [often] stopped . . . along the way and made to show my badge [as representative to the National Assembly]. More than once I was amused by these novices who spoke all manner of patois. Paris was full of countrymen arrived from every province, many of whom were in Paris for the first time."

> Owing to the railroads, they came from fifty leagues away, although the fighting had only begun the previous evening. During the following days they came from 100 and 200 leagues away. These men belonged to every social class. There were many peasants, many bourgeois, many big landholders and aristocrats—all merging within the same ranks. Their weapons were makeshift and insufficient, but they converged on Paris.

This convergence tipped the scales on the side of Cavaignac— the side of order and reaction. Tocqueville was right in believing that if the June uprising "had been less radical and wild, most bourgeois probably would have stayed at home, France would not have come to our aid, and the National Assembly itself might have yielded." But what is the purpose of repeating history if not better to explain it *a contrario*? If the insurrection failed, it was because it did not have revolutionary chiefs "leading the insurgents." Those potential leaders "were taken prematurely like fools on 15 May [the day for Poland], and only saw combat through the walls of the donjon of Vincennes."

The words "like fools" betray Tocqueville. He is on the side of order, too quick to underestimate the true revolutionaries of the time: Blanqui, "ill, evil, and disgusting"; Barbès, "the most sense-less, disinterested, and resolute of all." "I kept a constant eye on him" during the 15 May event. As to Ledru-Rollin (is he a true revolutionary?), the target is too good: "A fat guy, very sensual and very temperamental, lacking principles no less than ideas, with no real audacity of heart or soul, and even without evil." Obviously Tocqueville is not on their side, yet calling them "anti-revolutionary" would not be either fair or appropriate, since neither is he on the other side. His attitude is that of the unpenitent and honest observer, troubled by "the fearful speed [with which] the most peace-loving souls . . . rally behind civil wars" and allow "the taste for violence and contempt for human life to take over." He is no less troubled by his own reaction to this sight and "the promptness with which I became familiar with these inexorably rigid ideas which would normally have been foreign to me," accepting repression as a necessity.

On 3 June 1849, Tocqueville became head of the Department of Foreign Affairs in the short-lived Odilon Barrot cabinet. He would remain in this post only for a few months, until the government's resignation on 31 October 1849. This passage through power is the other strain in the book, of far lesser interest than its preceding pages. The counter-Revolution dramatically begun in June 1848 was established in December through the election of Louis Napoleon Bonaparte, was pursued through the elections in the Legislature in May 1849, and continued until the coup d'état of 2 December 1851 and the reestablishment of the Empire.

The formation, duration, and vicissitudes of the Odilon Barrot administration—so unstable that Tocqueville behaved "each day as if I were to cease being Minister the next day"—are only of passing interest. If this latter part of *Recollections* holds our attention, it is because it sheds light on the *witness* become *actor*, now forced to take a stand. He does not shy away. Yet his writings represent a clarification rather than a justification. He wants to see himself as he was during those few months of apparent power, during which he observed Europe at a distance while under his gaze, the astonishing and sad events in France wove its fate. Tocqueville weathers the challenge with flying colors.

From the outset he establishes a code of conduct and holds to it throughout: to serve the national interest to the best of his ability and in accord with the possibilities and demands of a changing political situation of which he is evidently not the master. There is an internal and external challenge, but the two are interdependent.

In France as in Europe, the revolutionary tide was ebbing. The winter 1848 revolutions had curiously sprung together; the reactions that followed were equally synchronized. It was a cosmic phenomenon of directional shift. While the first movement belonged to rebellious peoples, the second re-established the authority of yesterday's jostled princes. At one end of Europe was the tsar, masterminding and promoting reaction; at the other end was England, "more lukewarm" than ever, with only a "sterile goodwill." Seeking support from the latter was out of the question. For France it was a matter of "reducing itself to a modest living, day to day . . . but even that was difficult," since French public opinion "resisted this requirement of the times." What else could be done? To bet on the retreating Revolution would not rescue it for Europe, and it would certainly rekindle it in France. To bet on the counterrevolution would be tantamount to placing oneself under the patronage of tsarist Russia, causing France to lose "the liberal air that characterized its natural physiognomy among peoples." For Tocqueville, it would have to be a code of conduct of French leaders "not to let themselves be drawn into denying the principles of our Revolution—of liberty, equality, and clemency . . . [nor] play up to the passions of the old powers." Richelieu had both cut down the Protestants within and "helped them rise again in Germany." But such a choice was not available in 1849. Said Tocqueville to our ambassadors: "I know that France is not in a position either to be dominant in Europe or to prevail in terms of events taking place far away." All that could be done was save face and wait, navigate the best course, and avoid compromising a fragile France.

Internal politics, too, afforded only limited room for maneuver. Prince Napoleon at the Elysée represented the risk of a "bastard" monarchy, favored by the need for security, order, requital, and external glory of a peasant, working-class, and reactionary France. In the legislative elections of May 1849, the reactionary victory had been massive (450 representatives). But they were not content. Their goal was to eliminate the adversary. The "Montagnards" numbered 180, to their own surprise. Everything would fall into place on June 13, following a day of rioting that ended in failure. The "Montagnards" were completely finished. According to the president prince: "It is time for the good to feel reassured and for the evil to tremble."

What could be more "essential" for Tocqueville than to work toward the fragile preservation of the Republic? In September 1851 Tocqueville wrote: "I did not believe then any more than I do now that the republican government was better suited to the needs of France. By 'republican government' I mean elective executive power. . . . I have always believed that the Republic was a government without checks and balances. . . . [Yet] I wished to preserve it because there was nothing either good or ready to replace it. The old dynasty was profoundly revolting to the majority of the people. . . . Louis Napoleon alone was prepared to take the place of the Republic."

The political situation was thus triangular. The monarchist legislators were divided into two groups: the Legitimist minority and the Orleanists who knew that they could not seize power quickly, that they must compromise. Across from them was the president's clan, still lacking an established party. Between the two blocs there were a few men determined to save the Republic. Tocqueville bent over backward to show goodwill and conciliation. Being on easier terms with the Legitimists by reason of his family origins, he accepted the presence—even the friendship—of Falloux, who would soon bring to a vote the educational bill bearing his name (15 March 1850). Regarding the Orleanists he was cautious and skillful, having ties with the five-dozen or so moderates in the group. Finally, he was more than obliging toward the forbidding president prince. Tocqueville came to terms with the fact that governing was a day-to-day endeavor, and that the price of wisdom or weakness was often "dirty hands" (an expression he would have hated). For instance, upon assuming his post in the Department of Foreign Affairs, he learned that the French expedition sent against the Roman Republic with strict orders not to attack the city, was now about to do so. "The first thing I learned upon entering the cabinet was that three days hence our army had been ordered to attack Rome. During those two days [12-13 June] I was in an agonizing situation, I entirely disapproved . . . the manner in which the Roman expedition had been undertaken and conducted." Yet departmental solidarity tied his hands and he swallowed the bitter pill.

Compromise and conciliation will not go very far for a man who, like Tocqueville, is profoundly honest. Being a moderate, he was sure to lose, whether victory went to the president prince or to the Orleanists. Is it not often the fate of honest intellectuals to be forced to choose opposition? Tocqueville, always disappointed, would have to stand against the July monarchy, the Banquets campaign, the February Revolution, the days of June, the socialist hope, the Orleanist reaction, and the all-encompassing and underhanded ambition of Louis Napoleon Bonaparte. His self-respect forbade any other attitude. When all is said and done, it is fortunate that his political career was not too long—such as that of historians Thiers and Guizot—and that he devoted the remaining years of his life to writing *The Ancien Régime and the Révolution.*

Yet we would have loved more complete disclosures as a result of his sojourn through power. He did not try to define his own terms with power, or answer the kind of questions a psychoanalyst might ask of him today. The book is obviously unfinished. But an unfinished book can have great worth. Did not Tocqueville shed more light than many on the break of the European mid-nineteenth century? J.P. Mayer, admirably versed on Marx (he rediscovered and published the manuscript of youthful writings *and* Tocqueville, prefers *Recollections* to Marx's *Eighteenth Brumaire*. In his view Tocqueville is more scientific and objective than Marx. This is possible. Yet without seeking to reconcile all things: Is it not true that what fires our imagination in both works is to place Marx's or Tocqueville's thought?

George Lefebvre and I had the pleasure of talking about and singing the praises of Michelet. Lefebvre reminded me about Tocqueville. At the time his words surprised me. Must a historian always prefer a model that is not a mirror image of his passions? Georges Lefebvre represents the Revolution. Lucien Lefebvre should have leaned toward Tocqueville, who, as you have seen, belongs without difficulty on the side of the *Annales* school. Yet he chose Michelet. Must one choose between Tocqueville and Michelet? The latter is more romantic, more revolutionary. The former is more obstinate in weighing both sides and carefully analyzing the issues. If Michelet had presented the France of 1848—which he did not do—he would have chosen as his hero, either Blanqui or Barbès. Then, leaning over this hero's shoulder, he would have witnessed the unfolding of events. France, with its changing colors, would have revolved around a center chosen in advance, just as the France of our religious wars revolves, in Michelet's pathetic account, around Admiral de Coligny. In this game, a reconstituted history takes on dramatic and troubling facets. And the game of revolution has its risks: the historian engages in it with no interference. Tocqueville refused such engagement. Whether witness or participant, he stepped back from the arena. He could not entertain the thought, even for an instant, of seeing the history of France revolve around his person. "How hard is it to speak well of oneself!" he cried. "One is too close to see oneself clearly . . . I am naturally in great defiance of myself." Let us not regret this caution; it enables Tocqueville to give us an incomparable lesson in lucidity.

Let us imagine how these two ways of perceiving history, Tocqueville's and Michelet's, might put our politicians to the test in today's France. *A la Michelet—What politician would be at the center of French life?* A la Tocqueville—What would be the portraits of those who presumably govern us? What underlying phenomena could be perceived beneath the veneer of actuality? Do we have a tired and abusive dominant class, and, with the economic recession begun at least since 1974, do we have an opening for the emergence of turmoil and change, in short, signs (to use an unreasonable expression of the reasonable Tocqueville) "for he who can scent Revolutions from afar"? This is surely a question which the cautious will wait a few years to answer.

ADDITIONAL BIBLIOGRAPHY

Agulhon, M., *1848 ou l'Apprentissage de la République 1848-1852*, Paris, 1973. (important bibliographical indications.)

Agulhon, M., *Les Quarante-huitards*, Paris, 1975.

Amann, P.H., *Revolution and Mass Democracy. The Paris Club Movement in 1848*, Princeton, University Press, 1975.

Bastid, P., *Un juriste pamphlétaire: Cormenin, précurseur et constituant de 1848*, Paris, 1948. (important bibliographical indications.)

Chevalier, L., *Classes laborieuses et classes dangereuses à Paris pendant la première moitié du XIXe siècle*, Paris, 1958.

Dansette, A., *De 2 decembre au 4 septembre. Le Second Empire*, Paris, 1961.

Dolleans, E., *Histoire du mouvement ouvrier (1830-1971)*, vol. I, Paris, 1957.

Duveau, G., *La Vie ouvrière en France sous le Second Empire*, Paris, 1946.

Godechot, I., *Les Constitutions de la France depuis 1789*, Paris, 1970.

Jennings, L.C., *France and Europe in 1848*, Oxford, 1973.

Luna, F.A. de, *The French Republic under Cavaignac, 1848*. Princeton, 1969.

Price, R., *The French Second Republic. A Social History*, London, 1972. (See Index under Tocqueville.) (important bibliographical indications.)

Rudé, G., *Debate on Europe, 1815-1850*, Harper Torchbooks, 1972.

Stearns, P.N., *The Revolutions of 1848*, London, 1974. (important bibliographical indications.)

Tocqueville, A. de, *Democracy in America*, ed. J.P. Mayer, New York, 1982 (18th Edition).

INTRODUCTION (1969)

Tocqueville's *Recollections* were first published in France in 1893; the editor, Alexis de Tocqueville's grandnephew, the Count de Tocqueville, following his great-uncle's testamentary instructions, omitted certain important passages which were restored in the 1942 French edition published in Paris and edited by M. Luc Monnier. An English edition of the *Recollections*, translated by Alexander Teixeira de Mattos appeared in 1896, based on the French edition of 1893. This edition was for many years out of print. In 1949 I published another English edition of the *Recollections*, inserting and indicating the omitted passages in de Mattos' text. This edition was published in the United Kingdom by the Harvill Press and in the United States by the Columbia University Press. In 1959 I revised this edition and gave the reprint rights to Meridian Books. It ran through four printings and established itself as a college text in French studies, political science, history and sociology on both sides of the Atlantic.

In the meantime the definitive edition of Tocqueville's *Oeuvres Complètes*, which I am directing, included in 1964 another French edition of the *Recollections*, which presents the definitive text of Tocqueville's manuscript; the editor was again M. Monnier. It is this edition that forms the basis of the present book, whose text differs in various aspects from the 1942 edition: it includes Tocqueville's own comments, which he wrote into the manuscript, including his footnotes or marginal comments; moreover, a number of passages that appeared in the 1942 edition in the main text, had in this edition to be separated from it, because of evidence that Tocqueville wanted to remove or revise them. Thus the present edition gives a faithful image of the state of the manuscript and shows Tocqueville's historical and sociological thought in *statu nascendi*.

The French edition within the context of the *Oeuvres Complètes* gives all the variants; in this English edition we have inserted only those that give the text an additional meaning (purely verbal or stylistic variants have not been included). Since the publication of my 1959 Meridian edition, the complete correspondence between Tocqueville and Beaumont (3 vols., Paris, 1967) has become available as part of the *Oeuvres Complètes*, together with Tocqueville's correspondence with Gobineau (*Oeuvres Complètes*, vol. XI, 1959), both of which throw new light on the pages of the *Recollections*.

But there was also another reason why a new edition became necessary. The de Mattos translation did not stand the test of time. My slight revisions of 1949 did not satisfy me. I therefore asked George Lawrence, who has so firmly established himself as a Tocqueville translator, to prepare an entirely new English version.

Our notes and bibliographical indications attempt to help the reader set this great work in the context of its time. (Obvious or less important facts and names have not been annotated; our aim was to prepare a readable book, not overburdened by superfluous annotation or vain show of learning easily available elsewhere.)

So much for the text.

As to content, Tocqueville's *Recollections* should not be regarded as a work on the history of the 1848 Revolution. He deliberately wrote political memoirs, nothing else. Simpson's severe judgement in *Louis Napoleon and the Recovery of France* (p. 387) is wholly beside the point. The first three paragraphs of the *Recollections* make Tocqueville's autobiographical intention quite plain. In another passage (p. 80) he compares his intention in writing his *Recollections* with Cardinal de Retz when the latter was writing his *Mémoires*. Tocqueville's *Recollections* do for politics or political affairs what Pascal's *Pensées* or Montaigne's *Essais* had previously achieved in the realm of philosophy. Tocqueville writes in the same tradition.

The reader of the *Recollections* would do well, before he begins their study, to familiarise himself with a reliable history of the French Revolution of 1848. He might, for instance, profitably read Seignobos' *La Révolution de 1848–Le Second Empire* (*1848–1859*), published as the sixth volume of Lavisse's *Histoire de France contemporaine;* or if he chooses to look more to the right, he might consult Pierre de la Gorce's *Histoire de la Seconde République* and the same author's *Histoire du Second Empire.* These works (and many others) provide us with the historical background of the *Recollections.*

Tocqueville writes as a sociologist or political scientist. He observes events, ideas or men, he observes himself, his own actions, and attempts to analyse them in the perspective of French and European politics. He does not act like most of our contemporary politicians in the vacuum of the present. He knows that today is the result of many yesterdays, and that past and present make the future. Tocqueville's power of historical and sociological analysis is unsurpassed. His prediction of the 1848 Revolution, a few weeks before its beginning, is too well-known to be quoted here. There are other equally enduring passages.

Perhaps I should illustrate only how Tocqueville viewed the *one* revolutionary process that began in 1789 and that to this very hour—I am writing in 1969—is still not complete:

> It is no part of the plan of these *Recollections* to inquire into what gave the February Revolution this socialist character. I shall only say that it should not have surprised the world as much as it did. Had no one noticed that for a long time the people had been continually gaining ground and improving their condition, and that their importance, education, desires and power were all constantly growing? Their prosperity had also increased, but not so fast, and it was getting close to that limit which, in old societies, cannot be passed, when there are many candidates but few places. How could it have failed to occur to the poor classes, who were inferior but nonetheless powerful, that they might use their power to escape from their poverty and inferiority? For sixty years they had been working towards this end. . . .
>
> This natural restlessness in the minds of the people, with the inevitable ferment in the desires, thoughts, needs and instincts of the crowd, formed the fabric on which the innovators drew such monstrous and grotesque patterns. One may find their efforts ludicrous, but nothing merits the serious study of philosophers and statesmen more than the background on which they are working.

> Will socialism remain buried in the contempt that so justly covers
> the socialists of 1848? I ask the question without answering it. I am
> sure that in the long run the constituent laws of our modern society
> will be drastically modified; many of the main parts of them have
> already been substantially modified. But will they ever be abolished
> and replaced by others? That seems impracticable to me. I say no
> more, for the more I study the former state of the world, and indeed
> even when I see the modern world in greater detail, when I consider
> the prodigious diversity found there, not just in the laws but in the
> principles of the laws and the different forms that the right of property
> has taken and, whatever anybody says, still takes on this earth, I am
> tempted to the belief that what are called necessary institutions are
> only institutions to which one is accustomed, and that in matters of
> social constitution the field of possibilities is much wider than people
> living with each society imagine (pp. 75–6).

There are probably not many passages in Tocqueville's work
where he comes nearer to Karl Marx's teachings. Yet in my
opinion the *Recollections* are infinitely superior to Marx's *Eighteenth
Brumaire,* and even more to the *Class Struggles in
France.* Marx wrote with the understandable impatience of the
social revolutionary, whereas Tocqueville writes, favoured by his
aristocratic, conservative instincts, with a fairer appreciation of
the inherent brakes within his contemporary society. All the
same, both thinkers stated the fundamental problem that our
generation and the next will have to solve.

Both Marx and Tocqueville regarded the Revolution of 1848
as a phase in *one* revolutionary process, but while Marx abused
and ridiculed the revolutionaries of 1848 for having failed to
establish a socialist society, Tocqueville did not measure his
own time with norms that were not its own. Not that he did
not see those *new* norms towards which French (and indeed
European) society was moving, but he did not think that they
could be realised then.

Tocqueville's understanding of the structure of the historic
process was perhaps subtler than that of Marx:

> For my part [we read in the *Recollections* (p. 62)], I hate
> all those absolute systems that make all the events of history depend
> on great first causes linked together by the chain of fate and thus
> succeed, so to speak, in banishing men from the history of the human
> race. . . . Antecedent facts, the nature of institutions, turns of mind

and the state of mores are the materials from which chance composes those impromptu events that surprise and terrify us.

Tocqueville was a realistic sociologist; in comparison Marx was a Utopian. Yet there can be no doubt that the Utopianism of 1848 exerted a greater influence on later generations than the uncomfortable loneliness of the great Frenchman.

Tocqueville stood for the maintenance of what he believed to be the structure of the French society of his time. His traditions, his training as a lawyer and judge, in short his political philosophy, which he had formulated in the three volumes of *Democracy in America,* had led him to these conclusions:

> I did not then think, any more than I think now, that a Republican form of government was the one best suited to the needs of France, meaning by "Republican government" an elected executive branch. Where the habits, traditions and mores of a people have assured such a vast sphere of power for the executive, its instability will always, whenever troubled days come, lead to revolution, and even in peaceful times such instability will be uncomfortable. In any case, for me a republic is an ill-balanced form of government, promising more freedom and giving less than a constitutional monarchy. Nonetheless I sincerely desired to maintain the Republic; and, although there were, so to speak, no Republicans in France, I did not think maintaining it was an absolutely impracticable proposition (*Recollections,* pp. 200–201).

With such convictions he accepted the high office of Minister of Foreign Affairs. His directives and policies are clearly indicated in the remarkable addition to the old text of the *Recollections* (pp. 240–241) to which there is probably no parallel in French political literature since Richelieu's *Testament politique.* Nor should we forget to draw particular attention to Appendix VIII, Tocqueville's speech on the Roman Question, which, according to his Chef du Cabinet, Arthur de Gobineau, is "undoubtedly the best, the most firm, clear and adroit [speech] that he has yet made." (Cf. R. Pierre Marcel, *Essai politique sur Alexis de Tocqueville,* Paris, 1910, p. 426.) We have taken this speech from the *Moniteur* of 18 October 1849.

Tocqueville's account of the deliberations of the Committee of the Constitution of which he was a member is of special interest to the student of politics. (Again his account is not that of the historian. Cf. H. Michel, *Note sur la Constitution de 1848* in *La Révolution de 1848*, vol. I, pp. 41–56.) Here we see Tocqueville's political sociology at work. He formulates with brilliant clarity: "In France there is only one thing that we cannot make: a free government; and only one that we cannot destroy: centralization" (p. 170). In these sentences the fundamental tenets of his *Ancien Régime and the Revolution* are already made clear.

He relates with distress his and his friends' defeat on the question of whether the Second Republic ought to have a dual-Chamber system or not. Tocqueville was in favour of the dual system, though "public opinion in almost all the departments as well as in Paris had come out strongly in favour of a single Chamber" (p. 173). Moreover, he was not in doubt about the danger of having the President of the Republic elected directly by the people: ". . . we had lost our taste for monarchy but had preserved the spirit of it. In such conditions who could be the president elected by the people, unless he were a pretender to the throne?" Louis Napoleon's plebiscitarian dictatorship was the answer to Tocqueville's question.

In summing up the work of the Committee of the Constitution, Tocqueville believed that "the only part of our work that was handled with superior intelligence . . . was the part dealing with justice." The Committee maintained the irremovability of judges. Here, the example of the British constitution was evident, and it was not without satisfaction that Tocqueville wrote: "What we did there is a great improvement on all the attempts at the same task during the last sixty years. Probably it is the only part of the Constitution of 1848 that will survive" (*Recollections*, pp. 180–181).

Again Tocqueville was thinking in the perspective of the *one* revolution of which the '48 period was only a phase.

His judgements on his contemporaries are not always just. He is severe, if not unfair, to Louis Blanc and Blanqui. Perhaps he has given us an explanation of this part of his character in the extraordinary example of self-analysis (p. 84) of which only a few lines need be quoted:

> Does this extreme distrust of my own powers and this continual need to find some sort of test of myself in the thought of others spring from true modesty? I am more inclined to believe that their origin is a great pride as nervous and restless as the mind itself.

Indeed neither in Blanc nor in Blanqui could Tocqueville find the confirmation of his own thoughts.

The Revolution of 1848 and its surprising and terrifying results—Napoleon III's plebiscitarian dictatorship—mark a watershed in European political thought. In order to understand the shock the French revolutionary development exerted on its contemporaries, one must bear in mind that until 1848 there were less than 250,000 voters in France; the elections for the Constituent Assembly, however, had given voting rights to more than 9,000,000 voters "almost all of them," as Seignobos writes, "without any political idea, without any experience of voting, and most of them even illiterate." It was this sudden jump into universal manhood franchise that created such a confused political situation. Although "universal franchise" was severely restricted by the electoral law of 1850, the voting population was still more than twenty times as large as it had been before the Revolution. Such a confused mass electorate fell an easy prey to a plebiscitarian leader.

A comparison with English electoral history is perhaps revealing. British parliamentary representation, although no doubt feudal and corporative in its beginnings, began its development towards a democratic electoral system in 1832. Yet after 1832 not more than 250,000 voters were added to the 435,000 voters existing in England and Wales before the first Reform Bill. Even considering the difference in population figures—France in 1840, 32,000,000; England and Wales in 1840, 16,000,000—the English additional voting figures do not imply such a strain on the political organisation as must have been the case in France.

The French Republic, based on universal franchise, produced its dialectical antithesis—to use, for once, the Hegelian term. Donoso Cortès, the great Spanish political philosopher, prophesied to the liberal bourgeoisie, which he despised: "Behind the sophists the hangman will appear"[1]; Bismarck sent the young

[1] Donoso Cortès, *Ensayo sobre el Catolicismo, el Liberalismo y el Socialismo*, Madrid, 1851.

German lawyer Constantin Frantz to Paris, where he duly
fabricated the first "coherent" philosophy of the plebiscitarian
principle[2]; Bagehot[3] demonstrated his later brilliance by his
early reports from the Paris of 1851; Jacob Burckhardt, the
great Swiss historian, writing and teaching from Basle, whence
he could contemplate the policies of three European powers,
summed up the '48 period in his *Reflections on History*:

> At the same time, the events of 1848 had given the ruling classes
> a deeper insight into the people. Louis Napoleon had risked universal
> suffrage in the elections, and others followed his lead. The conservative
> strain in the rural populations had been recognised, though no attempt
> had been made to assess precisely how far it might be extended from
> the elections to everything and everybody. . . . With all business
> swelling into big business, the views of the businessman took the
> following line: on the one hand, the State should be no more than
> the protective guarantor of his interests and of his type of intelligence,
> henceforth assumed to be the main purpose of the world. Indeed,
> it was his desire that his type of intelligence should obtain possession
> of the State by means of constitutional adjustments. On the other
> hand, there prevailed a profound distrust of constitutional liberty in
> practice, since it was more likely to be used by destructive forces
> (London, 1943, p. 165).

Alexander Herzen fled from France to London to write his
equally disillusioned memoirs on the breakdown of the revolutionary hopes.[4] Yet in spite of his melancholic scepticism with
regard to European politics, Herzen believed firmly in the political future of the Russian people.

Moreover, there was Proudhon[5] who transmitted the conviction that the 1848–51 period was a watershed in European
political thought to Georges Sorel, who became the involuntary
teacher of Fascism. Similarly, through Marx's *Eighteenth Brumaire* and other historical writings, the powerful dynamics of the

[2] Cf. my edition, Potsdam, 1933, edited under pseudonym Franz Kemper.
[3] Cf. Walter Bagehot, *Literary Studies*, London, 1906, Vol. III, p. 1 sqq.
[4] Cf. *The Memoirs of Alexander Herzen*, 6 vols., London, 1924. See
particularly vol. IV, p. 167 sqq.
[5] Proudhon's *La Révolution sociale démontrée par le Coup d'État du
Deux Décembre* (*Oeuvres Complètes de P. J. Proudhon, Nouvelle Édition*,
Paris, 1936) may serve as an illuminating corrective to Tocqueville's
Recollections. Cf. particularly the suggestive introduction by MM. Dol-
léans and Duveau. See also the important book by Édouard Molléans:
Proudhon, Paris, 1948.

1848 period made the deepest impression on Lenin. But it was the *myth* of the Revolution, not its history, that was in Lenin's mind during the Russian revolutionary struggles in 1917. In Lenin's *State and Revolution,* the classic study of revolutionary Marxism, the simplified and more virulent form of Marxist interpretation prevails. When Lenin formulated the theoretical foundations of the Soviet State in Switzerland, he thought the knowledge of reading and writing and a little arithmetic was enough to qualify the proletarian revolutionary for the task of State administration. When the Russian State was conquered, he soon learned a different lesson.

Perhaps it is significant to remember that Marx himself to some extent corrected the simplified and, as it were, mythical picture he had drawn of the '48 period. When, as a political refugee in London, he re-edited *The Eighteenth Brumaire* in 1869, he had lived long enough in England to understand the slow and *evolutionary* progress towards universal franchise. The following sentences were omitted from the second edition:

> . . . in those momentous days the French nation committed a deadly crime against democracy, which, on its knees, now utters the daily prayer: "Holy Universal Suffrage, pray for us!" Naturally enough, the believers in universal suffrage will not renounce their faith in a wonder-working power which has transformed the second Bonaparte into a Napoleon, Saul into Paul, and Simon into Peter. The folk-spirit speaks to them through the ballot boxes as the god of the prophet spoke to the dry bones: *"Haec dicit dominus deus ossibus suis: Ecce ego intromittam in vos Spiritum et vivetis."*[6]

[6] Cf. my edition, Berlin, 1932, p. 10 sqq. In 1965, I had the opportunity of discussing these text variants with a Chinese Marx-scholar in Peking. When I asked my Chinese interlocutor why Chinese Communists have never printed the second edition of *The Eighteenth Brumaire,* he replied that the second edition did not exist. When I pointed out to him that I had published an edition in which these variants were indicated, he simply replied, "We have always regarded you as an incorrigible revisionist." It is evident that the myth of the European 1848 revolutions extends even to China.

This denial of the existence of the second edition, made in a tone of perfect Confucian courtesy, together with other facts which I observed when in China, indicates that ancient customs and traditions are partly, if imperfectly, integrated into the new socio-cultural framework of the modern Chinese State. Cf. J. P. Mayer, *Aufzeichnungen in Peking, in Geist und Tat,* 21, Jahrgang, April 1966.

In this respect, too, Tocqueville was the greater realist, for we read in the *Recollections:*

> Universal suffrage had shaken the land from top to bottom without bringing into prominence any new man deserving of attention. I have always thought that, no matter what procedure is followed in a general election, most of the exceptional men in the country will surely succeed in getting elected. The electoral system chosen influences only the type of ordinary individuals included in an assembly, who are bound to be at the base of any political body. The classes from which these ordinary members are drawn and their attitudes vary widely according to the electoral system used. The appearance of the Constituent Assembly confirmed me in this opinion. I knew almost all the men who played leading parts in it, but the crowd of other members was like nothing I had seen previously (p. 104).

Here, Tocqueville's subtle mind penetrates the *forms* of electoral mechanisms and lays bare the substance of the organisational structure of politics. Yet, ultimately, myth, not reason, is the driving force in history.

Thus, as long as Europeans choose to and are allowed to think freely, the *Recollections* remain the document of a man who, though ready to compromise as a politician, fully anticipated as a sociologist the trends of future societies whose principal difficulty was to be the synthesis of equality and freedom.

Tocqueville's free and independent mind drove him into melancholy isolation, an attitude with which we sympathise and which indeed we share.

Our own time has underlined the political and sociological significance of the 1848 Revolution. Everywhere, in France, in the United Kingdom, in the United States, plebiscitarian trends have become more distinct and more dangerous. The power of the mass media, in particular of television, has become a vital factor in shaping election results. The democratic processes are in danger of becoming undermined; hence everywhere new tendencies towards active local and regional participation are coming into being. Whether they will be able to dam the plebiscitarian waves remains to be seen. At the moment when these pages were being sent to the printers, General de Gaulle lost his referendum and subsequently resigned as President of the Fifth French Republic (27–28 April 1969). A fateful phase of French history came to its close. De Gaulle's last plebiscite combined an intended constitutional and institutional reform with an appeal for further confidence in his "charismatic" leadership. "One must seek support from the people rather than from the elites which tend to interpose themselves between the people and myself," wrote Charles de Gaulle in his *Mémoires*. But new French generations grew into men and women, for whom the power of the Gaullist myth—a strange mixture of romanticism and realism—faded. The plebiscitarian appeal was rejected by the assertion of the unfulfilled rational demands made by the present and the near future. The lesson is, perhaps, telling: the plebiscitarian trend of which I have written, can be checked, controlled and perhaps guided into the realm of rational politics. The lesson is important, not only for France.

Today as in 1848 the challenge of democracy by various kinds of plebiscitarian totalitarianisms remains a vital problem requiring the utmost vigilance: in consequence a profound study of Alexis de Tocqueville's *Recollections* may provide the younger generation with an indispensable guide.

J. P. Mayer

University of Reading
April 1969.

PART ONE

Written in July 1850, at Tocqueville

CHAPTER ONE

*Origin and Character of these Recollections – General
aspects of the period preceding the Revolution of
1848 – First symptoms of the Revolution*

Now that for the moment I am out of the stream of public life,
and the uncertain state of my health does not even allow me
to follow any consecutive study, I have in my solitude for a time
turned my thoughts to myself, or rather to those events of the
recent past in which I played a part or stood as witness. The
best use for my leisure seems to be to go back over these
events, to describe the men I saw taking part in them, and
in this way, if I can, to catch and engrave on my memory
those confused features that make up the uncertain physiognomy
of my time.

Along with this decision of mine goes another to which I
shall be equally faithful: these recollections are to be a mental
relaxation for myself and not a work of literature. They are
written for myself alone. These pages are to be a mirror,[1] in
which I can enjoy seeing my contemporaries and myself, not a
painting for the public to view. My best friends are not to know
about them, for I wish to keep my freedom to describe myself

[1] *Marginal Note (Tocqueville)*: Such memoirs cannot be a mirror where
no fault was found. These memoirs could not be read or shown except to a
friend in whom I would have no weakness to forgive (?) and before whom
I would agree to display my own weakness. Does such a one exist?
All pictures of one's friends which are painted in front of them, or
pictures of oneself shown to everyone, are inaccurate. The only true
pictures are those which are not intended to be shown.

and them without flattery. I want to uncover the secret motives that made us act, them and myself as well as other men, and, when I have understood these, to state them. In a word, I want to express myself honestly in these memoirs, and it is therefore necessary that they be completely secret.[2]

I do not intend to start my recollections further back than the Revolution of 1848, nor to carry them beyond the date when I left office, that is, 30 October 1849. It is only within this span that the events I want to describe had something of greatness in them, or that my position enabled me to see them clearly.

Although I was somewhat out of the stream of events, I did live in the parliamentary world of the last years of the July Monarchy,[3] but I would find it difficult to give a clear account of that time, which is so close, but which has left so confused an impression on my memory.[4] I lose the thread of my recollections amid the labyrinth of petty incidents, petty ideas, petty passions, personal viewpoints and contradictory projects in which the life of public men in that period was frittered away. Only the general physiognomy of that time comes readily to my mind. For that was something I often contemplated with mingled curiosity and fear, and I clearly discerned the particular features that gave it its character.

Seen as a whole from a distance, our history from 1789 to 1830 appears to be forty-one years of deadly struggle between the Ancien Régime with its traditions, memories, hopes and men (i.e. the aristocrats), and the new France led by the

[2] *Variant:* My only purpose in writing them is to give me a solitary pleasure, the pleasure of looking at a true picture of human affairs, of seeing man in the reality of his virtues and vices, his nature, of understanding and judging.

Beginning of a variant: Which would be experienced in the depths of the desert.

[3] This régime, called the July Monarchy from the month of its establishment in 1830, is particularly notable for the complete social and political ascendancy of the middle classes. The Duke of Orleans was declared king by the Chamber of Deputies, and took the title of Louis-Philippe I, King of the French. The régime lasted until February 1848. (Editors' Note.)

[4] *To this Tocqueville added the marginal note:* I confess that I am honest by instinct rather than from principle. But I have always found that instinct very useful, and it has continually struck me that I should have found it very difficult to live as a rascal, had I wished to do so.

middle class. 1830 would seem to have ended the first period of our revolutions, or rather, of our revolution, for it was always one and the same, through its various fortunes and passions, whose beginning our fathers saw and whose end we shall in all probability not see. All that remained of the Ancien Régime was destroyed forever. In 1830 the triumph of the middle class was decisive and so complete that the narrow limits of the bourgeoisie encompassed all political powers, franchises, prerogatives, indeed the whole government, to the exclusion, in law, of all beneath it and, in fact, of all that had once been above it. Thus the bourgeoisie became not only the sole director of society, but also, one might say, its cultivator. It settled into every office, prodigiously increased the number of offices, and made a habit of living off the public Treasury almost as much as from its own industry.

No sooner had this occurred than a marked lull ensued in every political passion, a sort of universal shrinkage, and at the same time a rapid growth in public wealth. The spirit peculiar to the middle class became the general spirit of the government; it dominated foreign policy as well as home affairs. This spirit was active and industrious, often dishonest, generally orderly, but sometimes rash because of vanity and selfishness, timid by temperament, moderate in all things except a taste for well-being, and mediocre; a spirit that, combined with that of the people or of the aristocracy, could work wonders, but that by itself never produces anything but a government without either virtues or greatness. Mistress of all, as no aristocracy ever has been or perhaps ever will be, the middle class, which must be called the ruling class, entrenched in its power and, shortly afterwards, in its selfishness, treated government like a private business, each member thinking of public affairs only in so far as they could be turned to his private profit, and in his petty prosperity easily forgetting the people.

Posterity, which sees only striking crimes and generally fails to notice smaller vices, will perhaps never know how far the government of that time towards the end took on the features of a trading company whose every operation is directed to the benefit that its members may derive therefrom. These vices were linked to the natural instincts of the dominant class, to its absolute power, and to the enervation and corruption of the age. King Louis-Philippe did much to make them grow. He was the accident that made the illness fatal.[5]

Although this prince sprang from the noblest family in Europe and had, buried in the depths of his soul, a full measure of hereditary pride, certainly not considering himself like any other man, he nevertheless shared most of the good and bad qualities associated primarily with the lower ranks of society. He had regular mores and wanted those around him to have the same. He was orderly in his behaviour, simple in his habits, and moderate in his tastes; he was naturally on the side of law and hostile to any excess; sober in all his acts if not in his desires; kind, although without sensitivity; greedy and soft. He had no raging passions, or ruinous weaknesses, or striking vices, and only one kingly virtue, courage. His politeness was extreme, but without discrimination or dignity—the politeness of a tradesman rather than of a prince. He had no taste for letters or the fine arts, but cared passionately for business. He had a prodigious memory which was capable of relentlessly recalling the smallest details. His conversation was prolix, diffuse, original, anecdotal, full of little facts and wit and meaning, in short of all the pleasures of the mind that are possible in the absence of delicacy and elevation of spirit. His mind was distinguished, but restricted and clogged by the meanness and narrowness of his soul. He was enlightened, subtle and tenacious, but all his thoughts turned to the useful, and he was filled with such a deep contempt for truth and such a profound disbelief in virtue that they clouded his vision, not only making it impossible for him to see the beauty that always goes with truth and honesty, but also preventing him from understanding their frequent usefulness. He had a profound understanding of men, but only in respect to their vices; in matters of religion he had the

[5] *The following passage appears in the two first editions, but since Tocqueville circled it in pen in the manuscript, he apparently intended it to be omitted:* That prince was a strange mixture and, to describe him in detail, one should have seen him much longer and closer than I ever did. But his principal characteristics were apparent even from a distance to any passer-by.

disbelief of the eighteenth century, and in politics, the scepticism of the nineteenth. Having no belief himself, he had no faith in the belief of others. He was by nature fond of power and of dishonest[6] courtiers, as if he really had been born on a throne. His ambition, which was limited only by prudence, never either satisfied or carried him away, but always remained close to the ground.

There have been many princes who resemble this portrait, but what was peculiar to Louis-Philippe was the analogy, or rather the kinship and consanguinity between his defects and those of his age; it was this that made him an attractive prince, but one who was singularly dangerous and corrupting for his contemporaries, and particularly for the class that held the power. Placed at the head of an aristocracy, he might perhaps have had a happy influence on it. At the head of the bourgeoisie, he pushed it down the slope that it was by nature only too inclined to go. It was a marriage of vices, and this union, which first provided the strength of the one and then brought about the demoralization of the other, ended by bringing both to destruction.

Though I was never admitted to that prince's councils, I had occasion to approach him fairly frequently. The last time I saw him at close quarters was shortly before the February catastrophe.[7] At that time I was director of the French Academy and I had to bring to the King's notice some matter or other concerning that body. Having dealt with the question that brought me, I was about to withdraw, but the King detained me, taking a chair and motioning me to another, saying affably, "As you are here, Monsieur de Tocqueville, let us chat; I would like you to tell me a little about America." I knew him well enough to realize that that meant: I want to talk about America. And so he talked tellingly at great length, without my having a chance or even the desire to put in a word, for he really did interest me. He described places as if he could see them; he recalled the distinguished men he had met forty years before as if he had left them yesterday; he remembered their names and Chris-

---

[6] *The following words are Xed out:* mediocre, facile, dull.
[7] The revolution of February 1848 which ended the July Monarchy and brought about the Second Republic. (Ed.)

tian names; mentioned their age at that time; and recounted their life stories, genealogies and descent with wonderful accuracy and infinite detail and without ever becoming boring. Without taking breath he came back from America to Europe and talked about all our affairs, foreign and domestic, with an incredible lack of restraint (for I had no right to his confidence), telling me much ill about the Emperor of Russia, whom he called Monsieur Nicolas, mentioning Lord Palmerston in passing as a scapegrace, and finally talking at length about the Spanish marriages, which had just taken place, and the trouble they had caused him from the point of view of England: "The Queen is at me about it," he said, "and gets very upset. But after all," he added, "all their outcry won't stop me *driving my own cab.*" Although that turn of phrase dated back to the Ancien Régime, I thought it was doubtful that Louis XIV had ever used it after he accepted the Spanish succession. I think too that Louis-Philippe was mistaken, and, to borrow his language, the Spanish marriages[8] played an important part in upsetting his cab.

After three quarters of an hour the King got up, thanked me for the pleasure our conversation had given him (I had not said four words) and dismissed me, clearly delighted with me, as one usually is by anyone in whose presence one feels one has talked well. This was the last time he received me.

[8] This was the name given to the culmination of French attempts to gain a preponderant influence in Spanish affairs, and as such was one of Guizot's more energetic efforts in diplomacy between 1840 and 1848. It consisted of a double marriage, which took place on 10 October 1846 between Queen Isabella of Spain and her cousin the Duke of Cadiz, and between her sister the Infanta and the Duke of Montpensier, youngest son of Louis-Philippe, thereby ensuring the continuance of the Bourbon dynasty in Spain. The success in achieving these dynastic matches caused a complete rupture of the *entente cordiale* between France and Great Britain and may be seen as a contributory cause of the 1848 revolution. Tocqueville is here drawing an analogy between the dynastic preoccupations of Louis-Philippe and those of Louis XIV who, in accepting the Spanish throne for his grandson, the Duke of Anjou (later Philip V of Spain), in 1700 brought upon himself the war of the Spanish Succession. Both these events show the continuing desire of the French Government to maintain its influence in Spain and the equally strong determination of other powers —notably Great Britain—to prevent it. For Tocqueville's comments on the Spanish marriages at the time, see *Le Moniteur* of 3 February 1847. (Ed.)

This prince really did improvise the answers he made, even at the most critical moments, to the great State bodies; he was as fluent on these occasions as in his conversation, but he spoke with less felicity and spice. Generally in such cases his utterances were a deluge of commonplaces weighed down by false and exaggerated gestures, a great effort to seem touched, and great thumps on his chest. At such times he was often obscure, for he would start off boldly, headfirst, so to speak, on long sentences whose duration he had not measured and whose end he had not foreseen, from which he would finally break his way out, smashing the grammar and leaving his meaning unfinished. Usually his style on these solemn occasions reminded one of the sentimental jargon of the late eighteenth century, copied with facile fluency and a singular lack of accuracy; Jean-Jacques refurbished by a vulgar nineteenth-century kitchenmaid. This reminds me of a day when the Chamber of Deputies was visiting the Tuileries; I was well in front and so in full view, and I nearly caused a scandal by bursting out laughing, because Rémusat,[9] my colleague in the Academy as well as in the Legislature, took it into his head, while the King was speaking, to whisper maliciously in my ear in a serious and melancholy tone of voice: "At this moment the good citizen should be agreeably moved, but the Academician suffers."

In a political world thus composed and led, what was most

[9] Charles de Rémusat (1797–1875), journalist, man of letters, politician, and member of the Académie Française, succeeding Royer-Collard in 1846. He was a deputy of the Haute-Garonne throughout the July Monarchy and represented the same department at the two assemblies of the Second Republic. From 1830 onwards he was a supporter of conservative policies, but in 1840 he joined the second Thiers cabinet as Minister of the Interior and remained in Thiers' left-centre group thereafter. Although by no means active in the reformist movement, he made frequent attempts between 1841 and 1848 to bring in measures of parliamentary reform, to curb the increasing number of public officials in the Chamber of Deputies. His writings include memoirs which begin with his childhood under the Directory and end with the first few years of the Third Republic. These *Mémoires de ma vie* have now received their first publication in five volumes, Paris, 1958–67. The fourth volume (1841–51) covers the period described by Tocqueville in these *Recollections*, and it is perhaps instructive to compare the two viewpoints. In view of its importance, it is regrettable that the editor, M. Charles Pouthas, did not see fit to publish this work in its entirety. (Ed.)

lacking, especially at the end, was political life itself. Such life could hardly emerge or survive within the sphere delineated for it by the constitution: the old aristocracy had been defeated, and the people were excluded. As every matter was settled by the members of one class, in accordance with their interests and point of view, no battlefield could be found on which great parties might wage war. This peculiar homogeneity of position, interest, and consequently of point of view which prevailed in what M. Guizot had called the legal country,[10] deprived parliamentary debates of all originality, all reality, and so of all true passion. I have spent ten years of my life in the company of truly great minds who were in a constant state of agitation without ever really becoming heated, and who expended all their perspicacity in the vain search for subjects on which they could seriously disagree.

On the other hand the preponderant influence Louis-Philippe acquired by taking advantage of the mistakes and, especially, the vices of his adversaries prevented anybody from straying very far from that prince's ideas, lest by doing so they lose all hope of success, and so reduced the differences between the parties to slight nuances, and the contest, to a quarrel over words. I doubt if ever a parliament (and I do not except even the Constituent Assembly of 1789) has ever contained more varied and brilliant talents than ours of the closing years of the July Monarchy. But I can assert that these great orators were very bored with listening to each other, and, what was worse, the whole nation was bored with hearing them. Gradually the nation became accustomed to regarding the debates in Parliament as exercises of wit rather than serious discussions, and to thinking of the differences between the parliamentary parties—majority, left-centre and dynastic opposition—as quarrels between the children of one family over the distribution of their

[10] *Pays légal* was the phrase by which Guizot was wont to describe those who had the right to vote under the 1831 electoral law. Under this law, voters had to show that they paid at least 200 francs in direct taxation. Such a condition ensured that political power remained in the hands of the propertied classes, and throughout the July Monarchy, the electorate never numbered more than 241,000 out of a total population of well over 30,000,000. (Ed.)

inheritance. Some glaring instances of corruption, accidentally discovered, suggested that other scandals lay hidden everywhere and convinced the nation that the entire governing class was corrupt. So the nation conceived a quiet contempt for that class, which was generally interpreted as a trusting and satisfied submission.

The country was at that time divided into two parts, or rather into two unequal zones: in the upper one, which was meant to contain the entire political life of the nation, languor, impotence, immobility and boredom reigned; but in the lower one an attentive observer could easily see from certain feverish and irregular symptoms that political life was beginning to find expression.

I was one of those observers, and although I was far from supposing that the catastrophe was so close and would prove so terrible, I felt an uneasiness forming and gradually growing in my mind; more and more the idea took root that we were marching towards a new revolution. This marked a great change in my thought. The universal calming down and levelling off that followed the July revolution made me suppose, for a long time, that I was destined to live my life in an enervated, tranquil society. Indeed anyone who looked only inside the structure of government would have been convinced of that. Provided with all the machinery of liberty, everything seemed to combine to produce an immense royal power, a power so absolute that it bordered on despotism, and that was effortlessly produced by the regular, peaceful movement of the machine. Proud of the advantage he derived from this ingenious mechanism, Louis-Philippe was convinced that, so long as he did not interfere with this beautiful instrument as Louis XVIII had done, but allowed it to work according to its rules, he was protected from every danger. He was concerned only with keeping it in order and using it in accordance with his own views, forgetting the society upon which the ingenious mechanism was poised; he was like a man refusing to believe that his house had been on fire because he had the key in his pocket. I did not have the same interests or cares, and this allowed me to penetrate the mechanism of institutions and the mass of petty daily occurrences and to consider the state of mores and opinions in the country. There I clearly noted the appearance of several of the signs that usually announce the approach of revolutions. And I began to think that in 1830 I had mistaken the end of an act for the end of the play.[11]

A short piece I wrote then, which has remained unpublished, and a speech I made at the beginning of 1848 bear witness to these preoccupations.

Several of my parliamentary friends had met in October 1847 to try to come to an agreement about the line to take during the next legislative session. We decided that we should publish a programme in the form of a manifesto, and this task was entrusted to me. Afterwards, the idea of such a publication was abandoned, but I had composed the required piece. I have found it among my papers, and I quote the following sentences.[12] After describing the languor of parliamentary life, I add[13]:

> The time is coming when the country will again be divided between two great parties. The French Revolution, which abolished all privileges and destroyed all exclusive rights, did leave one, that of property. Property holders must not delude themselves about the strength of their position, or suppose that, because it has so far nowhere been surmounted, the right to property is an insurmountable barrier; for our age is not like any other. When the right to property was merely the basis of many other rights, it could be easily defended, or rather, it was not attacked: it was like the encircling wall of a society whose other rights were the advance defence posts; the shots did not reach it; there was not even a serious intention to reach it. But now that the right to property is the last remnant of a destroyed aristocratic world, and it alone still stands, an isolated privilege in a levelled society; when it no longer has the cover of other more doubtful and more hated rights, it is in great danger; it alone now has to face the direct and incessant impact of democratic opinions . . .
> Soon[14] the political struggle will be between the Haves and the

[11] *Tocqueville added the marginal note:* Insert here a very brief summary of these symptoms if they do not come in later on.
[12] This manifesto was published by Beaumont in vol. IX (pp. 514–19) of his edition of Tocqueville's complete works, and was entitled *De la classe moyenne et du peuple.* (Ed.)
[13] *Marginal note (Tocqueville):* Instead of quoting the whole of this big extract which drags, a few words.
[14] *Marginal Note (Tocqueville):* Perhaps begin here.

Have-nots; property will be the great battlefield; and the main political questions will turn on the more or less profound modifications
of the rights of property owners that are to be made. Then we shall
again see great public agitations and great political parties.

Why is everybody not struck by the signs that are the harbingers
of this future? Do you think it is by chance, or by some passing
caprice of the human spirit, that on every side we see strange doctrines
appearing, which have different names, but which all deny the right
of property, or, at least, tend to limit, diminish or weaken the exercise
of that right? Who can fail to recognize in this the last symptom of
the old democratic disease of the times, whose crisis is perhaps approaching?

I was even more explicit and urgent in the speech I made to
the Chamber of Deputies on 29 January 1848, which can be
read in the *Moniteur* for the 30th.[15] Here are the main passages:

It is said that there is no danger because there is no riot, and
that because there is no visible disorder on the surface of society, we
are far from revolution.

Gentlemen, allow me to say that I think you are mistaken. True,
there is no actual disorder, but disorder has penetrated far into men's
minds. See what is happening among the working classes who are,
I realize, quiet now. It is true that they are not now tormented by
what may properly be called political passions to the extent they
once were; but do you not see that their passions have changed
from political to social? Do you not see that opinions and ideas are
gradually spreading among them that tend not simply to the overthrow of such-and-such laws, such-and-such a minister, or even such-
and-such a government, but rather to the overthrow of society,
breaking down the bases on which it now rests? Do you not hear
what is being said every day among them? Do you not hear them
constantly repeating that all the people above them are incapable
and unworthy to rule them? That the division of property in the
world up to now is unjust? That property rests on bases of inequity?
And do you not realize that when such opinions take root and
spread, sinking deeply into the masses, they must sooner or later (I
do not know when, I do not know how) bring in their train the most
terrifying of revolutions?

15 This speech was delivered in the debate on the Address in reply to the
Speech from the Throne. *Le Moniteur* was, as it had been before and was
after, the official organ of the régime, and all the debates of the two
Chambers were reported in full in its columns. Tocqueville is slightly inaccurate here as to the date of his speech. He in fact delivered it on
27 January 1848, and the text is to be found in *Le Moniteur* of the
28th. (Ed.)

Gentlemen, my profound conviction is that we are lulling ourselves
to sleep over an active volcano . . .

. . . I was saying just now that sooner or later (I do not know
when or whence) this ill will bring into the land revolutions of the
utmost seriousness: be assured that that is so.

When I come to study what has been, at different times and
epochs of history among different peoples, the effective reason why
ruling classes have been ruined, I note the various events and men
and accidental or superficial causes, but believe me, the real cause,
the effective one, that makes men lose power is that they have become unworthy to exercise it.

Consider the old Monarchy, gentlemen. It was stronger than you,
stronger because of its origin; it was better supported than you are
by ancient customs, old mores and old beliefs; it was stronger than
you, and yet it has fallen in the dust. And why did it fall? Do you
think that it was because of some particular accident? Do you think
it was due to one particular man, the deficit, the Tennis Court Oath,[16]
La Fayette or Mirabeau? No, gentlemen, there is another cause: the
class that was ruling then had, through its indifference, selfishness
and vices, become incapable and unworthy of ruling.

That is the real reason.

Gentlemen, feelings of patriotism should preoccupy us at all times,
but now more than ever. Have you no intuitive instinct, incapable
of being analyzed but certain, that tells you the ground is trembling
once more in Europe? Do you not feel—how should I say it—a revolutionary wind in the air? We do not know whence it comes, or
whither it goes, or what it will carry away; and at such a time you
remain calm in face of the degradation of public mores—for the expression is not too strong.

I am speaking here without bitterness, and I even trust that I am
speaking without party feeling; I am attacking men against whom
I feel no anger, but I am bound to disclose to my country my deep
and firm conviction. And that profound and fixed conviction is that
public mores are becoming degraded, and that this degradation will
lead you shortly, very shortly perhaps, into new revolutions. Are the
lives of kings supported by stronger threads, which are harder to
snap, than the lives of other men? Have you at this very moment
any certainty of the morrow? Do you know what may happen in

16 The so-called Tennis Court Oath was that taken on 20 June 1789
by every member of the newly constituted National Assembly, to unite and
to remain united until a constitution had been established. Working on
this project over the next two years, the Constituent Assembly, as it came
to be called, produced the Constitution of 1791, France's first attempt to
establish a constitutional monarchy, which lasted only a few months. The
Jeu de Paume, where the oath was taken, was a covered tennis court at
the château of Versailles. (Ed.)

France a year, a month, or perhaps a day from now? You do not know that, but you do know there is a tempest on the horizon, and it is moving towards you. Will you let it take you by surprise?

Gentlemen, I implore you not to do so; I do not ask, I implore. I would gladly go down on my knees before you, so real and serious do I think the danger, and so persuaded am I that it is no idle rhetorical flourish to point it out. Yes, the danger is great. Avert it while there is yet time; cure the ill with effective remedies, attacking the thing itself and not its symptoms.

There has been talk of legislative changes. I am very much inclined to believe that such changes are not only useful, but necessary: hence I consider electoral reform useful, and parliamentary reform necessary; but, gentlemen, I am not so mad as to be unaware that the destinies of people are not shaped by laws alone. No, gentlemen, great events do not spring from the mechanism of the laws, but from the very spirit of the government. Keep those laws if you like—keep them, though I think you would be making a great mistake—even keep the same men if that gives you any pleasure; but for God's sake change the spirit of the government, for, I repeat, it is the spirit that is leading you to the abyss.[17]

These sombre prophecies were received with insulting laughter by the majority. The opposition applauded energetically, but from party spirit rather than conviction. The truth is that no one yet seriously believed in the danger I foretold, although we

[17] It is significant that the complete text of this speech was appended to the thirteenth edition of *Democracy in America* by Tocqueville himself. This was the last edition to appear in his lifetime (Paris, 1850). It can be found appended to this work in the *Oeuvres Complètes* I. 2, pp. 368–79 (ed. J. P. Mayer, Paris, 1961). It may also be found in the George Lawrence translation pp. 722–30 (ed. J. P. Mayer and Max Lerner, New York, 1966). The passages quoted here have been added by the first editor of the *Recollections*, Count de Tocqueville in 1893. The manuscript of the *Recollections* gives at this point only a dotted line.

Since Tocqueville is critical of Thiers throughout these *Recollections*, it is worth noting Thiers' reaction to this speech, described by Rémusat in volume IV of his memoirs, p. 181, and his own view of relations between the two men—a view in part borne out in the *Recollections:* "I remember that this speech of Tocqueville upset Thiers. Being a fair and generous man, Thiers could not stomach overmuch talk of corruption. He remembered having been grossly slandered himself and suspected that those who took up the cause of offended morality were hypocrites. While Tocqueville was speaking, Thiers said to me 'He's a nasty man,' and, to back up his statement, pointed to the pallor of poor Tocqueville's complexion—and indeed he looked painfully sick. Thiers' mistake was great, and he has now changed his tune. At that time, however, he and Tocqueville had little to do with each other, and were not, I think, each without prejudice against the other." (Ed.)

were so near the brink.[18] Every politician had, during the long
parliamentary comedy, contracted an inveterate habit of colour-
ing the expression of his feelings outrageously and exaggerating
his thoughts out of all proportion, and in this way they had become unable to appreciate the real and the true. For several years
the majority had been saying that the opposition was endanger-
ing society, and the opposition had been constantly repeating
that the Ministers were ruining the Monarchy. Both sides had
asserted these things so often, without believing them very much,
that in the end they came not to believe them at all, just at
the moment when events were about to prove them both right.
Even my personal friends thought that a bit of rhetoric was
mixed with my facts.[19]

I recall that as I came down from the tribune, Dufaure[20]
took me to one side and said with the parliamentary intuition
that was his sole claim to genius: "You succeeded. But you
would have succeeded even better if you had not overshot the
feeling of the Assembly so much and tried to make us so
frightened." And now that I am here face to face with myself
and inquisitively searching my memory to see if I was as afraid
as I seemed to be, I find that I was not; and I clearly see that
the event justified me more promptly and completely than I
had foreseen.[21] No, I did not expect such a revolution as we

18 Tocqueville was not the only one to foresee dangers for the régime in
the climate of opinion prevalent among the underprivileged classes of
French society. For a similar, although not identical opinion, see Rémusat's
memoirs, vol. IV, pp. 164–66. (Ed.)

19 That I had overshot the mark and: *words marked for omission.*

20 Jules Dufaure (1798–1881), a lawyer from Bordeaux, he was deputy
of the Charente-Inférieure from 1834 to 1848, and was Minister of Public
Works in the Soult cabinet of May 1839 to March 1840. He belonged, as
did Tocqueville, to the small independent group of deputies who politically
were situated between Thiers' left-centre group and the dynastic left led
by Odilon Barrot. He rallied to the Second Republic and was a representative in both assemblies. He became Minister of the Interior in Cavaignac's provisional government, and supported Cavaignac's bid to become
President of the Republic. He, however, accepted office, again as Minister
of the Interior, in the second Barrot cabinet which was formed after the
election of Louis Napoleon Bonaparte as President. For a complete account
of Dufaure's political career, see G. Picot, M. Dufaure, sa vie et ses discours,
Paris, 1883. (Ed.)

21 Which has perhaps happened to other political prophets with better
credentials than I for foretelling the future: *sentence marked for omission.*

were going to have; who could have expected it? I think I did see clearer than the next man the general causes that tilted the July Monarchy towards its ruin. But I did not see the accidents that were to topple it over. However, the days that still separated us from the catastrophe slipped away fast.

The Banquets – Sense of security entertained by the Government – Anxiety of the Leaders of the Opposition – Arraignment of Ministers

I did not want to get involved in the excitement about the banquets.[1] I had both trivial and serious reasons for keeping away; some of these trivial reasons I frankly admit were bad, though honourable, and, if it had been a private matter, excellent —I mean my irritation at and distaste for the character and manoeuvres of those conducting the business; for I admit that one's private feelings about men are a bad guide in politics.

At that time M. Thiers[2] and M. Barrot[3] had just formed a

---

[1] This was the name given to the campaign for electoral and parliamentary reform of 1847–48. The campaign took the form of banquets, in order to avoid suppression by the authorities as an infringement of the law limiting public assembly. The campaign opened with a banquet in Paris on 9 July 1847; subsequently, banquets were held in some of the larger provincial towns, and the campaign was to have culminated in the Paris banquet of 22 February 1848. The campaign was organized by members of all the opposition nuances, but a preponderant influence was exercised by Ledru-Rollin and the radical opposition. This led to the campaign's adopting an increasingly radical and republican tone, which the various groups of constitutional opposition were powerless to prevent. (Ed.)

[2] Louis Adolphe Thiers (1797–1877), journalist, historian and politician, he began his career as a journalist under the Restoration. He contributed largely to *Le National*, established as a weapon against the reactionary policies of Charles X in 1830, and it was in this organ that his well-known aphorism "Le roi règne et ne gouverne pas" (The king reigns and does not govern) was first stated. He was instrumental in gaining the consent of the Duke of Orleans (later King Louis-Philippe) to take advantage of the situation created by the July revolution of 1830. He headed the cabinet

close alliance, that brought about a fusion between the two
fragments of the opposition that in our political jargon we call
the left centre and the left. Almost all of the many stubborn,
intractable spirits in the latter party had been tamed, soothed
and made pliable; each in turn was softened by M. Thiers' lavish
promises of offices. I even believe that, for the first time, M. Barrot allowed himself not exactly to be captured, but to be taken
off his guard by arguments of this type. At any rate, whatever
the reason, the closest intimacy linked the two great leaders
of the opposition, and M. Barrot, who is pleased to mix a touch of
silliness with his weaknesses and his virtues, did his best to secure
his ally's triumph even at his own expense. M. Thiers had allowed
him to get involved in the business of the banquets (I think he
may even have pushed him into it without getting entangled
himself) because he was eager to have the result of this danger-

of October 1832, together with Guizot and Broglie. He subsequently
formed two cabinets, one in 1836, the other in 1840, but in each case was
forced to resign after disagreement with the King, who disapproved of
Thiers' energetic handling of foreign affairs. From 1840 onwards, Thiers
led his own left-centre group in opposition to Guizot and was not called
upon by Louis-Philippe to form a cabinet until the monarchy was *in
extremis*. During the Second Republic, he adopted a more conservative
attitude, and supported the candidature of Louis Napoleon Bonaparte to
the presidency of the Republic, but he was one of those imprisoned and
then exiled after the coup d'état of December 1851. His writings include
two monumental histories—*Histoire de la Révolution* (Paris, 1823–27), and
Histoire du Consulat et de l'Empire (Paris, 1845–62). (Ed.)

3 Odilon Barrot (1791–1873), a member of the Paris bar, he took a prominent part in the July revolution of 1830 as a member of the National
Guard. Throughout the July Monarchy he was a leading member of the
dynastic left, supporting a policy that united a desire for reform, particularly
a wider franchise, with a determination to remain within the framework
of the constitution, to maintain the constitutional monarchy. He played a
leading part in the banquet campaign of 1847–48. When the 1848 revolution broke out, he attempted to rally support for the regency of the
Duchess of Orleans during the minority of the Count of Paris, her
eldest son. This attempt proving fruitless, he rallied to the Second Republic.
He formed his first ministry in December 1848, and his second, in which
Tocqueville became Minister of Foreign Affairs, in June 1849. This second
ministry lasted only until the 31st October of the same year. Barrot's own
view on his career may be found in his four volume *Mémoires Posthumes*,
edited by Duvergier de Hauranne, Paris, 1875–76. See also C. Alméras,
Odilon Barrot, Avocat et Homme Politique (1791–1873) Paris, 1951, which
has an important bibliography. (Ed.)

ous agitation, but not the responsibility for it. He himself stayed quietly in Paris surrounded by his friends, while Barrot spent three months going up and down the country alone, giving long speeches in every town he stopped at and, to my mind, acting like a beater who makes a great noise to drive the game within easy reach of the hunter in the covert. I felt little inclination to join that shoot. But the main reason that held me back was the one that I kept expounding to all who tried to drag me to political meetings:

"For the first time in eighteen years," I used to say, "you are going out to speak to the people and to seek support outside the middle class; if you do not succeed in working up a popular agitation (which seems to me the most probable result), you will make yourselves even more odious than you already are in the eyes of the government and of the middle class, most of which supports the government, and thus you will reinforce the administration you wish to overthrow; if, however, you do start a popular agitation, you have no more idea than I have where it will take you."

As the campaign for the banquets dragged on, the second hypothesis, contrary to my expectation, became the more likely. Even the leaders began to feel some anxiety, but it was only a vague foreboding that crossed their minds without taking root. I was told by Beaumont,[4] who was then one of the main leaders, that the agitation in the country about the banquets surpassed

[4] Gustave de Beaumont (1802–66), Tocqueville's close friend and his companion on the latter's journey to America in 1831. He was elected deputy for the Sarthe in 1839, and, like Tocqueville and Dufaure, was a member of the intermediary group of independent deputies between the left-centre and the dynastic left. Elected representative to both assemblies of the Second Republic, he was appointed ambassador to London by Cavaignac in August 1848—giving up the post on the election of Louis Napoleon Bonaparte as President of the Republic. He was appointed ambassador to Vienna in 1849, but resigned on the dismissal of the second Barrot cabinet on 29 October 1849. His diplomatic career was definitively cut short by the coup d'état of December 1851. On his return from America, he published two works, *Le Système Pénitentiaire aux États-Unis,* in collaboration with Tocqueville, in 1833, and *Marie, ou l'Esclavage aux États-Unis,* in 1835. He later published *L'Irlande sociale, politique et religieuse,* in 1839 and 1842, very probably his most important work. Beaumont's complete correspondence with Tocqueville is now available in the Tocqueville *Oeuvres Complètes* (ed. J. P. Mayer) VIII, 1, 2, 3, Paris, 1966. (Ed.)

not only the expectations, but also the desires of those who had started it; they began to work more to calm than to increase it. They did not intend to have a banquet in Paris and did not want to have any anywhere after the Chambers had been convened. Actually they were trying to find some escape from the bad road down which they had started. Certainly the decision to hold the final banquet was against their wishes; they were associated with it only under constraint, because the matter was already in progress and, especially, because their vanity was compromised. The government, too, by its defiance, pushed the opposition into this dangerous proceeding, hoping to lead it to destruction. Bravado and unwillingness to retreat carried the opposition forward, with the government urging and goading it on; in this way both sides pressed towards the common abyss and reached it without even then seeing where they were going.[5]

Two days before the February revolution I recall meeting Duvergier de Hauranne[6] at a great ball given by the Turkish Ambassador. I had a real esteem and affection for him; although he had almost every defect that party spirit can inspire, he also had at least a kind of disinterestedness and sincerity such as one finds when passions are true, and these are rare advantages in our day when one hardly ever finds a true passion except for a man's self. With a familiarity warranted by our friendship, I said to him: "Courage, dear friend, you are playing

[5] *Marginal note* (*Tocqueville*): Here some details about the simultaneous movement of government and opposition towards the abyss, each *goading* and pushing the other. Look up the *Moniteur.*

[6] Prosper Duvergier de Hauranne (1798–1881), political journalist, distinguished historian, and politician. He was deputy for the Cher during the July Monarchy. Like his friend Rémusat, he upheld conservative policies up to 1840 when he supported the formation of Thiers' second cabinet and thereafter was an active member of the left-centre group until 1848. He proposed in 1847 a measure of electoral reform, which would have brought about a marginal increase in the franchise, and was one of the prime movers in the banquets campaign, unlike other prominent members of the left-centre. He was elected to both assemblies of the Second Republic, but his political career came to an end with the coup d'état of December 1851. Apart from other works, he was the author of an *Histoire du Gouvernement Parlementaire en France 1814–1848*, 10 vols., Paris, 1857–72. A work of primary importance, it deals with the history of parliamentary government up to 1830. (Ed.)

a dangerous role." To which he answered gravely, but without any trace of fear: "Believe me, all this will come out all right; besides one must risk something. No free government has escaped such tests." This answer gives an accurate impression of that resolute but limited man. For although he was very intelligent, he was limited; his intellect could clearly see each detail on its horizon, but could not imagine that the horizon might change. He was learned, disinterested, ardent, bilious and vindictive, a member of that scholarly clique that regulates its politics by imitating past examples and by its historical memory, confining its thought to a single idea, which both warms and blinds it.

Moreover, the government was even less uneasy than the opposition leaders. A few days before this conversation, I had had another with Duchâtel, the Minister of the Interior. I was on good terms with him in spite of the fact that for eight years I had carried on lively warfare (even, I confess, too lively where foreign affairs were concerned) against the administration of which he was one of the leaders. It could be that this error of mine helped me with him, for I think that in the depths of his heart he had a soft spot for those who attacked his colleague at the Ministry of Foreign Affairs, M. Guizot.[7] Some years before M. Duchâtel and I had made common cause supporting the penitentiary system, and that had brought us together and established a sort of bond between us. He bore no resemblance to the other man I just mentioned; his person and his manners were as eupeptic as those of the other were dyspeptic, angular, bitter and cutting. In him, ample scepticism took the place of the other's ardent convictions, and soft indifference, the other's feverish activity. Within his heavy body, his mind was supple, shrewd and subtle, and while he talked condescendingly about business, he actually understood it very well. He was well acquainted with the stuff of men's evil passions, especially those of his own party, and always knew how to play on them. He had no prejudices or spite and was warm

[7] For further details on Guizot see D. Johnson, *Guizot. Aspects of French History 1787–1874*, London, 1963—the standard work on Guizot, with a valuable bibliography. (Ed.)

and easy and ready to oblige when it was not against his own interest. He had the full measure of both contempt and good-will for his fellow men. In short, a man whom one could neither esteem nor hate.

A few days before the catastrophe, I took M. Duchâtel to one side in a corner of the conference room and told him the government and the opposition seemed to be working together to push things to an extreme that might harm everyone; I asked him if he could find some good way out of such an annoying situation, some honourable arrangement that would allow each side to retreat. I added that my friends and I would be very happy to be shown such a path and would do our best to persuade our colleagues in the opposition to accept it. He listened attentively and assured me that he understood my meaning, but I could see that he had not got my point. Things, he said, had reached such a point that one could not find the expedient I was seeking—the government was within its rights and could not yield; if the opposition persisted in its course, there might be a fight in the streets, but such a fight had been long foreseen, and, if the government was animated by the evil passions attributed to it, it would desire rather than fear such a struggle, since it would be assured of success. He then went on complacently to tell me the details of all the military measures that had been taken, the extent of their resources, the number of the troops, the stores of munitions . . . I left him convinced that the government, without actually trying to stir up a rising, was far from fearing one, and that the administration, assured of victory, saw the trouble brewing as perhaps its last chance to rally its scattered friends and reduce its enemies to impotence. I confess that I thought as he did: his unfeigned assurance had infected me.

The only people in Paris who were really worried at that time were the radical leaders and those sufficiently near the people and the revolutionary party to know what was going on. I have reason to believe that most of them did fear the oncoming troubles, perhaps because for them the passions of the past were traditions, not feelings; or perhaps because they were getting accustomed to a state of affairs in which, after cursing it so often, they had taken a position; or perhaps because they doubted success; or, more probably, because, having a close view of their allies and knowing them well, they were afraid at this decisive moment of the victory, of what they would owe to them. On the very eve of the outbreak, Madame de Lamartine called on Madame de Tocqueville in such an extraordinary state of anxiety—excited and almost deranged by such sinister thoughts—that the latter became alarmed and told me of it the same evening.

One of the oddest features of this singular revolution was that the incident that started it was brought about and almost desired by those who were to be ousted from power, and it was only the future victors who foresaw and feared it.

At this point I had better recapitulate the historical sequence, so that I can more easily fit my personal memories around it.

It will be remembered that in his speech from the throne at the opening of the session of 1848, King Louis-Philippe described the sponsors of the banquets as men animated by "blind" or "hostile" passions.[8] This put the Throne into direct conflict with more than a hundred members of the Chamber. Such an insult added anger to all the other ambitious passions seething in most of their hearts, and so made them lose their senses. A violent debate was expected, but it did not take place at once. The first speeches answering the Address were calm, both the government side and the opposition held themselves back at first, like two men who know they have lost their tempers and so are afraid of doing or saying something silly.

But in the end passion broke through, bursting out with unusual violence. For anyone who could sniff the scent of revolution from afar, the unaccustomed fire of the debate was already a foretaste of civil war.

Speakers for the moderate opposition were led by the heat of the argument to assert that the right of assembly at the banquets was one of the most assured and necessary of rights[9]; that to

[8] Louis-Philippe's last speech from the throne was delivered on 28 December 1847. (Ed.)
[9] See the speech of M. Duvergier de Hauranne, 7 February 1848. (Note of the Editor of the 1893 edition)

dispute it was to tread liberty itself under foot and to violate the Charter—not seeing that by talking in this manner they were unintentionally making an appeal not to argument but to arms. M. Duchâtel on his side, though usually very adroit, in these circumstances showed consummate clumsiness.[10] He absolutely denied the right to assemble at any banquet, but did not at the same time state clearly that the government had decided to prevent any such demonstration; on the contrary, he seemed to invite the opposition to risk it again, so that the matter could be tested in the Courts. His colleague at the Ministry of Justice, M. Hébert, was even clumsier, but that was usual with him. I have always observed that magistrates can never become politicians, but I have never met one who was less of a politician than M. Hébert; on becoming a minister he remained attorney general to the marrow of his bones, and he had the icy character and face for it. You must picture a narrow, shrunk, weasel face compressed at the temples; forehead, nose and chin all pointed; cold, bright eyes and narrow, drawn-in lips; add to this a long quill usually held across his mouth, which at a distance looked just like a cat's bristling whiskers, and you have the portrait of a man more like a carnivorous animal than any other I have seen. Nevertheless he was not stupid or even spiteful, he simply had a stiff, ill-articulated mind, with no tact to bend or turn in time, so that he would tumble into violent acts without meaning to, because he did not grasp the nuances. M. Guizot cannot have cared much about conciliation if he put that speaker forward on such an occasion[11]; his language was so exaggerated and provocative that Barrot, beside himself and scarcely knowing what he did, cried in a voice stifled with rage that Charles X's

10 The Minister replied to M. Léon de Malleville. He invoked the laws of 1790 and 1791, which empowered the authorities to oppose any public meetings that seemed to threaten public order; quoting precedents, he declared that the government in doing its duty would not give way before demonstrations of any description. At the end of his speech he again used the words "blind or hostile passions" and attempted to justify them. (Note of the Editor of the 1893 edition)

11 Replying to M. Odilon Barrot, M. Hébert maintained that, since the right of public meeting was not laid down in the Charter, it did not exist. (Note of the Editor of the 1893 edition)

ministers, Polignac and Peyronnet,[12] had never dared to talk
like that. I could not help shuddering as I sat there in my
place, when I heard this normally moderate man exasperated
into bringing back, for the first time, the terrible memories of
the 1830 revolution, in a sense holding it up as an example
and involuntarily suggesting it be imitated.

We all know that this heated debate ended in a sort of
challenge to a duel between the government and the opposition
with the rendez-vous in the Courts. It was tacitly agreed that
the opposition should hold one last banquet, and that the authorities, without preventing its assembly, should prosecute the
sponsors in the Courts, leaving them to decide.

The debates on the Address ended, if I remember correctly,
on the 12th February, and it was really from that moment that
the revolutionary movement burst out. From that day on, the
constitutional opposition, which had for some months past been
pushed forward by the Radical party, was directed and led by
that party. And the leaders were not so much the members of
that party in the Chamber (most of whom had cooled off
and become enervated in the atmosphere of Parliament), as
younger, bolder and less responsible men writing for the demagogic press. The change affected two matters that influenced
events predominantly: the programme for the banquet and the
impeachment of ministers.[13]

On the 20th February almost all the opposition newspapers
published a programme for the forthcoming banquet, which was
really a proclamation calling on the schools and the National
Guard itself to attend the ceremony as a body.[14] One might
have taken it for a decree of the Provisional Government, which

[12] Jules de Polignac (1780–1847), and Charles de Peyronnet (1778–
1854), respectively Prime Minister and Keeper of the Seals (*Garde des
Sceaux*) in the last ministry of Charles X's reign, were generally considered
to represent reactionary ideas more forcibly than the other members of
the cabinet who signed. with Charles X, the ordinances of 25 July 1830,
which, in dissolving the newly elected Chamber of Deputies, reducing
the franchise, and re-establishing press censorship, brought about the downfall of the Restoration. (Ed.)
[13] *Marginal note (Tocqueville)*: This should be checked.
[14] *Marginal note (Tocqueville)*: (Is that the date?)—look all this up in
the newspapers of the time.

was formed three days later. The administration, already under criticism from many of its supporters for tacitly allowing the banquet, now felt justified in changing course and officially announced that it forbade the banquet and would prevent it by force.

It was this declaration by the government that provided the battlefield. I am in a position to state that, incredible though it may seem, this programme, which instantly turned the banquet into a rebellion, was composed, approved and published without the help and against the will of the parliamentarians who imagined that they still led the movement they had created. The programme was hastily drafted at night by a meeting of journalists and radicals, and the leaders of the dynastic opposition, like the rest of the public, learned about it when they woke the next morning.

See how human affairs are pushed forward on the rebound. M. Barrot, who was as critical of the programme as anyone, dared not disavow it for fear of offending those who, until then, had been marching with him; and when the government, frightened by the publication of this document, forbade the banquet, M. Barrot, finding himself faced by civil war, retreated. He withdrew from the dangerous demonstration; but while making this concession to moderate opinion, he allowed the extremists to impeach the Ministers. He accused the latter of violating the Constitution by forbidding the banquet, thus providing an excuse for those who were ready to take up arms in defence of the violated Constitution.

Consequently the leaders of the radical party, who considered a revolution premature and did not want one yet, felt obliged, in order to make some distinction between themselves and their allies of the dynastic opposition, to speak in revolutionary terms at the banquets and fan the flames of insurrection. The dynastic opposition on its part, though it wanted no more banquets, was also forced to follow this unfortunate path in order not to appear to retreat before the government's threats. Finally, the mass of Conservatives, who thought that great concessions must be made and were ready to make them, were led by the violence of their adversaries and the passions of some of their leaders to deny

even the right to assemble at private banquets, and to refuse
the country any hope of reform whatsoever.[15]

One has to have spent long years in the whirlwind of party
politics to realize how far men drive each other from their intended courses, and how the world's fate is moved by their
efforts, but often in opposite directions from the wishes of those
who produced the current, like a kite which flies by the opposing action of the wind and the string.

[15] *Marginal note (Tocqueville) at the head of this paragraph:* Perhaps to be placed elsewhere.

CHAPTER THREE

Troubles of the 22nd February — The Sitting of the 23rd — The New Ministry — Opinions of M. Dufaure and M. de Beaumont

There was nothing to cause me serious alarm on the morning of the 22nd. The streets were packed with people, but they seemed more prone to gape and jeer than to rebel. Soldier and civilian made good-natured quips when they met, and there were more jokes than outcries from the crowd. I know one must not trust appearances too far. It is the street urchins of Paris who generally start rebellions, and they usually do so gaily, like schoolboys off for the holidays.

The Chamber, when I returned there, was apparently impassive, but under the surface one sensed the seething of a thousand repressed passions. It was the only place that morning where I heard no open talk about the things that then preoccupied the whole of France. There was a listless discussion about starting a bank at Bordeaux, but only the speaker and the member who was to reply were paying any attention to it. M. Duchâtel told me that everything was going very well. His manner seemed simultaneously assured and worried, which struck me as suspicious. I observed that he was twisting his neck and shoulders, which was a nervous habit with him, much more violently and frequently than usual, and I remember that this small observation gave me more food for thought than anything else.

I learned that there had been serious trouble in several places I had not visited; a certain number of men had been killed and wounded. At that time, one was not used to such incidents, as one had been a few years before and was to be, even more, a few months later, and the excitement was great.

I was invited to dine that evening at the house of a fellow member of the opposition in Parliament, M. Paulmier, the deputy for Calvados. I had some difficulty in reaching his house because of the troops who were still guarding the streets. I found the house in great disorder; Madame Paulmier, who was pregnant and who had been frightened by a skirmish beneath her window, had gone to bed. It was a splendid meal, but the dinner table was deserted; only five of the twenty invited guests appeared; either physical obstacles or the day's worries kept the rest away. And it was a pensive party that sat down to that pointless plenty. I felt we were living in strange times when one was never sure, between ordering and eating one's dinner, whether a revolution might not intervene. Among the guests was M. Sallandrouze, the heir of the great business house of that name, which has grown so rich manufacturing textiles. M. Sallandrouze was one of those young conservatives, more notable for their money than their distinction, who occasionally made some show of opposition, or rather criticism, chiefly, I think, to call attention to themselves. In the final debate on the Address, this man had proposed an amendment[1] which would have compromised the cabinet if it had been adopted. Just when this incident was most in men's minds, M. Sallandrouze went to a reception at the Tuileries, hoping that this time at least he would not be unnoticed in the crowd. And indeed, as soon as King Louis-Philippe saw him, he approached him with an air of eagerness, and, pointedly taking him aside, he at once started talking with warm interest about the branch of industry that

[1] M. Sallandrouze de Lamornaix' amendment proposed to modify the expression "blind or hostile passions" by adding the words: "Amid these various demonstrations, your government will know how to recognize the real and lawful desires of the country; it will, we trust, take the initiative by introducing certain wise and moderate reforms called for by public opinion, among which we must place parliamentary reform. In a Constitutional Monarchy, the union of the great powers of the State removes all danger from a progressive policy, and allows every moral and material interest of the country to be satisfied." (Note of the Editor of the 1893 edition)

brought the young deputy his fortune. The latter was not at first surprised, thinking that the King, who was clever at managing men, had chosen this private path to reach great affairs by a short detour. But he was mistaken, for after a quarter of an hour the King changed not the subject, but the person addressed, leaving our friend all in a muddle with his woollen goods and carpets. Sallandrouze had still not got over the trick played on him, but he was beginning to be very much afraid that he would be too well avenged. He told us that the day before M. Émile Girardin had said to him: "In two days the July Monarchy will be no more." We all took that for a journalist's hyperbole, as perhaps it was, but events turned it into an oracle.

The next day, the 23rd February, I heard when I got up that the agitation in Paris was not dying down, but growing worse. I went early to the Chamber. Silence reigned there; the approaches were occupied and closed by battalions of infantry, while squadrons of cuirassiers were drawn up beside the palace walls. Inside there was a feeling of excitement without any clear cause.

The sitting had opened at the ordinary time, but the Assembly, unwilling to repeat the parliamentary comedy of the day before, had suspended its business; it listened to reports of incidents in the town, awaited events and counted the hours in feverish idleness. At one moment a loud blare of trumpets was heard outside. We soon learned that cuirassiers guarding the building had been amusing themselves by sounding fanfares. These joyful notes of triumph contrasted so bitterly with the secret thoughts of the deputies that a hasty stop was put to the unwelcome, tactless music, for it had the painful effect of making each man face himself.

Eventually a decision was made to talk out loud about things everybody had been discussing in whispers for several hours. A Paris deputy, M. Vavin, began to question the Cabinet about the state of the city. It was three o'clock when M. Guizot appeared at the door of the House. He entered with his firmest step and haughtiest bearing, silently crossed the gangway and mounted the tribune, almost throwing his head over backwards for fear of seeming to bow it; in two words he announced that the King had entrusted M. Molé with the formation of a new government. I have never seen such a piece of melodrama.

The opposition remained seated, most of them uttering cries of victory and satisfied vengeance. Only the leaders kept silent, turning over in their minds what use they could make of this triumph and being careful not to insult a majority on whom they might soon have to rely. The majority, struck by such an unexpected blow, trembled like an oscillating weight which may fall on either side; then the members tumbled down tumultuously into the semicircle, some crowding round the ministers, seeking further information or paying their last respects, but most of them raising their voices to insult them. "To leave the government and abandon your political friends in such circumstances is," they said, "a piece of gross cowardice." Others shouted that they must go in a body to the Tuileries and force the King to go back on such a fatal decision. There was nothing surprising in such despair when one remembers that, for most of these men, it was not only their political opinions but also the most sensitive of their private interests that were struck down. The overthrow of the Ministry put the whole of one man's fortune in danger, another risked losing his daughter's dowry, and yet another feared for his son's career. It was such considerations that held almost all of them. Most of them had not only bettered themselves by supporting the government, one might say they had lived by it; they still were living by it, and they hoped to go on doing so, for since the government had lasted eight years, people had become accustomed to the idea of its going on forever, and it inspired much the same honest, tranquil fondness one feels for one's own lands. I watched this agitated crowd from my seat and saw the mixture of astonishment, anger, fear and greed that came and went over their frightened faces; in my private thoughts I compared them to a pack of hounds whose prey has been snatched from their half-full mouths.

One must admit that a great many members of the opposition would, if put to a like test, have shown up as badly. While many Conservatives defended the Ministry only in order to keep their salaries and positions, many of the opposition, I think, attacked only to gain these. The deplorable truth is that a taste for jobs and a life at the public expense is not, with us, confined to any single party, but is the great and permanent weakness of the nation itself; it is the combined effect of the democratic constitution of our civic society and the excessive centralization of our government. This is the hidden illness that has gnawed away every ancient authority, and will do the same to all others in the future.[2]

In the end the riot calmed down. It became clearer what had happened: one battalion of the fifth legion had shown rebellious inclinations, and a direct appeal to the King by several high-ranking officers of that guard had started it.

As soon as he knew what was happening, King Louis-Philippe, who could change his opinions less, but his conduct more easily than any man I have ever known, immediately came to a decision, and the Ministry, after eight years of complacency, found itself dismissed in two minutes without ceremony or polite phrases.

The Assembly broke up without delay, each man thinking about the change of ministry, forgetting the revolution.

I went out of the Chamber with M. Dufaure; I saw at once that he was constrained as well as preoccupied; clearly he was in the critical and complicated position of an opposition leader about to become a minister who, conscious of the help his friends have been to him in the past, begins to consider the embarrassment their pretensions may cause him in the future.

There was a slightly sly turn to M. Dufaure's mind which made it easy for him to entertain such thoughts, and a sort of natural homeliness combined with integrity that made it almost impossible for him to conceal them. Besides he was the most sincere and by far the worthiest of those who then stood a chance of becoming minister. But believing that power lay within his reach, he longed for it with a passion all the more intense because it was suppressed and discreet. In his place, M. Molé

2 *Marginal note* (*Tocqueville*)—*Variant:* it has gnawed away like an internal illness . . . it had gnawed the government away from within . . . inside, while leaving it its outward form. Until was nothing but façade (sic)

would have felt much more egotism and ingratitude, *but* his manner would have been much more open and agreeable.

I left him soon and went to M. de Beaumont's, where I found every heart rejoicing. I was far from sharing their joy and, being with people to whom I could speak freely, gave my reasons. "The National Guard of Paris," I said, "has just destroyed a cabinet; therefore the new ministers will conduct affairs subject to its good pleasure. You are delighted that the Ministry is overthrown, but don't you see that it is authority itself that lies on the ground?" Beaumont had no taste for this gloomy view.[3] "You always see the black side of everything," he told me. "Let us enjoy our victory first, and worry about the consequences later."

Madame de Beaumont,[4] who was present, seemed to share completely her husband's elation, which was the clearest proof I have ever seen of the irresistible power of party spirit. For self-interest and hatred were foreign to the nature of this distinguished and attractive lady who was one of the most truly and consistently virtuous people I have ever known, and one moreover who made virtue something touching and delightful.[5]

I nonetheless continued to press my thesis against her, maintaining that, all in all, the incident was unfortunate, or rather that it was more than an incident, indeed something that would change the whole face of affairs. I felt free to philosophize in this manner, for I did not share my friend Dufaure's illusions. I thought the political machine had been given too violent a jolt for power to remain in the hands of the intermediate party to which I belonged, and I foresaw that it would slip into hands almost as hostile to me as those who had lost it.

I was dining with another friend, M. Lanjuinais, of whom I shall have much to say later on; it was a fairly large party and politically very mixed; several of the guests were delighted at

[3] The words "bitterness and ambition carried him away" follow here in the first edition. They do not occur in the manuscript, but two lines in the margin have been blocked out and cannot be read. (Ed.)

[4] Gustave de Beaumont had married Clémentine de Lafayette, the General's granddaughter, in June 1836. (Ed.)

[5] "With the La Fayettes' nobility of heart, she had a mind that was acute, refined, kindly and fair": those words in the manuscript have been marked for omission. Several lines have also been blocked out. (Ed.)

the day's doings, while others were alarmed; but they all thought that the rebellious movement would stop of its own accord, to break out again elsewhere and in another form. All the rumours reaching us from town seemed to confirm this belief; shouts of joy were replacing war cries. Portalis, who was to become Attorney General of Paris a few days later, was one of the party, the nephew, not the son, of the first president of the Court of Appeal. This Portalis had neither his uncle's brains and exemplary mores, nor his platitudinous piety. His coarse, violent, cross-grained mind readily absorbed every false idea and extreme opinion current in our day. In spite of links with most of those who were later said to be the authors and leaders of the Revolution of 1848, I can testify that on that evening he did not expect the revolution any more than the rest of us. I am convinced that even at that supreme hour the same could be said of most of his friends. It is a waste of time to seek secret conspiracies that bring about such events. Usually revolutions brought about by the emotions of the mob have been desired, but not premeditated. Those who boast of conspiracies have done no more than take advantage of them. They spring spontaneously from some general malady of men's minds suddenly brought to a crisis by an unforeseen chance incident. And those who claim to be the originators and leaders of these revolutions do not originate or lead anything; their sole merit is identical with that of the adventurers who have discovered most of the unknown lands, namely the courage to go straight ahead while the wind blows.

I took my leave early and went straight to bed. Though my house was quite near the Foreign Office, I did not hear the firing which so greatly changed our fate, and I went to sleep unaware that I had seen the last day of the July Monarchy.

CHAPTER FOUR

*The 24th February – The Ministers' Plan of Resistance
– The National Guard – General Bedeau*

As I left my bedroom the next day, the 24th February, I met
the cook who had been out; the good woman was quite beside
herself and poured out a sorrowful rigmarole from which I could
understand nothing but that the government was having the
poor people massacred. I went down at once, and as soon as
I had set foot in the street I could for the first time scent revolution in the air: the middle of the street was empty; the shops
were not open; there were no carriages, or people walking; one
heard none of the usual street vendors' cries; little frightened
groups of neighbours talked by the doors in lowered voices;
anxiety or anger disfigured every face. I met one of the National
Guard hurrying along, rifle in hand, with an air of tragedy. I
spoke to him but could learn nothing save that the government
was massacring the people (to which he added that the National
Guard would know how to put that right). It was always the
same refrain which, of course, explained nothing to me. I knew
the vices of the July government all too well, and cruelty was
not among them. I consider it to have been one of the most
corrupt, but least bloodthirsty, that has ever existed, and I repeat that rumour only to show how such rumours help revolutions
along.

I hurried to M. de Beaumont's house in the next street and
learned that the King had summoned him during the night. I
was told the same at M. de Rémusat's where I called next. Fi-

nally I met M. de Corcelle who gave me an account of what was happening; but it was a confused account, for in a city during a revolution, as on a battlefield, each man tends to accept what he has seen himself as the event of the day. I heard about the firing on the Boulevard des Capucines and the rapid spread of the insurrection for which that senseless act of violence was cause or pretext; of M. Molé's refusal to take office in these circumstances; and finally how MM. Thiers, Barrot and their friends were summoned to the palace with definite instructions to form a cabinet—all well-known facts that I need not dwell on. I asked M. de Corcelle how the ministers thought they would set about calming people down. "I have it from M. de Rémusat," he told me, "that the plan adopted is to withdraw all the troops and *flood Paris with national guards.*" Those were his actual words. I have always noticed in politics how often men are ruined by having too good a memory.

The men charged with suppressing the Revolution of 1848 were the same men who had made the Revolution of 1830. They remembered that then the army's resistance had failed to stop them, whereas the National Guard, so imprudently disbanded by Charles X, might have caused them great embarrassment and prevented their success. They took the opposite course to that of the government of the elder branch, and reached the same result. For it is very true that, although humanity is always the same, people's outlooks and the incidents that make history vary constantly.[1] One time will never fit neatly into another, and the old pictures we force into new frames always look out of place.

After discussing the dangerous state of affairs for a few moments, M. de Corcelle and I went on together to look for M. Lanjuinais, and then we all three went to M. Dufaure's house in the rue Le Peletier. The boulevard along which we passed presented a strange sight. There was hardly anyone to be seen, although it was nearly nine o'clock in the morning; no sound of a human voice could be heard; but all the little sentry boxes the whole way along that great street seemed on the move, oscillating on their bases and occasionally falling with a crash, while the

[1] *Variant:* All historical events differ, that the past teaches one little about the present . . .

great trees along the edge came tumbling into the road as if of
their own accord. These acts of destruction were the work of isolated individuals who set about it silently, methodically and fast,
preparing materials for the barricades that others were to build.
It looked exactly like some industrial undertaking, which is just
what it was for most of those taking part; an instinct for disorder had given them the taste for it, and experience of past
revolutions had taught them the theory. Nothing that I saw later
that day impressed me so much as that solitude in which one
could, so to speak, see all the most evil passions of humanity at
work, and none of the good ones. I would rather have encountered a furious mob there. Calling Lanjuinais' attention to the
tottering buildings and falling trees, I remember for the first time
saying what had long been on the tip of my tongue: "Believe me
this time it is not another riot, but a revolution."

M. Dufaure told us all that concerned himself in the events of
the previous evening and night.[2] First M. Molé had come to
ask for his help in forming the new Cabinet; the increasing
seriousness of the situation had soon made them both realize
that the time for intervention by either was past. M. Molé told
the King this about midnight, and the latter sent for M. Thiers
who in turn refused to accept office without M. Barrot's support. After that time M. Dufaure knew no more than I. We
dispersed without deciding anything about our future line of
conduct beyond agreeing to meet at the Chamber as soon as it
opened.

M. Dufaure did not come there, and I have never known
exactly why. Weakness was certainly not the reason, for I have
subsequently seen him very calm and unmoved in much more
dangerous circumstances. I think that in his concern for his family he must have wanted to put them in safety outside Paris
first. His private and his public virtues, for he had both in great
measure, did not march in step, for the former always came first;
we saw things go that way more than once. In any case, I
cannot count that as a great crime. Virtues of any sort are rare

[2] *Marginal note* (*Tocqueville*): Go over all this again with Dufaure.
Id. with Beaumont.

There are a great many small details which their conversation brings
back almost as if I could see them.

enough, and we can ill afford to quibble about their type and relative importance.

During the time we were at M. Dufaure's, the rioters had been able to put up many barricades across the route we had traversed, and they were adding the last touches to them as we returned. These barricades were skilfully constructed by a small number of men who worked industriously—not like criminals fearful of being caught *in flagrante delicto,* but like good workmen who wanted to do their job expeditiously and well. The public watched them passively, without either disapproving or helping. Nowhere did I see the seething unrest I had witnessed in 1830, when the whole city reminded me of one vast, boiling cauldron. This time it was not a matter of overthrowing the government, but simply of letting it fall.

On the boulevard we met a column of infantry falling back towards the Madeleine. No one said a word to the men, yet their retreat seemed a rout. Their ranks were broken and disorderly, and they marched with hanging heads, shamefaced and frightened. Whenever one of them left the main body for an instant, he was immediately surrounded, caught, clasped, disarmed and sent back; all this in the twinkling of an eye.

On my return home I found my brother Édouard with his wife and children there. They were living in the Faubourg de Montmartre. There had been rifleshots round their house all through the night. Frightened at the tumult they had decided towards morning to leave home. They reached ours on foot, passing through the barricades. Characteristically, my sister-in-law had lost her head. She already saw her husband dead and her daughters raped. My brother, although one of the staunchest men alive, was at his wit's end and did not know what to do, being no longer his normal self. Never before did I realize so vividly that, while a brave helpmate is a great support in times of revolution, a craven, even if she has the heart of a dove, is a cruel embarrassment. What made me most impatient was that my sister-in-law had no thought for the country's fate in the lamentations she poured out concerning her dear ones. There was neither depth of feeling nor breadth of sympathy in her demonstrative sensibility. She was, after all, very kind and even intelligent, but her mind had contracted and her heart frozen as both were restricted within the narrow limits of a pious egotism, so that both mind and heart were solely concerned with the good God, her husband, her children and especially her health, with no interest left over for other people. She was the most respectable woman and the worst citizen one could find.

I was anxious to rescue her from this predicament and myself from the embarrassment she caused me. I suggested taking her to the station for Versailles, which was not far away. She was terrified to stay in Paris, but also terrified to go away, and continued to fill my ears with her lamentations without deciding anything. In the end I took her almost by force and conducted her and her family to safety as far as the train platform at Versailles, where I left her to return to the town.

Back in town, as I was crossing the Place du Havre, I encountered for the first time a battalion of that National Guard which was to have flooded Paris: bewildered fellows marching uncertainly and surrounded by street urchins shouting "Reform forever!"—a slogan they echoed, but with hoarse constrained voices. This battalion came from my district, and most of the men in it knew me by sight, though I recognized hardly a single one. They crowded around me and greedily asked for news; I told them that we had gained all we could desire, for the government was changed and all the abuses complained about would be corrected; that the only danger now was that we might let ourselves be carried too far, and that it was up to them to prevent that. It was obvious that they did not follow my last point. "That's all very well, sir," they said, "the government has got itself into this fix by its own fault; so let it get itself out as best it can . . ." "Poor fools," I answered, "can you not see that now the brunt will fall, not so much on the government, but on you? Do you think that, if Paris is in anarchy and the whole kingdom in confusion, it is only the King who will suffer?" This cut no ice, and the only answer I could get was this prize nonsense: it is the government's fault, and therefore its risk; we don't want to get shot for people who have managed affairs so badly. And what was speaking was that very middle class whose greedy desires had been pampered for eighteen years; it, too, had been carried away by the tide of public opinion in the end, and that tide threw it against those whose constant flattery had led to its corruption.

This led me to a reflection that has often come to my mind since: in France a government is always wrong to base its support on the exclusive interests and selfish passions of a single class. Such a policy could succeed only in a nation where self-interest counts for more and vanity for less than with us; with us, when a government so constituted becomes unpopular, the members of the very class for whose sake it becomes unpopular will prefer the pleasure of joining with everybody else in abusing it to the enjoyment of the privileges it preserves for them. The old French aristocracy, which was more enlightened than our contemporary middle class and had a much stauncher *esprit de corps*, had already illustrated that rule; in the end it found it clever to criticize its own prerogatives and thunder against the abuses on which it lived. So I think that, all things considered, the best way for a government of ours to keep itself in power is to rule well and, especially, to govern in the interest of everybody. Nevertheless I must admit that, even if it does follow this path, it is still none too certain that it will last long.

I soon set out for the Chamber although it was still too early for the time fixed for the sitting; I think it was about eleven o'clock. I found no civilians but several regiments of cavalry filling the Place Louis XV. When I saw so many troops in such good order, I began to think that the streets had been deserted in order to mass force around the Tuileries and the Chamber and hold out there. The staff was mounted and at the foot of the obelisk; at their head was a lieutenant general whom, as I came closer, I recognized as Bedeau, his unlucky star having brought him back from Africa in time to bury the July Monarchy. The year before, I had spent a few days with him at Constantine, and a sort of intimacy had sprung up between us, which has continued since. As soon as he saw me, Bedeau dismounted and came and shook my hand in a way that immediately betrayed his nervousness. His talk gave even stronger evidence of nerves, and this did not surprise me; for I have always noticed that it is military men[3] who lose their heads first and show up as weakest in a revolutionary situation. Being accustomed to face an organized force of the enemy with an obedient army behind them, they are easily upset by the unruly shouts of a crowd of harmless, unarmed citizens, and by the sense that their own men are hesitating and sometimes conniving with the crowd. There is no doubt that Bedeau was nervous, and everybody knows the result of this: how the Chamber was invaded by a handful of men within pistolshot of the squadrons guarding it; and how, in consequence, the fall of the Monarchy was proclaimed and the Provisional Government elected. Unluckily for him, Bedeau's part in that day's events was of such major importance that I would like to stop for a moment to consider his character and the reasons for his behaviour. The links between us, both before and after that fatal day, were sufficiently close for me to be able to speak of him with understanding. It is certain that he had received an order not to fight. But why did he obey such an extraordinary order, and one that circumstances had rendered so impracticable?

Bedeau certainly was not craven nor even, strictly speaking, undecided; once he had made up his mind, you would find him making for his goal with the calmest and staunchest courage. But his mind was exceedingly methodical, not at all self-reliant or adventurous, and as pliable as one could imagine. It was his way to consider anything he was to do in all its aspects first, beginning with the gloomiest, and to waste precious time diluting his thought in a flow of words. For the rest, he was fair, reasonable, and liberal, with a kindness unaffected by eighteen years spent fighting in Africa, and also modest, moral, honest, even sensitive and religious; in short, the sort of worthy man that is very seldom found in uniform, or for that matter anywhere else. It was certainly not cowardice that made him do things that had that colour, for his courage would stand any test; still less was treachery his motive, for, although he had no ties with the Orleans family, he was as incapable of betraying them as were any of their best friends, and much more so than their

[3] *Marginal note (Tocqueville)*: Ask Bedeau for circumstantial details about this.

creatures turned out to be. His single misfortune was to be drawn into events beyond his powers, being a man of parts when a genius was needed, and not only a genius but one of the particular sort that can cope with revolutions, supremely gifted to fit actions to facts and knowing when to disobey opportunely. Memories of that February poisoned General Bedeau's life, leaving a deep wound in the depths of his soul. His endless accounts and explanations of the events of those days betrayed the extent of his grief.

While he was explaining his perplexities to me and pointing out that the opposition's duty was to go in a body into the street and make speeches to calm the people, a crowd slipping between the trees of the Champs Elysées was bearing down in our direction along the great avenue. Bedeau, seeing these people, took me with him in their direction on foot, leaving his cavalry more than a hundred yards behind, and began to harangue them; I have never known another man with a sword at his side who had quite such a taste for making speeches.

While he was addressing them, I noticed that the listening throng was gradually spreading out round us and that very soon we would be surrounded; moreover, behind a first row of casual loiterers I clearly saw the movement of some men of more dangerous aspect, while from somewhere in the depths of the crowd I could hear the dull murmur of these dangerous words, "It is Bugeaud."[4] So I leaned over and whispered into the general's ear: "I have more experience than you of popular uprisings; trust me and get back to your horse at once, for if you stay here, you will be killed or taken prisoner within five minutes." It was well that he did believe me. A few minutes later these men whose conversion he had undertaken murdered the occupants of the guard post in the rue des Champs Elysées; and I had some difficulty myself in forcing a passage through them. One of them, a short, thickset man who seemed to belong to the lower ranks of the working class, asked me where I was going. I answered,

[4] Bugeaud was the man widely considered to have been responsible for the massacre of the rue Transnonain, which occurred in 1834, and as such, he was detested by the Paris populace. Bedeau was thus in great danger in being mistaken for him at such a time. (Ed.)

"To the Chamber," and added to show that I belonged to the opposition, "Reform forever! You know that Guizot's ministry has been dismissed?" "Yes, sir, I know," he answered with a mocking look and pointing towards the Tuileries, "but we want more than that."

CHAPTER FIVE

The Sitting of the Chamber – the Duchess of Orleans
– The Provisional Government

I went into the Chamber; the sitting had not started; the deputies were wandering to and fro in the corridors like men distraught; it was a crowd rather than an assembly, for no one
was leading it.

The leaders of both parties were absent; the former ministers
were in flight; the new ones had not appeared; there were
shouts for the sitting to begin, but they were more the expression
of some vague longing for action than of any firm plan; the
President refused that; he was used to doing nothing without
orders, and now that no one had given orders since the morning,
he did not know what decision to make. I was asked to go and
find him and persuade him to take the chair, which I did. He
got easily excited over the smallest matter, so you can imagine
what state he was in then. I found this excellent man—for such
he was in spite of well-meaning bits of trickery, pious fibs and all
the other petty sins that a timid heart and vacillating mind
could suggest to an honest soul—I found him, I say, walking
about in his room, a prey to strong emotions. M. Sauzet had
handsome but undistinguished features, the dignity of a cathe-
dral verger, and a large fat body with very short arms. When
he was restless or upset, as he nearly always was, he would
waggle his little arms convulsively in all directions like a drown-
ing man. His manner, while we talked, was strange; he walked
about, stopped and then sat down with one foot tucked under

his fat buttocks, as he usually did in moments of great agitation; then he got up and sat down again without coming to any conclusion. It was a great misfortune for the House of Orleans to have a respectable man of that sort in charge of the Chamber on such a day; a bold rogue would have been more use.

M. Sauzet gave me many reasons for not opening the sitting, but it was one that he did not give that convinced me. Seeing him so without direction and so incapable of finding one for himself, I thought he would make the confusion worse if he attempted to lead others. So I left him and, thinking it more important to find defenders for the Chamber than to open the sitting, I set out towards the Ministry of the Interior in search of help.

Crossing the Place du Palais Bourbon on the way, I saw a very mixed crowd loudly cheering two men whom I recognized as Barrot and Beaumont. Both had their hats pushed down over their eyes, clothes covered with dust, hollow cheeks and tired eyes; never did men led in triumph look so much as if they were going to be hanged. I ran up to Beaumont and asked him what was going on. He whispered that he had seen the King abdicate and that that prince had fled; that to all appearances Lamoricière had just been killed when he went to announce the abdication to the rebels (in fact an A.D.C. had come to say that he had seen him in the distance fall from his horse); that everything was adrift; and finally that he and Barrot were on their way to the Ministry of the Interior to take possession of it and try to establish a centre of authority and resistance somewhere.

"What about the Chamber?" I said. "Have you taken any precautions for its defence?"

Beaumont looked annoyed at this suggestion, as if I had been talking about the defence of my own house. "Who is thinking about the Chamber?" he answered impatiently. "Whom could it help or harm in the present state of affairs?"

I felt then that he was wrong to speak like that, and indeed he was. It is true that at that moment the Chamber had been reduced to singular impotence, since the majority was despised and the minority outstripped by public opinion. But M. de Beaumont forgot that it is especially in times of revolution that everything that keeps the concept of law before the people, everything, that is, from its least important instruments to its most important external symbols, takes on a special value. For it is particularly at a time of anarchy and universal collapse that one feels the need to cling to the smallest simulacrum of tradition or broken fragment of authority, in order to preserve what remains of a half-destroyed constitution or to clear it away completely. If the deputies had been able to proclaim the Regency, perhaps in the end in spite of its unpopularity it might have prevailed; on the other hand, the Provisional Government clearly owed a great deal to the chance that brought it to birth between the four walls so long occupied by the representatives of the nation.

I followed my friends to their destination at the Ministry of the Interior. The crowd around us entered, or rather poured tumultuously in, and penetrated with us right up to the small office M. Duchâtel had just left. Barrot immediately tried to free himself by dismissing this cohort, but with no success.

These people who, as I then discovered, held two widely opposed points of view, some being Republicans and others Constitutionalists, started an energetic discussion with us and between themselves about the measures to be taken. And as we were all crammed against each other in a very narrow space, the heat, dust, confusion and noise soon became frightful. Barrot, who could always find long pompous phrases in the most critical moments, and who preserved an air of dignity, almost of mystery, even in the most ridiculous circumstances, delivered a fine peroration *in angustiis* (in a narrow space). Sometimes his voice dominated the uproar, but never stopped it. In despair and disgust at this violent and ridiculous scene, I quit the place where almost as many blows as arguments were being exchanged, and went back to the Chamber.

I was almost at the door, still without any suspicion of what was going on inside, when I saw people running and shouting that the Duchess of Orleans, the Count of Paris and the Duke of Nemours had just arrived. At this news I flew up the palace stairs four at a time and rushed into the Chamber.

There indeed I saw those three members of the royal family at the foot of the tribune and with their backs to it. The Duchess of Orleans was seated, dressed in mourning, pale and calm; obviously she was profoundly upset, but her emotion seemed to me that of a courageous soul and more likely to turn into heroism than fright.

The Count of Paris had a boy's thoughtlessness combined with a prince's precocious impassivity. Beside them stood the Duke of Nemours, buttoned up in his uniform, erect, stiff, cold and silent: a post painted to look like a lieutenant general. In my view he was the only man in real danger that day. All the time that I watched him exposed to this peril, his courage remained the same: taciturn, sterile and uninspired. Courage of that nature was more likely to discourage and dishearten his friends than to impress the enemy; its only use would be to enable him to die honourably, if die he must.

These unhappy royalties were surrounded by the national guardsmen who had come with them, some deputies and a few, but not many, of the common people. The galleries were empty and closed, except for the press gallery into which an unarmed but noisy crowd had forced its way. I was more struck by the shouts that came off and on from that quarter than by all the rest of the proceedings.

Such a sight had not been seen for fifty years. Since the time of the Convention, the galleries had been silent, and their silence had become part of parliamentary mores. In any case, at the moment in question, though the House may have felt its movements hampered, it was not yet subject to compulsion; the deputies were fairly numerous; the main party leaders were always absent. On all sides I heard people asking where M. Thiers and M. Barrot were; I did not know what had become of M. Thiers, but I knew only too well what M. Barrot was doing. I hastily sent one of our friends to warn him of what was happening, and he hurried along with all speed, for I can confidently assert that he did not know what fear was.

After a moment spent looking at this extraordinary sitting, I hurriedly went to my usual place on the upper benches of the left-centre; I have always made it a rule to be sure, at moments of crisis, not only to be found in the Assembly of which one forms part, but also to be in the seat where people expect to see you.

Some sort of confused and noisy argument was in progress; I heard M. Lacrosse, who was later my colleague in the administration, shouting through the uproar:

"M. Dupin wishes to speak."

"No, no," the latter replied, "I did not ask that."

"No matter," came the answer from all sides, "Speak! Speak!"

So urged, M. Dupin got up into the tribune and in two words proposed that we should go back on the law of 1842 and proclaim the Duchess of Orleans Regent.[1] This was received with cheers in the Assembly, exclamations in the galleries, and murmurs in the lobbies. The lobbies, which at first had been fairly clear, began to be alarmingly crowded; the people were not yet flooding into the Chamber, but they were coming in little by little as separate individuals; each time you looked, you could see a new face; it was a flood by infiltration. Most of the new arrivals belonged to the lowest classes; many of them were armed.

From early on, I began to be afraid of this growing invasion and felt the danger increasing minute by minute; I looked round the whole House, searching for the man best able to withstand the torrent; only Lamartine seemed to have both the standing and the ability to attempt it; I remembered that in 1842 he had been the only one to propose the Regency of the Duchess of Orleans. On the other hand his recent speeches and, especially, his writings had won him popular favour. Moreover his kind of

[1] The Duke of Orleans, Louis-Philippe's eldest son and heir apparent, died after a driving accident on 13 July 1842. Since the Duke's eldest son, the Count of Paris, was then only four years old, it was necessary to make provision for his minority, should his grandfather die before he was of age to rule for himself. The government therefore proposed a bill whereby the regency should be exercised by that member of the royal house closest in line of succession who was also of age. This implied that the regency would go to the Duke of Nemours, Louis-Philippe's second son who was considered to be very conservative in his outlook. The Duchess of Orleans was considered to be much more liberal, and her claim was supported by Lamartine and less forcefully by Odilon Barrot. Tocqueville himself opposed the bill, since it sought to introduce a general law, where constitutionally, only a law dealing with this particular situation was appropriate. Thiers, however, rallied to the government measure, thereby causing a split between the left-centre and the dynastic left. The bill became law on 30 August 1842. (Ed.)

talent suited the popular taste.[2] I saw him standing in his place and forced my way through the crowd to reach him:

"We are going to ruin," I hastily whispered to him. "You alone at this supreme moment can make yourself heard. Go up into the tribune and speak."

As I write this now, I think I can still see his face, so striking was it then: I see his tall, straight, thin figure, and his eyes turned towards the semicircle; but he was absorbed in inward contemplation and his fixed, vacant stare did not take in what was going on around him. He did not turn on hearing my voice but merely pointed to where the royal family was standing, and said, in answer to his own thoughts rather than mine:

"I will not say a word as long as that woman and that child are there."

I asked nothing further; I knew enough and went back towards my seat, passing Lanjuinais and Billault seated in the right centre:

"Don't you see anything we could do?" I asked.

They shook their heads sadly, and I went on.

Meanwhile such a crowd had piled up in the semicircle that the royal party was in danger of being crushed or suffocated at any moment.

The President vainly tried to clear the House; failing in that, he asked the Duchess to withdraw; that brave princess refused; then her friends with great difficulty extricated her from the crowd and escorted her up to the top of the left centre where she sat down with her son and the Duke of Nemours.

Marie and Crémieux had just announced the establishment of a provisional government to the silent disapproval of the deputies and the cheers of the people, when Barrot finally appeared; he was out of breath but not frightened. He went up the steps of the tribune and announced:

"Our duty is clear before us. The crown of July rests on the head of a child and a woman."

[2] *The following passage is marked for omission in the manuscript:* I did not know that half an hour before, at a meeting of journalists and deputies in one of the offices of the Chamber, he had given his sanction to the Republic.

At that the House plucked up courage and took heart to cheer, while the people in their turn were silent. The Duchess got up in her place and seemed to wish to speak, but listened to timid advice and sat down again; thus the last glimmer of her luck was put out. Barrot finished his speech but without regaining the effect of his first words; all the same the House was a little more confident, and the people wavered.

At that moment, the crowd filling the semicircle was driven up into the now mostly empty benches of the centre by the pressure of a flood from outside; it scattered and spread over the benches. Such deputies as had remained either slipped away and left the House or climbed up from row to row like wretches who, caught by the tide, climb up from rock to rock as the waters continue to rise. The impetus responsible for all this confusion came from two bands of men, mostly armed, who were marching down either lobby with officers of the National Guard and flags at their head. The two officers with the flags—one of whom was a swaggering half-pay colonel called, as I learned afterwards, Dumoulin—marched theatrically up into the tribune waving their flags, prancing about, gesticulating melodramatically, and bawling some revolutionary balderdash or other. The President announced that the sitting was suspended, and wanted, as the custom is, to put on his hat; but, with his knack of making the most tragic situations ridiculous, in his haste he seized a secretary's hat instead of his own and pulled it down over his eyes.

Such sittings obviously cannot be suspended, and the President's attempt only made this one more disorderly.

From that moment, one continuous uproar was broken by occasional intervals of quiet, and the tribune was filled, not by individuals, but by groups of speakers; finally, Crémieux, Ledru-Rollin and Lamartine all rushed up into it at the same time. Ledru-Rollin chased Crémieux out and himself held on with his large hands, while Lamartine, neither fighting nor quitting, waited till his colleague should have finished speaking. Ledru-Rollin began speaking and wandered from the point, interrupted constantly by the impatience of his own friends. "Finish! Finish!" shouted Berryer who had more experience than he and who controlled his dynastic rancour more warily than the other his republican passion. Finally Ledru-Rollin asked for the immediate appointment of a provisional government and descended the stairs.

Then Lamartine came forward; he obtained silence and began with a splendid eulogy of the Duchess of Orleans' courage, and even the people, who are never insensitive to generous feelings expressed in fine language, applauded. The deputies breathed again.

"Wait," I said to my neighbours. "That is only the prelude."

In fact Lamartine did soon turn sharply and march towards Ledru-Rollin's conclusion.

So far, as I have already mentioned, all the galleries except the journalists' had been empty and shut, but while Lamartine was speaking, great blows could be heard against one of the doors, and it broke and scattered in fragments. Immediately a shouting band of armed men invaded that gallery, and all the others soon afterwards. One of the common people put his foot on the cornice and pointed his gun at the President and the speaker; others seemed to be aiming at the Assembly. Some devoted friends escorted the Duchess of Orleans and her son out of the House and into the lobby behind. The President murmured something intended to signify that the sitting was closed, and stepped, or rather slid, off the platform on which his chair was placed. I saw him pass, a shapeless mass, before my eyes; never would I have believed that fear could accelerate such a fat body so much, or, rather, suddenly transmogrify it into a sort of liquid. All the remaining Conservative deputies then scattered, and the mob sprawled over the centre benches, shouting: "Let's take the corrupt ones' places."

Throughout this tumultuous scene I had remained fixed in my place, watching very attentively but surprisingly little excited. And now, when I come to wonder why I felt no acuter emotion in the face of events bound to exercise great influence over France's fate and my own, I find that the shape this great adventure took greatly diminished its impact on me.

During the February Revolution I had two or three times seen sights with something of grandeur in them (I will be describing these later), but there was absolutely no grandeur in this one, for there was no touch of truth about it.[3] We French, Parisians especially, gladly mingle literary and theatrical reminiscences with our most serious demonstrations. This often creates the impression that our feelings are false, whereas in fact they are only clumsily tricked out. In this case the quality of imitation was so obvious that the terrible originality of the facts remained hidden. It was a time when everybody's imagination had been coloured by the crude pigments with which Lamartine daubed his *Girondins*. The men of the first revolution were still alive in everybody's mind, their deeds and their words fresh in the memory. And everything I saw that day was plainly stamped with the imprint of such memories; the whole time I had the feeling that we had staged a play about the French Revolution, rather than that we were continuing it.

Despite the naked swords, bayonets and muskets, I could not for a moment persuade myself that anybody, let alone myself, could be in danger of death. And I sincerely believe that no one was in fact in danger. Bloodthirsty hatreds only came later; they had not then had time to germinate; one could not yet distinguish the particular taste of the February Revolution. In the interval, we tried without success to warm ourselves at the hearth of our fathers' passions; their gestures and attitudes as seen on the stage were imitated, but their enthusiasm could not be copied, nor their fury felt again. A tradition of violent action was being followed, without real understanding, by frigid souls. Though I foresaw the terrible end to the piece well enough, I could not take the actors very seriously; the whole thing seemed a vile tragedy played by a provincial troupe.

I confess that the only thing that really touched me during the whole of that day was the sight of the woman and child on whose heads had fallen the weight of faults they did not commit. I kept looking pityingly at that foreign princess thrown into the midst of our civil discords; and when she had fled, the memory of that sad, gentle, stalwart face looking towards

---

[3] *Marginal note (Tocqueville)*: M(arie) finds all this bit somewhat laboured and coloured; in fact the thought is not developed in a way to be properly understood. Must begin by putting strong emphasis on the *imitation* and the frigidity resulting therefrom.

the Assembly throughout the long day's agony came back to me
so vividly, and I felt so touched by pity at the thought of the
dangers of her flight, that I got up in a hurry and rushed towards
the place that my knowledge of the topography led me to
suppose she and her son would have chosen for a refuge. I
threaded my way quickly through the crowd, crossed the floor,
passed through the cloakroom and reached the private staircase
that leads from the side door in the rue de Bourgogne up to
the top floor of the palace. A messenger, whom I asked as I
ran past, told me that I was on the track of the royal party,
and in fact I could hear people hurrying up to the top of those
stairs. So I went on and reached a landing; the noise of foot-
steps in front of me had just that moment stopped. I found
a closed door in front of me, knocked, and it was not opened.
So I halted, not ashamed but a little astonished to find myself
there; for after all I had no reason to cling so to that family's
fortunes. They had done me no kindness, nor even given me
any sign of confidence. It was with regret that I saw that
family installed on the throne, and if I loyally helped to keep it
there, the public interest, not any affection for them, was my
motive. Its only attraction in my eyes was that which great
fortunes bring. If princes were like God who reads hearts and
accepts the will for the act, they would certainly have been
grateful for what I did that day; but they will never know,
for nobody saw me and I told nobody.

I went back to the House and took my place; almost all
the deputies had left. The benches were occupied by men of
the people. Lamartine was still in the tribune haranguing the
crowd, or rather conversing with them, for the speakers seemed
as numerous as the audience. The confusion was at its height;
during one moment of half silence, Lamartine began to read
the list of names of various people proposed by I don't know
whom to form part of a provisional government that had just
been decreed, nobody knows how. Cheers greeted most of the
names, but some were rejected with groans and others were
the target for jokes, for, as in Shakespeare's plays, when the
people play a part, burlesque and tragedy jostle together, and
jokes are intermingled with revolutionary fervour. When Garnier-

Pagès' name was proposed, I heard somebody shout: "You are making a mistake, Lamartine. It was the dead one who was the good one." For Garnier-Pagès had a famous brother, to whom he bore no resemblance save in name. M. de Lamartine began, I think, to get very embarrassed by his position, for in a riot, as in a novel, the most difficult thing to invent is the ending. When it came into somebody's head to say: "To the Hôtel de Ville!"[4] Lamartine echoed, "To the Hôtel de Ville," and went out, there and then, taking half the crowd with him.

The others stayed with Ledru-Rollin who, I suppose in order to keep a leading part, thought he ought to start this ghost of an election over again, after which, he too left for the Hôtel de Ville. There the same electoral display was gone through once more, and here I cannot resist repeating a story I heard some months later from M. Marrast. It interrupts the thread of my story a little, but it gives a wonderful picture of two men who at that moment played important parts, and points the difference, if not between their feelings, then at least between their education and mores. "A list of candidates for the Provisional Government," Marrast told me, "had been hastily prepared; the question was how to announce it to the people. I gave it to Lamartine, asking him to read it aloud from the top of the steps.

"'I can't do that,' Lamartine answered when he read it, 'my name is there.'

"I passed it to Crémieux to read, and when he had done so, he said: 'You are laughing at me, asking me to read a list to the people without my name on it.'"

When I saw M. Ledru-Rollin leave the House, where only the dregs of the insurrection were left, I saw that there was no more for me to do there; so I started to leave. But, as I did not want to get involved with the band marching on the Hôtel de Ville, I turned in the opposite direction, going down the narrow, steep cellarlike stairs, which lead down to the inner court of the palace. I then saw an armed column

---

4 The Hôtel de Ville was, and still is, the centre of municipal administration in Paris. It came to be a tradition for revolutionaries to use it as their first platform. (Ed.)

of the National Guard coming towards me and running up that same staircase with fixed bayonets. There were two men in civilian dress in front who seemed to be leading them, who were shouting at the top of their voices:

"Long live the Duchess of Orleans and the Regency!"

I recognized one as General Oudinot and the other as Andryane, the man who was shut up in the Spielberg[5] and wrote his *Memoirs* in imitation of Silvio Pellico's. I did not see anybody else, and nothing shows more clearly how difficult it is for the public to discover the truth about events that happen in the tumult of a revolution. I know there is a letter of Marshal Bugeaud in which he recounts how he succeeded in getting together a few companies of the 10th Legion, rousing them in favour of the Duchess of Orleans and leading them at the double from the courtyard of the Palais Bourbon up to the doors of the Chamber, which he found empty. This account is correct except for the Marshal's own presence, for, had he been there, I should certainly have noticed that important fact. There was no one there, I repeat, except General Oudinot and M. Andryane. The latter, seeing me standing still and saying nothing, excitedly took me by the arm and said:

"Sir, you must join us in rescuing the Duchess of Orleans and saving the Monarchy."

"Sir," I answered, "your intention is good, but you come too late: the Duchess has disappeared and the House is dispersed."

Now, where should we find that mettlesome defender of the Monarchy that very same evening? The story is worth telling and noting as a conspicuous example of the greedy versatility that abounds in the history of all revolutions. He was in M. Ledru-Rollin's office, acting in the name of the Republic as Secretary General to the Ministry of the Interior.

To return to the column he was leading: I joined it, but without hope it could succeed any longer. In mechanical obedience to its first impulse, it went right up to the doors of the Chamber. Then each man discovered what had been happening. They turned about as a body, and almost at once dispersed

---

[5] A castle in the town of Brünn, Austria (now Brno in Czechoslovakia). It was used as a political prison. (Ed.)

in every direction. Half an hour earlier that handful of men of the National Guard could, as happened on the following 15th May, have changed the destiny of France. I let this fresh crowd disperse and then, alone and very thoughtful, turned homewards, still casting one last glance on the empty and deserted building where for nine long years I had heard so many eloquent vain words.

M. Billault, who left the Chamber a few minutes before me, by the side door on to the rue de Bourgogne, told me that he met M. Barrot in that street, and that:

"He was rushing along unconscious that he had no hat and that his grey hair, usually so carefully brushed over his temples, was fluttering untidily over his shoulders. He seemed beside himself."

All day long that man had made heroic efforts to save the Monarchy from the slope down which he himself had pushed it, and its fall seemed to have left him crushed. I heard from Beaumont, who never left him all that day, that he had faced and passed twenty barricades; he went up unarmed to each of them, sometimes facing insults and often fire, but always in the end his words conquered those who were guarding them.

For his words did have power over the multitude; he had every requisite for influencing them at a given moment: a strong voice, turgid eloquence and an intrepid heart.

At the same moment M. Barrot was leaving the Chamber in this state, M. Thiers, even more distraught, was wandering round Paris afraid to go home. He had been seen for a moment in the Assembly before the Duchess of Orleans' arrival, and he had vanished at once giving the signal for many others to do the same. The next day I learned the details of his flight from M. Talabot, the man who had helped him accomplish it. I had fairly close party links with M. Talabot, and M. Thiers, I think, had long-standing business relations with him. M. Talabot was a man of powerful resource and resolution, most helpful in such an emergency. This is what he told me, with nothing, I hope, left out or added:

"As M. Thiers was passing through the Place Louis XV, he was insulted and threatened by some of the common people;

he was very agitated and upset when I saw him come into the House; he came up to me, took me by the hands and told me that he was going to be massacred by the people unless I helped him escape. I immediately took him by the arm and asked him to go along with me, fearing nothing. M. Thiers wanted to avoid the Pont Louis XVI for fear of the crowd there. We went to the Pont des Invalides, but when we got there, he thought he saw a gathering on the other side of the river and again refused to cross. We then made for the Pont de Jena, which was free, and crossed it without difficulty. Once on the other side, M. Thiers noticed some urchins yelling on the foundations of what was to have been the palace of the King of Rome, and he immediately turned down the rue d'Auteuil and made for the Bois de Boulogne. There we had the good luck to find a cab prepared to take us around by the outer boulevards to the neighbourhood of the Barrière de Clichy, whence we were able to get back to his house by roundabout streets. Throughout the journey," M. Talabot added, "but especially at the beginning, M. Thiers struck me as being almost out of his senses; he gesticulated, sighed and murmured incoherent phrases. His troubled, wandering thoughts were ever roaming through a chaotic mixture of the catastrophe he had witnessed, the country's future, and his own danger."

So of the four men most responsible for the events of the 24th February—Louis-Philippe, M. Guizot, M. Thiers and M. Barrot—the two former were exiles by the end of the day, and the two latter were half-mad.

PART TWO

---◆---

Everything contained in this notebook (that is chapters 1 to 11 inclusive) was written at odd moments at Sorrento in November and December 1850 and in January, February and March 1851

My view of the reasons for the events of the 24th February, and my thoughts concerning its effects for the future

So the July Monarchy had fallen, fallen without a struggle, not under the victors' blows, but before they were struck; and the victors were as astonished at their success as the losers at their defeat. After the February Revolution I often heard M. Guizot and even M. Molé and M. Thiers say that it was all due to surprise and should be considered pure accident, a lucky stroke and nothing more. I have always felt tempted to answer them as Molière's Misanthrope answers Oronte: *"Pour en juger ainsi, vous avez vos raisons,"*[1] for for eighteen years those three men had directed the affairs of France under Louis-Philippe, and it was hard for them to admit that that prince's bad government had prepared the way for the catastrophe that threw him from the throne.

Obviously I, not having the same reasons to believe it, was not quite of their opinion. I am not asserting that accidents played no part in the February Revolution, for they played a very great one; but they were not the only thing.

In my life I have come across literary men who wrote histories without taking part in public affairs, and politicians

---

[1] "You have your private reasons for such a view." Molière. *Le Misanthrope.* Act I, Scene II, line 169.

Tocqueville is not entirely accurate in his quotation here; the line in fact runs as follows: *"Pour les trouver ainsi, vous avez vos raisons."* (Ed.)

whose only concern was to control events without a thought of describing them. And I have invariably noticed that the former see general causes everywhere, whereas the latter, spending their lives amid the disconnected events of each day, freely attribute everything to particular incidents and think that all the little strings their hands are busy pulling daily are those that control the world's destiny. Probably both of them are mistaken.

For my part I hate all those absolute systems that make all the events of history depend on great first causes linked together by the chain of fate and thus succeed, so to speak, in banishing men from the history of the human race. Their boasted breadth seems to me narrow, and their mathematical exactness false. I believe, *pace* the writers who find these sublime theories to feed their vanity and lighten their labours, that many important historical facts can be explained only by accidental circumstances, while many others are inexplicable. Finally, that chance, or rather the concatenation of secondary causes, which we call by that name because we can't sort them all out, is a very important element in all that we see taking place in the world's theatre. But I am firmly convinced that chance can do nothing unless the ground has been prepared in advance. Antecedent facts, the nature of institutions, turns of mind and the state of mores are the materials from which chance composes those impromptu events that surprise and terrify us.

In common with all other great events of this sort, the February Revolution was born of general causes fertilized, if I may put it so, by accidents. And to make the whole thing depend on the former is as superficial as attributing it solely to the latter.

The industrial revolution, which for thirty years had been making Paris the leading manufacturing city in France, attracting a whole new population of workmen, not to mention the work on the fortifications,[2] which had brought in a flood of labourers now out of work; the passion for material pleasures, which, spurred on by the government, was getting a firmer and

[2] Fortifications of Paris, the construction of which was begun in 1841. (Ed.)

firmer hold over the whole of this multitude, the democratic disease of envy silently at work; economic and political theories, which were beginning to attract notice and which tended to encourage the belief that human wretchedness was due to the laws and not to providence and that poverty could be abolished by changing the system of society; the contempt felt for the ruling class, especially its leaders—a contempt so deep and general that it paralyzed the resistance even of those who stood to lose most by the overthrow of authority; the centralization, thanks to which control of Paris and of the whole machinery of government was kept in working order, was all that was needed to complete a revolution; and lastly, the mobility of everything—institutions, ideas, mores and men—in a society on the move, which had lived through seven great revolutions within sixty years, not to mention numerous small secondary upheavals: such were the general causes without which the February Revolution would have been impossible. The main accidents that brought it on were the clumsy passions of the dynastic opposition, which prepared the ground for a riot when it wanted a reform; the attempts to suppress that riot, excessive at first, then abandoned; the sudden disappearance of the former ministers, which snapped the threads of power, threads that the new ministers, in their confusion, could neither pick up nor retie; the mistakes and mental disorientation of these ministers who were so inadequate in rebuilding what they had been strong enough to throw down; the vacillation of the generals; the absence of the only members of the royal family who had either popularity or energy[3]; and above all the senile imbecility of King Louis-Philippe, a weakness nobody could have foreseen, and which even now after the event seems almost incredible.

I sometimes wonder what in the King's soul could have produced this unanticipated sudden collapse. Louis-Philippe's life had been passed amid revolutions, and he certainly lacked neither experience, nor courage, nor intelligence, although all

[3] Tocqueville is referring here to two other sons of Louis-Philippe, the Prince of Joinville and the Duke of Aumale, who were both in Algeria at that time. (Ed.)

those qualities deserted him on that day. I think his weakness was due to the intensity of his astonishment; he was knocked flat, unaware of what had hit him. The February Revolution was *unforeseen* by everybody, but by him most of all; no warning from the outside had prepared him for it, for his mind had retreated long ago into the sort of haughty loneliness inhabited by almost all kings whose long reigns have been prosperous, who mistake luck for genius, and who do not want to listen to anybody, because they think they have no more to learn. Besides, Louis-Philippe, like his ministers, had been misled, as mentioned before, by the will-o'-the-wisp light past history cast on the present. One could make a weird collection of all the utterly dissimilar mistakes that have been fathered one by the other. There is Charles I, being driven into arbitrary behaviour and violence by seeing how the spirit of opposition flourished under the kindly rule of his father; Louis XVI, determined to put up with everything because Charles I had perished unwilling to put up with anything; then Charles X provoking a revolution because he had witnessed Louis XVI's weakness; and finally Louis-Philippe, the most perspicacious of them all, who imagined that all he had to do to remain on the throne was, without violating the law, to pervert it, and that provided he himself observed the letter of the Charter, the nation would never go beyond it. To corrupt the people without defying them and to twist the spirit of the Constitution without changing the letter; to play off the country's vices one against the other; and gently to drown revolutionary passion in the love of material pleasures: this had been his idea throughout his life, and it gradually became, not just his main, but his only thought. He shut himself up in it; he lived inside it; and when he suddenly saw that it was wrong, he was like a man awakened at night by an earthquake, who, seeing his house falling down in the darkness and even the ground giving way under his feet, remains distracted and lost amid the universal unforeseen ruin.

I now sit back very comfortably to argue about the causes leading up to the 24th February, but on the afternoon of that day I had quite other thoughts in my head; the event itself filled my thoughts, and I was more concerned with what would follow than with what had produced it.[4]

This was the second revolution within the space of seventeen years that I had seen accomplished before my eyes.

Both pained me; but how much more bitter were the impressions left by the second! Right up to the end I had felt some remnants of hereditary affection for Charles X, but that king fell because he had violated rights that were dear to me, and I was able to hope that my country's freedom would be revived rather than extinguished by his fall. Today that freedom seemed dead to me; the fugitive royal family meant nothing to me, but I felt that my own cause was lost.

I had spent the best years of my youth in a society that seemed to be regaining prosperity and grandeur as it regained freedom; I had conceived the idea of a regulated and orderly freedom, controlled by religious belief, mores and laws; I was touched by the joys of such a freedom, and it had become my whole life's passion; I had felt that I could never be consoled for its loss, and now I clearly saw that I must give it up forever.

I had had too much experience of men to accept payment in idle words this time; I knew that, while one great revolution may be able to found a nation's liberty, several revolutions on top of each other make the enjoyment of an orderly liberty impossible there for a long time.

I still did not know what would come out of this one, but I was already certain that it would not be any result satisfactory to me; and I foresaw that, whatever might be the fate of our posterity, it was our lot to spend a wretched life between alternate swings to licence and to oppression.

4 *The following passage is marked for deletion in the manuscript:* I went slowly home. Briefly I explained to Madame de Tocqueville what I had just seen, and settled into a corner to dream sadly. I do not think I have ever felt my heart so full of bitter feelings, or my mind so enveloped by sombre thoughts.

At daybreak on 30 July 1830 I had seen Charles X's carriages pass along the outer boulevards of Versailles with escutcheons already scratched, moving slowly in file as at a funeral; I could not hold back my tears at the sight. The nature of my feelings at this time was very different, but they were still more acute.

Mentally I reviewed the history of our last sixty years and smiled bitterly to myself as I thought of the illusions cherished at the end of each phase of this long revolution; the theories feeding these illusions; our historians' learned daydreams, and all the ingenious false systems by which men sought to explain a present still unclearly seen and to foresee the unseen future.

The Constitutional Monarchy had succeeded the Ancien Régime; the Republic followed the Monarchy; the Empire the Republic; after the Empire the Restoration; then there had come the July Monarchy. After each of these successive changes it was said that the French Revolution, having achieved what was presumptuously called its work, was finished: men had said that, and they had believed it. Under the Restoration, I, too, unfortunately hoped for that, and I continued to hope after the Restoration government had fallen; and here was the French Revolution starting again, for it was always the same one. As we go on, its end seems ever farther off and hazier. Shall we reach, as other prophets as vain perhaps as their predecessors assure us, a more complete and profound social transformation than our fathers ever foresaw or desired, and which we ourselves cannot yet conceive; or may we not simply end up in that intermittent anarchy which is well known to be the chronic incurable disease of old peoples? I cannot tell, and do not know when this long voyage will end; I am tired of mistaking deceptive mists for the bank. And I often wonder whether that solid land we have sought for so long actually exists, and whether it is not our fate to rove the seas forever!

I passed the rest of that day with Ampère, my colleague at the Institute and one of my best friends.[5] He came to find out what had become of me in the scuffle and to ask me to dinner. At first I wanted to console myself by getting him to share my

[5] *Ampère's name is left blank in the manuscript.*

In a first version of this passage Tocqueville admits that he had asked Ampère to dinner and had forgotten about him:

So the rest of that day glided sadly away. No one came to see me, and I went to see nobody. We had reached the stage when everything is uncertain except the futility of efforts, and when there is nothing to do but wrap one's head in one's cloak.

Some time before I had invited A. to dinner on that day. The day's events had made me forget it. But A. remembered and came in spite of the revolution.

grief. But almost at once I found that his impressions were not the same as mine, that he looked with other eyes on the revolution that was taking place. Ampère was an intelligent man, and what counts for more, a warm-hearted man, gentle and reliable in behaviour. He was loved for his good nature, and his versatile, intelligent, amusing, satirical conversation was a pleasure; he would throw out a whole lot of remarks [none of which, it is true, rose very high, but][6] which passed the time very agreeably. Unluckily, he was too much inclined to carry the spirit of a salon over into literature, and that of literature into politics. What I call the literary spirit in politics consists in looking for what is ingenious and new rather than for what is true, being fonder of what makes an interesting picture than what serves a purpose, being very appreciative of good acting and fine speaking without reference to the play's results, and, finally, judging by impressions rather than reasons. I need not say that this peculiarity is not confined to Academicians. To tell the truth, the whole nation shares it a little, and the French public as a whole often takes a literary man's view of politics. Ampère, who was kindness itself and had not adopted the life of the coterie to which he belonged except to become too indulgent to his friends, absolutely despised the government that had fallen, and its last acts on behalf of the Swiss ultramontanes had irritated him very much.[7] His hatred for the latter, and

6 *The words between brackets are printed in the first edition, but crossed out in the manuscript.* (Ed.)

7 This refers to Guizot's support of the Sonderbund, a separatist movement of seven Catholic cantons formed in opposition to the Swiss Federal Government in 1845. It came into being as a consequence of violent reaction in other parts of Switzerland to the decision of the canton of Lucerne to entrust the Jesuits with the direction of its educational establishments. Those hostile to the Jesuits were in the main radicals. Feeling rose so high that each side took to arms, and the Sonderbund's forces were defeated in 1847. Guizot's moderate policy had tended to support the Sonderbund, as did Austria, whereas Palmerston, hostile to Guizot since the Spanish marriages, had supported the radicals. Although ineffectual, Guizot's policy had earned for him the opprobium of having apparently supported the Jesuits and of having allied himself with Austria. Hence, Ampère's attitude is not untypical. Guizot's vindication of his policy may be found in volume VIII of his *Mémoires pour servir à l'histoire de mon temps*, Paris, 1867. For the general historical and constitutional background, see W. E. Rappard, *La Constitution Fédérale de la Suisse, 1848–1948*, Neufchâtel, 1948. (Ed.)

especially their French friends, was his only feeling of that sort of which I am aware. He was mortally frightened of bores, but the only people he detested from the depths of his soul were the devout. The latter had, it is true, wounded him very cruelly and clumsily, for he was not naturally their adversary, and nothing is better proof of their blind intolerance than that they should have roused such flaming hatred in so Christian a man as Ampère. I am not saying that he was a Christian by belief, but through goodwill, taste and, if I dare to put it so, temperament. Thus Ampère needed little consolation for the fall of a government that had served them so well. Moreover he had just witnessed instances of unselfishness, even generosity and courage among the insurgents; and he was carried away by the general emotion.

I saw that he not only failed to share my feelings but was inclined to take the opposite view. Such an attitude made all the indignation, grief and anger that had been piling up in my heart since the morning suddenly erupt against Ampère; and I addressed him with a violence of language that makes me a little ashamed whenever I think of it, and which only such a true friend as he would have excused. Among other things, I remember saying:

"You don't understand anything of what is happening; you judge it like some Parisian idler, or a poet. You call this the triumph of freedom when it is its final defeat. I tell you that this people whom you so naïvely admire has just proved that it is incapable and unworthy of living in freedom. Show me what it has learned from experience? What new virtues has it discovered, and what old vices has it discarded? No, I tell you, it is always the same; just as impatient, careless and contemptuous of the law as ever; just as easily led and as rash in the face of danger as its fathers before it. Time has wrought no change in it, but has left it as frivolous in serious matters as it used to be in trifles."

After a lot of shouting, we both agreed to leave the verdict to the future, that enlightened and just judge who, unfortunately, always arrives too late.

Paris the day after the 24th February, and the days that followed – Socialist character of the new revolution

Started again at Sorrento in November 1850

The night passed without mishap for, although gunshots could be heard until morning, they were sounds of triumph, not of war. As soon as it was light I went out to see how the town looked and to find out what had happened to my two nephews. At the little seminary where they were being educated, they were being given no training to prepare them to live in a time of revolution such as ours, and it was not safe there with revolution abroad. The seminary was in the rue de Madame behind the Luxembourg, and so I had to go through a large part of Paris to get there.

I found the streets quiet and even half-deserted, as they usually are in Paris on a Sunday morning when the rich are still asleep and the poor resting. One did, of course, meet some of yesterday's victors from time to time along the walls, but[1] most of them were on their way home and took no notice of passers-by. In the few shops that were open one saw frightened and, still more, astonished shopkeepers, looking like an audience at a theatre who, after the play is finished, still wonder what it was about. Soldiers were the commonest sight in these empty streets, some alone, others in small groups, all unarmed and homeward

[1] *The following words are marked for omission in the manuscript:* Wine, more than political passions, filled them and

bound. Their recent defeat had left an acute sense of shame and anger in their souls, as became obvious later, but at the time it did not show; these lads' joy at finding themselves free seemed to swamp every other feeling; they went gaily along without a care in the world, like schoolboys home for the holidays.

No attack, or even insult, had disturbed the little seminary, and my nephews were not even there, having been sent the day before to their maternal grandmother's house. So I turned homewards, passing by the rue du Bac to find out if Lamoricière, who was then living there, had in fact been killed the day before, as his A.D.C. had said after seeing him fall. It was only after they had recognized me that his servants admitted he was at home and allowed me in to see him.

I found this uncommon man, of whom I shall have occasion to speak more than once later, stretched immobile on his bed, an unnatural and distasteful state for such as he. His head was half-broken open, his arms riddled with bayonet thrusts, and all his limbs bruised and crippled; but for the rest he was always the same, with his brilliant mind and indomitable heart. He told me all that had happened to him the day before, when only a miracle had saved him from a thousand dangers. I strongly urged him to stay quiet until he was recovered, and for a long time after that, so as not to risk his person and reputation uselessly in the ensuing chaos. Good advice, no doubt, to give to a man so much in love with action and so accustomed to act that, having accomplished things necessary and useful, he is always ready to undertake harmful and dangerous ones rather than do nothing at all, but as futile as advice that goes against the grain always is.

I spent the whole afternoon wandering about Paris and was particularly struck by two points: first, I will not say the mainly, but the uniquely and exclusively popular character of the recent revolution, and the omnipotence it had given the so-called people, that is to say, the classes who work with their hands, over all other classes. Secondly, how little hatred, or indeed any other acute feeling, was shown in this first moment of victory by the humble people who had suddenly become the sole masters of power.

Although the working classes had often played the principal part in the events of the first Republic, they had never been the leaders and sole masters of the State, in fact or in law; there was probably not a single man of the people in the Convention; it was full of the middle class and men of letters. The fight between the Mountain and the Gironde was between bourgeois on both sides, and the triumph of the former never brought power down into the hands of the people alone. The July Revolution was effected by the people, but they had been stirred up and led by the middle class who reaped the major advantages from it. But the February Revolution seemed to be entirely outside and against the bourgeoisie.

In the shock of conflict the two main parties composing the French body social had somehow separated, and the people, standing alone, remained in full possession of power. This was something completely new in our history. It is true that similar revolutions had taken place in other countries at other times; however new and unexpected contemporaries may find the particular events of any age, including our own, they are always part of the age-old history of humanity.[2] In particular, Florence at the close of the Middle Ages presents many analogies with our condition now; first the middle class had succeeded the nobility, and then one day the latter were driven out of government in their turn, and a barefoot *gonfalonier* marched at the head of the people and thus led the republic. But this popular revolution in Florence was the result of transitory and peculiar circumstances, whereas ours was due to very permanent and general causes, which, having thrown France into agitation, might be expected to stir up all the rest of Europe. For it was not just a party that triumphed this time; men aimed at establishing a social science, a philosophy, and I might almost say a common religion to be taught to all men and followed by them. Therein lay the really new element in the old picture.

Throughout this day in Paris I never saw one of the former agents of authority: not a soldier, or a gendarme, or a policeman;

2 *The following words are marked for omission in the manuscript:* For what we call new facts are most often only forgotten ones. *Tocqueville added in the margin:* Has not this been said by others?

even the National Guard had vanished. The people alone bore arms, guarded public buildings, watched, commanded and punished; it was an extraordinary and a terrible thing to see the whole of this huge city, full of so many riches, or rather the whole of this great nation, in the sole hands of those who owned nothing; for, thanks to centralization, whoever reigns in Paris controls France. Consequently the terror felt by all the other classes was extreme; I do not think that it had ever been so intense at any other moment of the revolution, and the only comparison would be with the feelings of the civilized cities of the Roman world when they suddenly found themselves in the power of Vandals or Goths.

Since nothing of the sort had happened before, many people anticipated unheard-of acts of violence. For my part, I never shared these fears. I noticed things that made me foresee strange perturbations and peculiar crises in the immediate future, but I never expected the rich to be looted. I knew the common people of Paris well enough to realize that their first impulses in times of revolution are usually generous, and that they like to pass the days immediately following their triumph in boasting about it, parading their authority and playing at being great men; during this interval some sort of authority is usually established, the policeman returns to his beat, and the judge to his bench. And when those great men of ours finally choose to come down again to the familiar, common ground of petty, evil human passions, they are no longer free to do so and are forced to live as simple honest people. Moreover we have passed through such long years of insurrections that a particular kind of morality of disorder and a special code for days of riot have evolved. These exceptional laws tolerate murder and allow devastation, but theft is strictly forbidden, which, whatever anybody says, does not prevent a lot of robbery on such days, for a society of rioters cannot be different from all others, and there are always rascals everywhere who jeer at the morality of the main body and are very contemptuous of its conception of honour when nobody is looking. I was further reassured by the feeling that the victors had been as surprised by their success as the losers by their defeat; there had been no time for passions to be enflamed and embittered in the fight; the government had fallen undefended by itself or others. Even those who in the depths of their hearts most regretted its fall had for a long time either fought against it or at least criticized it severely.

For the past year the dynastic opposition and the republican opposition had been living in deceptive harmony, performing the same acts for opposite reasons. This misunderstanding, which had facilitated the revolution, now made it more gentle. The Monarchy vanished, and the battlefield seemed empty; the people no longer saw clearly what enemies remained to be hunted down and defeated; the former objects of their anger were not there; the clergy had never been completely reconciled to the new dynasty and saw it fall without regret; the old nobility cheered, whatever the consequences might be. For the clergy had suffered from the intolerance of the middle classes, and the nobility from their pride. And both despised and feared their rule.

This was the first time in sixty years that priests, nobility and people had shared a common feeling—a longing for revenge, it is true, and not one of mutual affection. But in politics that is already much, for shared hatreds are almost always the basis of friendships. The real and only party defeated was the bourgeoisie, but even they had little to fear. Their rule had been exclusive rather than oppressive, and being corrupt rather than violent, it aroused more contempt than hatred. Moreover the middle class is never a compact body within the nation, nor does it form any very distinctive party within the whole. There is always something it shares with all the others, and in some places it becomes merged with them. This lack of homogeneity and of precise boundaries makes the rule of the middle class weak and vacillating. But it also makes it impossible to come to grips with that class, or even to see it, when it no longer rules, and others seek to strike it.

It was all these causes combined that resulted in the languor that, combined with omnipotence, struck me as so odd. And this languor stood out the more clearly in contrast with the overblown language used, language that brought back terrible memories.[3] M. Thiers' *History of the Revolution,* M. de Lamartine's *Girondins,* and other less famous but nonetheless well-known works, and especially some theatrical productions rehabilitated the Terror, and in a sense made it fashionable.[4] So the tepid passions of our day were expressed in the burning language of '93, and the names and deeds of illustrious villains were continually on the lips of men who had neither the energy nor even the sincere desire to imitate them.

It was those socialist theories, which I have previously called the philosophy of the February Revolution, that later kindled real passions, embittered jealousies, and finally stirred up war between the classes. While at the beginning passions were less disorderly than one might have feared, on the morrow of the revolution there was certainly an extraordinary ferment and unheard-of disorder in the people's ideas.

After the 25th February a thousand strange systems poured from the impetuous imaginations of innovators and spread through the troubled minds of the crowd. Everything except Throne and Parliament was still standing; and yet it seemed that the shock of revolution had reduced society itself to dust, and that there was an open competition for the plan of the new edifice to be put in its place; each man had his own scheme; one might publish his in the papers; another might use the posters that soon covered the walls; a third might proclaim his to the listening winds. One was going to abolish inequality of fortunes; another that of education; while a third attacked the oldest inequality of all, that between men and women. There were remedies against poverty, and against that disease called work which has afflicted man since the beginning of his existence.

There was great variety in these theories; sometimes they

[3] *The following passage is marked for omission in the manuscript:* The truth is that such a great change in the government, let alone in the whole condition of a nation, had never before been the work of citizens who cared so little.
[4] *Marginal note (Tocqueville):* This has been said already in connection with the capture of the Chamber. See which is the best place for this idea, and express it once only.

were contradictory and sometimes hostile to one another. But all of them, aiming lower than the government and attempting to reach society itself, on which government stands, adopted the common name of socialism. Socialism will always remain the most essential feature of the February Revolution, and the one that left the most frightening memory. Seen from afar, the Republic will appear as a means, not an end.

It is no part of the plan of these *Recollections* to inquire into what gave the February Revolution this socialist character. I shall only say that it should not have surprised the world as much as it did. Had no one noticed that for a long time the people had been continually gaining ground and improving their condition, and that their importance, education, desires and power were all constantly growing? Their prosperity had also increased, but not so fast, and it was getting close to that limit which, in old societies, cannot be passed, when there are many candidates but few places. How could it have failed to occur to the poor classes, who were inferior but nonetheless powerful, that they might use their power to escape from their poverty and inferiority?[5] For sixty years they had been working towards this end. At first the people hoped to help themselves by changing the political institutions, but after each change they found that their lot was not bettered, or that it had not improved fast enough to keep pace with their headlong desires. Inevitably they were bound to discover sooner or later that what held them back in their place was not the constitution of the government, but the unalterable laws that constitute society itself; and it was natural for them to ask whether they did not have the power and the right to change these too, as they had changed the others. And to speak specifically about property, which is, so to speak, the foundation of our social order, when all the privileges that cover and conceal the privilege of property had been abolished and property remained as the main obstacle to equality among men and seemed to be the only sign thereof, was it not inevitable, I do not say that it should be abolished

[5] *The following passage is marked for omission in the manuscript:* Especially at a time when the prospect of the other world has become hazier, and the miseries of this one are more apparent and seem more intolerable.

in its turn, but that at least the idea of abolishing it should strike minds that had no part in its enjoyment?

This natural restlessness in the minds of the people, with the inevitable ferment in the desires, thoughts, needs and instincts of the crowd, formed the fabric on which the innovators drew such monstrous and grotesque patterns. One may find their efforts ludicrous, but nothing merits the serious study of philosophers and statesmen more than the background on which they are working.

Will socialism remain buried in the contempt that so justly covers the socialists of 1848? I ask the question without answering it. I am sure that in the long run the constituent laws of our modern society will be drastically modified[6]; many of the main parts of them have already been substantially modified. But will they ever be abolished and replaced by others? That seems inpracticable to me. I say no more, for the more I study the former state of the world, and indeed even when I see the modern world in greater detail, when I consider the prodigious diversity found there, not just in the laws but in the principles of the laws and the different forms that the right of property has taken and, whatever anybody says, still takes on this earth, I am tempted to the belief that what are called necessary institutions are only institutions to which one is accustomed, and that in matters of social constitution the field of possibilities is much wider than people living within each society imagine.

[6] *Marginal Note* (*Tocqueville*): All this is basically similar to what I have written before on pp. 65–66.

Uncertainty of the members of the old Parliament about what attitude to adopt – My own reflections about what I ought to do and the resolutions I made

For a few days after the 24th February I neither sought nor saw the politicians from whom that day's events had separated me. I felt no need to do so and, to tell the truth, had no taste for it. I felt an instinctive repugnance against the memory of that wretched parliamentary world in which I had spent ten years of my life and seen the seeds of revolution sprouting.

Moreover I saw the utter futility at that moment of any sort of political talk or combination. However feeble the first impetus that set the crowd in motion may have been, that movement had now become irresistible. I felt that we were caught in one of those great democratic floods that drown those individuals, and those parties too, who try to build dikes to hold them. So for a time there is nothing better to do than observe the general characteristics of the phenomenon. Accordingly I spent my whole time in the streets with the victors, like any timeserver. I paid no homage to the new sovereign, however, and asked nothing from him. I did not even talk, merely listened and looked.

But after a few days I did get in touch with the vanquished again, meeting former deputies and peers, literary men, businessmen, financiers, landlords and those whom it was fashionable to call men of leisure. The revolution, I found, looked just as odd seen thus from above as it had when first seen from below. I did find much fear, but as little real passion as I had found elsewhere; there was a strange sense of resignation and, especially, no hope and, one might almost say, no idea of returning to a government that had after all only just fallen. Though the February Revolution had been the shortest and the least bloody of all our revolutions, it inspired in the minds and hearts of the defeated a much profounder sense of its almighty power than any of the others had done. I think the main reason for this was that those minds and hearts were empty of political beliefs and aspirations and that, after so many miscalculations and futile excitements, nothing but a taste for well-being was left, and that is a very tenacious and exclusive taste, but also a very gentle one that easily comes to terms with any type of government that allows it to find satisfaction.

So I perceived a universal inclination to fit in with fortune's improvisations and to tame the new master. Great landlords delighted to recall that they had always been hostile to the middle class and well disposed to the humble; priests again found the dogma of equality in the Gospel and assured us that they had always seen it there; even the middle classes discovered a certain pride in recalling that their fathers had been workers, and when the inevitable obscurity of their pedigrees prevented them from tracing descent from somebody who actually worked with his hands, they tried at least to unearth some boorish fellow who had made his own fortune. As much trouble was taken to give prominence to such a type as would until recently have been taken to hide him, for human vanity can take fantastically different shapes without changing its nature. It has an obverse and reverse face, but it is always the same medal.

Fear being the only real feeling in all hearts, far from breaking with those of their kin who had thrown in their lot with the revolution, men strove to get on good terms with them. This was the moment to turn every black sheep in the family to advantage. If one had a cousin, brother or son ruined by a disorderly life, one could be sure that he was on the road to success, and if he also had some extravagant theory knocking about in his head, he might get anywhere. Most government commissioners and undercommissioners were men of this type.

So those relations whom one used to avoid mentioning, those who in the old days would have been put away in the Bastille and, more recently, sent as officials to Algiers, suddenly became the glory and support of their families.

As for King Louis-Philippe, he could not have been more out of the picture if he had been a member of the Merovingian dynasty. Nothing struck me more than the complete silence surrounding his name. I did not hear it mentioned once, either by the people or by the upper classes. Those of his former courtiers whom I met did not speak of him, and I believe that they really did not think of him either. The revolution distracted their thoughts so violently that it drove out the memory of that prince. This, I shall be told, is the usual fate of fallen kings; but it is more worth noting that his enemies, too, had forgotten him; they did not fear him enough to abuse him, perhaps not even to hate him, and that may not be a greater insult of fate, but it is certainly a rarer one.

I do not want to write a history of the 1848 Revolution. I am merely trying to retrace my own actions, thoughts and impressions during that time. I shall therefore skip all that took place in the first weeks following the 24th February and go straight to the moment immediately before the general election.

The time had come to decide whether we wished to be plain spectators of this peculiar revolution or to take part in events. I found the former party leaders divided on this point: indeed to judge by the incoherence of their talk and their rapidly changing recommendations, they seemed even more divided in their own minds. These politicians, almost all of whom had formed their conception of public affairs within the regular framework of constitutional freedom and who were astonished amid their customary manoeuvres by the advent of a great revolution, seemed like river boatmen suddenly thrown into the open sea. The skills acquired in their little journeys were more hindrance than help in this great adventure, and they were often more inhibited and unsure of themselves than even the passengers.

M. Thiers several times expressed the opinion that one should stand for election and get chosen, and he also several times advised standing aside. I am not sure whether the reason for his hesitation was fear of what might happen after the election, or fear of not being elected.

Rémusat, who always sees so clearly what one might but so dimly what one should do, expounded good reasons for staying at home, and other equally good reasons that should have led to going out. Duvergier was bewildered. The revolution had smashed the system of the balance of powers that had kept his thoughts immobile for so many years, and he felt suspended in the void. As for the Duke of Broglie, he never poked his head out from under his cloak after the 24th February, but stayed waiting for the end of society, which he thought imminent. Only M. Molé, although he was by far the oldest of the parliamentary leaders, or perhaps for that very reason, remained resolute in the opinion that we ought to take part in affairs and try to lead the revolution; perhaps his longer experience had taught him that even a spectator's role is dangerous in troubled times; or perhaps the hope of once more having something to control cheered him and hid the danger of the enterprise from him; or, perhaps because, having had to bend so often this way and that under different régimes, his mind had become firmer as well as suppler and indifferent to what kind of master he served. Of course I gave very careful consideration to the part I ought to play.

At this point I should very much like to discover the reasons that then determined my conduct and, having discovered them, to set them out here without evasion; but how difficult it is to speak well about oneself! I have noticed that most of those who have left us their memoirs have recorded their bad actions and inclinations only when, as does sometimes happen, they have mistaken them for brave deeds or worthy instincts. Thus Cardinal de Retz, to gain credit, as he thought, for being a good conspirator, confesses his scheme for assassinating Richelieu and tells us about his devotions and his hypocritical charities, lest we should not think him a clever fellow. In such cases it is not love of truth that makes men speak, but the warped mind that unintentionally betrays the heart's vices.

But even when one wishes to be sincere, it is very rare to succeed therein completely. In the first place the public is to blame, for it likes to hear one accuse oneself but cannot stand self-praise; even one's friends usually call it amiable candour when one speaks ill of oneself, and awkward vanity when one claims some credit; thus on this reckoning, sincerity becomes an unrewarding trade, all losses and no gains. But the main difficulty is in the subject himself; one is too near to oneself to see oneself clearly and easily loses sight of oneself among all the views, interests, ideas, tastes and instincts that make one act. This tangle of little paths imperfectly known even by those who use them, prevents one from seeing clearly those main roads followed by the will, which led to its most important resolutions.

Nevertheless I want to try and discover myself in the midst of this labyrinth. For it is only right that I should take the same liberties with myself as I have taken, and will often take again, with so many others.

So then I must say that when I come to look carefully into the depths of my heart, I find with some surprise a certain relief, a sort of joy, mixed with all the sorrows and fears engendered by the revolution. This terrible event made me suffer for my country, but it is clear that I did not suffer for myself; on the contrary, I seemed to breathe more freely after the catastrophe. I had always felt constrained and oppressed within the parliamentary world just destroyed; I found it full of disappointments about others, and about myself; and, to begin with the latter, I was not slow to discover that I lacked the qualities needed to play the brilliant role of which I dreamed; both my good qualities and my defects proved obstacles. I was not sufficiently virtuous to command respect, but I had too much integrity to adapt myself to all those petty practices then necessary for quick success. And one must realize that there was no remedy for this integrity, for it was as much part of my temperament as of my principles, and without it I could get nothing whatsoever out of myself. When by chance I have been obliged to speak in a bad cause or to take a wrong path, I have immediately found myself completely bereft of talent as well as enthusiasm. And I confess that my greatest consolation for the frequently poor success of my integrity has been the conviction that I

should have made a very mediocre and clumsy rascal. I wrongly
supposed that as a speaker I should have the same success that
my book had had.[1] But skill as a writer is more hindrance
than help to a speaker, and vice versa. For a well-written chapter
is about as different as possible from a good speech. I soon
noticed that and saw that I was classed among those speakers
who are correct, straightforward and sometimes profound, but
always cold and consequently powerless. I have never been
able completely to cure myself of this defect. Certainly my
trouble is not any lack of passionate feelings, but on the
rostrum a passion for expressing myself well has always momentarily driven out all other passions. In the end I also discovered
that I completely lacked the art of holding men together and
leading them as a body. It is only in a tête-à-tête that I show
any dexterity, whereas in a crowd I am constrained and dumb.
Not but what on some particular occasion I may be capable
of doing and saying what pleases the crowd, but that is far
from sufficient; for great battles are rare in political warfare.

The basic craft for a party leader necessitates his mixing
continually with his own side, and even with his opponents,
with a universal geniality and accessibility, lowering or raising
the tone of his remarks so as to be understood by men of every
grade of intelligence; continually discussing and arguing, repeating
the same things a thousand times in different forms, and always
rousing himself to excitement about the same subjects. All things
of which I am profoundly incapable: I find discussion about
things that don't interest me much, awkward, and about things
for which I care acutely, painful. For me truth is something so
precious and rare that once I have found it, I do not want
to risk it in the hazard of an argument; I feel it is like a light
that might be put out by waving it to and fro. And as to getting
on good terms with people, I could not do so in any general
or systematic fashion, for there are so few whom I recognize.
Whenever there is nothing in a man's thoughts or feelings that
strikes me, I, so to speak, do not see him. I have always supposed
that mediocrities as well as men of parts had a nose, mouth and
eyes, but I have never been able to fix in my memory the forms

---

[1] Tocqueville alludes here to *Democracy in America*. (Ed.)

that those features take in each particular case. I am constantly asking the names of these unknown people whom I meet every day and constantly forget. It is not that I despise them, but I have little truck with them, feeling that they are like so many clichés. I respect them, for they make the world, but they bore me profoundly.

My distaste was completed by the mediocrity and monotony of the parliamentary events of my time, combined with the petty passions and vulgar perversity of the men who thought they were shaping or leading the same.

Sometimes I have thought that, though the mores of different societies varied, the morality of the politicians in charge of affairs was the same everywhere. What is certain is that in France all the party leaders I have met in my time have struck me as being more or less equally unworthy to command, some for lack of character or true enlightenment, most for lack of any virtues whatsoever. Hardly ever have I seen in any of them that disinterested concern for the good of mankind that I think I do find in myself, in spite of all my defects and weaknesses. So to join with others or to be self-sufficient was equally difficult for me, and in the end I came to live in morose isolation as a distant and badly judged character. I was continually conscious that imaginary qualities and defects were attributed to me. I was credited with a tactical skill, a peculiar profundity and a cunning ambition which I never had; while on the other hand my dissatisfaction with myself, my weariness and reserve were taken for arrogance, a defect that makes more enemies than any vice. I was thought sly and underhanded because I kept quiet; I was supposed to have an austere, vindictive, bitter temperament, which is not mine, for I often glide between good and evil with a soft indulgence that borders on weakness; and my quickness to forget grievances seems more like a lack of spirit, an inability to suffer the memory of an affront, rather than any virtuous effort to efface such impressions.

This cruel misunderstanding not only brought me suffering, but also reduced my capacities well below their natural level. For no man is approval more healthy than for me, and no one needs public esteem and confidence more to help him rise to the actions of which he is capable. Does this extreme distrust of my own powers and this continual need to find some sort of test of myself in the thought of others spring from true modesty? I am more inclined to believe that their origin is a great pride as nervous and restless as the mind itself.

But what preyed most on my hopes and my nerves throughout the nine years spent in public affairs, and what still remains the most frightful memory of that time, was the constant doubt in which I was forced to live about what was best to do each day. With me, I think, vacillation is due to intellectual doubts, not to a weak heart, and I never hesitate or find any trouble in taking even the thorniest path when I see clearly where it should lead me. But surrounded by all these petty dynastic parties, so little different in their aims and so much alike in the evil methods employed, what path clearly led to honesty or even to usefulness? Where was truth? Where was falsehood? Or which side were the evil ones? And on which the well-intentioned? I never could, at that time, fully answer those questions, and indeed I could not do so properly even now. Most party politicians do not let their spirits or nerves suffer from such doubts; there are even some who never knew them, or know them no longer. They are often accused of acting without conviction; but my experience goes to show that this is much less frequent than is supposed. It is just that they have a faculty, which is precious and indeed sometimes necessary in politics, of creating ephemeral convictions in accordance with the feelings and interests of the moment; and in this way they can with a tolerably good conscience do things that are far from honest. Unluckily I have never been able to illuminate my mind with such peculiar and contrived lights, or to persuade myself so easily that my advantage and the general weal conformed.

It was that parliamentary world, which brought me all the miseries just described, that the revolution had just smashed; it had jumbled and confounded the old parties in one common ruin, deposed their leaders and shattered their discipline. It is true that the society emerging therefrom was disorderly and confused, but it was one in which craft was less needed and less prized than disinterestedness and courage; where character was more important than the art of speaking well or managing men; and, especially, where there was no room left for moral hesitation: the choice lay between salvation or destruction for the country. One could no longer make a mistake about what path to follow; we were to walk in broad daylight sustained and encouraged by the crowd. It is true that the road looked dangerous, but my spirit is so constituted that I am less afraid of danger than of doubt. Moreover I felt that I was still in the prime of life; I had no children; my wants were few and, above all, I could count at home on the support of a devoted wife of penetrating insight and staunch spirit, whose naturally lofty soul would be ready to face any situation and triumph over any setback.

I therefore decided to plunge headlong into the fray, risking wealth, peace of mind and life to defend, not any particular government, but the laws that hold society itself together. The first necessity was to get elected, and so I left at once for my native Normandy to present myself to the electors.

CHAPTER FOUR

My candidature in the department of La Manche –
Characteristics of that province – The general election

The department of La Manche has of course an almost entirely
rural population. There are no large towns and few factories
and, with the exception of Cherbourg, no place in which workers come together in large numbers. At first the revolution was
hardly noticed there. The upper classes immediately bent beneath the blow, and the lower classes scarcely felt it. Agricultural
populations are usually less quick than others to receive political
impressions but more stubborn in retaining them; they are the
last to rise and the last to settle down again. My steward, who
is half-peasant, wrote telling me what was happening in the
country immediately after the 24th February:

"People are saying that if Louis-Philippe has been turned out,
that is well done, and he thoroughly deserved it . . ."

For them that was the whole moral of the play. But when
they began to hear talk of the disorder prevailing in Paris, new
taxes to be imposed, and the fear of a general war; when, too,
they saw trade coming to a standstill and money apparently
vanishing underground, and especially when they heard that the
principle of property was being attacked, they realized that
something more than Louis-Philippe was at stake.

The fear, which in the beginning had been confined to the
upper stratum of society, now descended to the lowest of the
working class, and a universal terror gripped the countryside.
That is the state of affairs I found on my arrival in the middle

of March. There was something that immediately struck me
with astonished pleasure. For although some sort of demagogic
agitation prevailed among the workers in the towns, in the
country all the landowners, whatever their origin, antecedents,
education, or means, had come together and seemed to form
a single unit: all the old political hatreds and rivalries of caste
and wealth had vanished. Neither jealousy nor pride separated
the peasant from the rich man any longer, or the bourgeois
from the gentleman; instead there was mutual confidence, respect and goodwill. Ownership constituted a sort of fraternity
linking all who had anything, the richest were the elder brothers
and the less prosperous the younger; but all thought themselves
brothers, having a common inheritance to defend. As the French
Revolution had divided up ownership of the land *ad infinitum*,
the whole population seemed part of one vast family. I have
never seen anything like it, and nobody had seen anything of
the sort in France within the memory of man. Experience has
proved that the union was not as close as it seemed to be and
has shown that the old parties and the various classes were
juxtaposed rather than mingled; fear had acted upon them as
physical pressure might on very hard substances, forcing them
to hold together while the compression continued, but leaving
them to fall apart when it was relaxed.

Besides, at this first moment, I could see no trace of what
are properly called political opinions. One would have said that
the republican form of government had suddenly become not
only the best but the only imaginable sort of government for
France: dynastic hopes and fears were so deeply buried in the
depths of men's souls that one could not even see the place
where they had been. The Republic respected persons and property, and it was accepted as legitimate. But the next point that
struck me was the universal hatred combined with terror felt
towards Paris for the first time. French provincials have the
same feelings about Paris and the central government of which
it is the seat as the English have about their aristocracy, sometimes impatiently complaining about it and often regarding it
with jealousy, but fundamentally liking it because they always
hope to make its power serve their particular interests. This time,

Paris and those who spoke in her name had so abused her power and seemed to set so little store by the rest of the country that the idea of shaking off her yoke and at last acting on their own entered the heads of many who had never thought of it before; these, it is true, were but timid, vague desires and clumsy ephemeral feelings, and I never thought there was much to hope or fear from them. But these new sentiments did convert themselves into electoral ardour. People wanted to attend the elections, and voting for enemies of the Parisian demagogy struck them not so much as the regular use of a right but rather as the least dangerous means available for confronting the master.

I stayed in the little town of Valognes, which is the natural centre of my influence, and, as soon as I had taken in the state of the country, set about my candidature. I noticed then something that I have observed in a thousand other contexts, namely that nothing makes for success more than not desiring it too ardently. I did very much want to be elected, but in circumstances of such critical difficulty I could easily reconcile myself to the idea of defeat; and this placid anticipation of a setback made my mind calm and limpid, and gave me a respect for myself and a contempt for the follies of the time that I could not have enjoyed to the same extent if nothing but a passion to succeed had filled my thoughts.

The country began to fill with roving candidates hawking their republican protestations from hustings to hustings. I refused to present myself before any other electoral body than that of the place where I lived.[1] Each little town had its club, and each club asked the candidates to given an account of their views and acts and imposed formulations of policy on them. I refused to answer any of these insolent questions. Such refusals might have seemed contemptuous, but in fact they were regarded as dignity and independence in dealing with the new sovereign authority, and I got more credit for my revolt than others did for their obedience.

I limited myself to publishing an address and having it posted everywhere throughout the department.

[1] See E. L'Hommedé, *Un Départment Français sous la Monarchie de Juillet. Le Conseil Général de la Manche et Alexis de Tocqueville*, Paris, 1933. (Ed.)

Most of the candidates had resumed the old usages of '92. In letters they addressed people as "Citizens" and signed themselves "Fraternally yours." My circular began by calling the electors "Messieurs" and I ended it by proudly assuring them of my respect.

"I do not come," I said, "to solicit your votes, but only to put myself under my country's orders. I asked to be your representative in quiet, easy times. Honour forbids me to refuse to represent you in a time of present trouble with many possible dangers ahead.[2] That is what I must tell you first."

I added that I had been faithful to the end to the oath I had sworn to the Monarchy, but that the Republic, which had come into being without my help, would have my energetic support, for I did not wish merely to tolerate its existence but to sustain it. I then went on:

"But what republic is in question? There are those who mean by a republic a dictatorship exercised in the name of freedom; who think that the Republic should not only change political institutions, but reshape society itself; there are those who think that the Republic should be aggressive and propagandist. I am not that kind of Republican. If that were your way of being one, I could be of no use to you, for I should not share your opinion. But if you understand the meaning of a republic in the same sense as I, you can count on my devoting my soul to a cause which is mine as well as yours."

In times of revolution, people who do not feel fear are like members of the royal family in an army, producing a great effect by very ordinary actions, for their peculiar position naturally allows no rivals and gives them great prominence.[3] I was myself astonished at the success of my circular. In a few days it made me the most popular man in the department of La Manche and the cynosure of all eyes. My former political ad-

[2] *The following passage has been marked for omission in the manuscript:* So then I do not ask for your votes, but am ready to consecrate my time, my fortune and my life to you.

[3] *Variant:* They produce a great effect . . . because the special position which they occupy takes them inevitably out of the crowd and puts them in a position of great prominence. It is very easy to be without rival in times of revolution. One has only to continue to be oneself to become a very unusual person.

versaries, the Conservatives and the agents of the old government, who had attacked me most and who had been overthrown
by the Republic, came in a body to assure me that they were
ready not only to support me but to follow my advice in everything.

Meanwhile the first meeting of the electors of the *arrondisse-
ment* of Valognes took place. I appeared together with the other
candidates. The forum was a shed serving as a hall. The chairman's platform was at the bottom, and at the side of this a
professor's chair had been provided as a rostrum for the candidate. The chairman, a teacher at the college of Valognes, addressed me in a loud, authoritative voice, but very respectfully:

"Citizen de Tocqueville, I am going to put to you the questions
requiring your answer." To which I answered in a slightly off-
hand way: "Mr. Chairman, I am listening."

A parliamentary speaker whose name I would rather not mention once said to me:

"You see, my dear friend, there is only one way of speaking
well from the rostrum, and that is to persuade yourself as you
go up that you have more brains than anybody else."

I always thought that easier said than done in the presence
of our great political assemblies. But I admit that here it seemed
easy advice to follow, and I successfully did so. Not that I went
to the length of thinking that I had more brains than anybody
else. But I soon saw that I was the only one well acquainted
with the facts they brought forward and even with the language
they wished to speak. It would have been difficult to appear
clumsier or more ignorant than my adversaries. They overwhelmed me with questions that they thought very knotty, but
that left me very free; and my replies, not always very brilliant,
invariably struck them as crushing. The ground on which they
especially hoped to bring me down was the question of the
banquets. I had not, as mentioned, wanted to take any part in
those dangerous demonstrations; my political friends criticized
me strongly for abandoning them in these circumstances, and
some of them still bore me a grudge, although the revolution
proved me right, or perhaps it was because the revolution proved
me all too right.

"Why did you desert the opposition at the time of the banquets?" I was asked.

I replied boldly: "I could find an excuse, but I prefer to give you my real reason. I did not want the banquets because I did not want a revolution. And I make bold to say that hardly any of those who sat down at those banquets would have done so if, like me, they had known what the result would be. So the only difference that I see between you and me is that I knew what you were doing, but you did not know."

This bold profession of anti-revolutionary faith had been preceded by one of faith in the Republic. The sincerity of the one seemed to attest to the sincerity of the other, and the assembly laughed and cheered. My adversaries were ridiculed, and I came out triumphant.

In my minutes of this meeting I have also found this question and answer, which I reproduce because they clearly show the preoccupations of the moment and the true state of my own mind.

Question: "If a riot threatens the National Assembly and bayonets invade it, do you swear to stay at your post and, if necessary, die there?"

Answer: "My presence here is my answer. After nine years of unremitting, useless labour trying to steer the government that has just fallen into more liberal and honest paths, I would have preferred to retire into private life and wait till the storm was over. But my honour forbade me to do so. Yes, like you, I think that perils await those who want to represent you faithfully. But with the danger there is glory, and it is because of the danger and the glory that I am here now."

I had won over the farming population of the department by my circular; it was a speech that won over the workers of Cherbourg. Two thousand of them had come together for a patriotic dinner. I received a very polite and pressing invitation to attend, and I did so.

When I arrived, the procession was ready to leave for the banquet hall, with, at its head, my old colleague Havin, who had come expressly from Saint-Lô to take the chair. It was the first time I had met him since the 24th February. On that day

I had seen him giving his arm to the Duchess of Orleans, and
the next morning I had learned that he was a commissioner of the
Republic in the department of La Manche. That had not surprised me, for I knew him to be one of those footloose men of
ambition who found themselves trapped for ten years in the opposition, whereas they had intended only to pass through that
way. What a lot of men of that type I saw round me, tormented
by their own virtue and in despair because the best part of
their lives was spent in criticizing the vices of others without
a chance to give play to their own, nourished by nothing but
imaginary abuses of power! The long fast had given most of
them such an appetite for places, honours and money that one
would naturally expect them to rush at power gluttonously at
the first opportunity, not waiting to choose their time or their
titbit. Havin was true to this type. The Provisional Government
had given him as colleague, or even superior, another of my
fellow deputies in the old Chamber, M. Vieillard, who has
since become famous as a particular friend of Prince Louis Napoleon. Vieillard had a right to serve the Republic, for he had
been one of the seven or eight republicans in the old Chamber
under the Monarchy. Before he became a demagogue, he had
been at home in the drawing rooms of the Empire; in literary
questions he was an intolerant classicist; in religion a Voltairean;
a bit vain, very kindly, an honest man and even an intelligent
one, but in politics strangely foolish. Havin had made him his
tool; whenever he wanted to strike down one of his own adversaries or to reward a friend, he almost invariably made Vieillard, who let him do what he liked, responsible. Thus Havin
advanced under cover of Vieillard's integrity and republicanism,
always making the latter go in front of him, like a miner with
his gabion.[4]

Havin hardly seemed to recognize me and gave me no invitation to join the procession. I modestly retreated into the crowd
and when I arrived at the banquet took a place at one of the
lower tables. Soon the speeches started; Vieillard read a very

[4] Webster's Dictionary gives the following definition of gabion: "A hollow
cylinder of wickerwork or strap iron like a basket without a bottom that is
filled with earth and used in building fieldworks or in mining as revet-
ments or as shelter from an enemy's fire." (Ed.)

suitable address, and Havin read another, which was fairly well received. I very much wanted to speak, but I was not on the list, and besides I did not quite see how to begin. A reference by one of the orators (all the speakers there were called orators) to the memory of Colonel Briqueville gave me my chance. I asked to speak, and the meeting chose to hear me. When I found myself mounted on the rostrum, or rather on the professor's chair raised twenty feet above the audience, I felt a little confused. But I soon recovered my presence of mind and delivered a touching little obituary address, which I should find impossible to remember now. I know only that it was somehow *à propos* and had the warmth that shows through in an improvised speech, however muddled, which is quite enough to make it a success with a popular assembly, or indeed any other assembly; for one cannot repeat too often that speeches are made to be heard, not read, and the only good ones are those that move the audience.

This one was universally and noisily acclaimed; and I must confess that I found it a treat to be avenged in this way for my former colleague's attempt to abuse what he took to be fortune's favours.

If I am not mistaken, it was between this time and the election that I made my journey to Saint-Lô as a member of the General Council. The Council had been summoned in extraordinary session; it still had the same composition it had had under the Monarchy. Most of its members had bowed to the wishes of Louis-Philippe's officials, and they had been among those who did the most to bring that King's rule into contempt in our part of the country. My only memory from that journey to Saint-Lô is the peculiar servility of those former conservatives. It was not just that they offered no opposition to Havin, whom they had loaded with insults for the past ten years, but that they proved themselves his most attentive courtiers. They praised him, voted for him and smiled on him; even among themselves they spoke well of him, for fear of indiscretion. I have often seen human baseness on a greater scale, but I have never seen a more perfect picture of it; and so, although it is so petty, I think it is worth bringing into the open, and I would like to train the light of subsequent events on it. For some months

later, when the turn of the popular tide had brought them back
to power, they immediately started attacking this same Havin
with a violence and sometimes an unfairness that were unbelievable. All their old hatred burst through their last shuddering
fears, and memories of their flattery made it the more bitter.

Meanwhile the date of the general election was getting close,
and the outlook was becoming daily gloomier; all the news
reaching us from Paris showed that great city continually on
the verge of falling into the hands of armed socialists. It was
doubtful whether these socialists would leave the electors alone
or, at least, whether they would not react violently against the
National Assembly. Already officers of the National Guard were
everywhere being made to swear that they would march against
the Assembly if a conflict arose between it and the people. The
provinces became more and more alarmed, but they also gathered their forces at the sight of danger.

I spent the last days before the general election at my poor,
dear Tocqueville; this was the first time I had been back there
since the revolution, and I was perhaps going to leave it forever.
On entering the house I was flooded with such an intense and
peculiar sadness that the memory of it still remains firmly engraved on my mind, although much else happened to remember
then. I arrived unexpectedly. The empty rooms with no one but
my old dog to welcome me, the uncurtained windows, the piles
of dusty furniture, fires gone out, clocks run down, the mournful
look of the place, the damp walls—all these things seemed witnesses of neglect and prophets of doom. This little isolated
corner of the world among the fields and hedges and woods of
our Norman landscape, which had often been the most delightful
retreat for me, now seemed a deserted wilderness. But through
the desolation of the present I could see, as if looking out from
the bottom of a tomb, the tenderest and gayest memories of my
life. It is wonderful how much brighter and more vivid than
reality are the colours of a man's imagination. I had just seen
the Monarchy fall; since then I have witnessed the most terrible
scenes of bloodshed. All the same I declare that neither at the
time nor now in recollection do I feel such deep and poignant
emotion about any of those disasters as I felt that day at the

sight of the ancient home of my ancestors and at the memory of the quiet, happy days I passed there without realizing how precious they were. Believe me, it was then and there that I most fully understood the utter bitterness of revolutions.

The local people had always been kindly disposed to me, but this time I found them positively affectionate, and I never had so much respect shown to me before a crass equality was placarded on every wall. We had to go in a body to vote at the town of Saint-Pierre, a league away from our village. On the morning of election day all the electors, that is to say the whole male population over twenty years old, assembled in front of the church. They formed themselves into a double column in alphabetical order; I preferred to take the place my name warranted, for I knew that in democratic times and countries one must allow oneself to be put at the head of the people, but must not put oneself there.[5] The crippled and sick who wished to follow us came on pack horses or in carts at the end of this long procession. Only the women and children were left behind. We were in all a hundred and seventy persons. When we got to the top of the hill overlooking Tocqueville, there was a momentary halt; I realized that I was required to speak. I climbed to the other side of a ditch. A circle formed around me, and I said a few words appropriate to the occasion. I reminded these good people of the seriousness and importance of the act they were going to perform; I advised them not to let themselves be accosted or diverted by people who might, when we arrived at the town, seek to deceive them, but rather to march as a united body with each man in his place and to stay that way until they had voted. "Let no one," I said, "go into a house to take food or to dry himself (it was raining that day), before he has performed his duty." They shouted that they would do this, and so they did. All the votes were given at the same time, and I have reason to think that almost all were for the same candidate.

As soon as I had voted myself, I said good-bye to them and got into a carriage to go to Paris.

[5] *Sentence crossed out in the manuscript:* Like me, the priest and curate were in their place.

CHAPTER FIVE

*First meeting of the Constituent Assembly – Appearance
of that Assembly*

I stopped at Valognes only to say good-bye to some of my
friends; several of them had tears in their eyes as we parted,
for there was a widespread belief in the countryside that the
deputies would face great dangers in Paris. Several of these
worthy people told me: "If the National Assembly is attacked,
we will come to defend you." I am sorry to remember that at
the time I thought these merely empty words, for they actually
did come, they and many others, as will be seen later on.

It was only when I got to Paris that I learned that I had been
elected with 110,704 votes out of about 120,000. Most of the
colleagues elected with me had belonged to the old dynastic
opposition; only two had professed republican opinions before
the revolution and were, as it was called in the slang of the day,
"republicans of yesterday." It was the same in most parts of
France.

There have been more mischievous revolutionaries than those
of 1848, but I doubt if there have been any stupider. They did
not know how to make use of universal suffrage or how to manage without it. If they had held the elections immediately after
the 24th February when the upper classes were stunned by
the blow they had just received and the people were more astonished than malcontent, they might perhaps have got an Assembly after their own hearts. If they had boldly seized dictatorship, they might have retained it for some time. But they handed

themselves over to the nation while doing everything best calculated to alienate it; they threatened it while they put themselves at its mercy; they frightened it by the boldness of their plans and the violence of their language, while the feebleness of their deeds invited resistance; they flaunted the airs of instructors at the very moment when they put themselves at the nation's disposal. Instead of opening their ranks after the victory, they jealously closed them; in a word, they seemed bent on solving this insoluble problem: how to govern through the majority but against its inclinations.

Following examples from the past without understanding them, they gullibly imagined that to summon the people to political life was enough to attach them to their cause; and that, if they gave the people rights but no advantages, it was enough to make the Republic popular. They forgot that their predecessors at the same time that they gave every peasant a vote did away with tithes, abolished the *corvée*[1] and other seignorial privileges, and divided the nobles' land among their former serfs, whereas there was nothing similar that they could do. By establishing universal suffrage they thought they were summoning the people to support the revolution, whereas they were only arming them against it. I am, however, far from believing that it was impossible for revolutionary passions to have been roused even in the country districts. In France every farmer owns some part of the soil, and most of their small holdings are encumbered with debt; therefore the creditor rather than the noble was their enemy, and it was he who should have been attacked. Not the abolition of property rights, but the abolition of debts should have been promised. The demagogues of 1848 did not think of this scheme; they proved themselves much clumsier than their predecessors, but that did not make them any more honest; they were just as violent and unfair in their desires as the others

[1] During the Ancien Régime, the corvée was an obligation placed on the unprivileged classes of society to spend a certain number of days in the year working on the main roads of the kingdom. The work was either of construction or maintenance, and was unpaid. For further information on the dues and obligations of pre-revolutionary France, see M. Marion, *Dictionnaire des Institutions de la France*, Paris, 1923, or the reimpression of 1968. (Ed.)

had been in their acts. But to commit acts of violent injustice, it is not enough for a government to desire them, or even to have the ability to do them; it is essential that the mores, ideas and passions of the time lend themselves to the enterprise.

Accordingly most of the elections went contrary to the wishes of the party that had made the revolution, and rightly so. None-theless that party found it a painful surprise. Its sorrow and its anger grew as its candidates were turned down. And one could hear it complaining, sometimes gently, sometimes stridently, about the nation, which is regarded as ignorant, ungrateful, mad and hostile to its own good. I was reminded of Molière's Arnolphe saying to Agnès:

"Pourquoi ne m'aimer pas, madame l'impudente?"[2]

It was, however, no laughing matter but something sinister and frightening to see the state of Paris when I returned there. In that city there were a hundred thousand armed workmen formed into regiments, without work and dying of hunger, but with heads full of vain theories and chimerical hopes. Society was cut in two: those who had nothing united in common envy; those who had anything united in common terror. There were no longer ties of sympathy linking these two great classes, and a struggle was everywhere assumed to be inevitable soon. There had already been physical clashes with different results between the *bourgeois* and the *people*—for these old names had been revived as battle cries—at Limoges and at Rouen. In Paris hardly a day passed without some attack or threat to the propertied classes' capital or income. Sometimes the demand was that they should provide employment without selling anything; some-times that they should let their tenants off their rent, when they themselves had no other income to live from. The landlords bent as they could before this tyranny, trying to get at least some advantage from their weakness by publishing it. I recall among several advertisements in the papers this one, which struck me as a perfect example of vanity, cowardice and stu-pidity artistically blended:

"Mr. Editor," it ran, "I make use of your paper to inform my

---

[2] "Why not love me, you brazen bit?" Molière. *L'École des Femmes.* Act V, Scene IV, line 52. (Ed.)

tenants that, desiring to put into practice in my relations with them those principles of fraternity that should guide true democrats, I will give any of those tenants who ask for it a receipt for their next quarter's rent."

A dull despair had descended on the oppressed and threatened middle classes, but imperceptibly that despair was turning into courage. I had always thought that there was no hope of gradually and peacefully controlling the impetus of the February Revolution and that it could only be stopped suddenly by a great battle taking place in Paris. I had said that immediately after the 24th February, and what I now saw persuaded me that the battle was not only inevitable but imminent, and that it would be desirable to seize the first opportunity to start it.

The National Assembly finally met on the 4th May. Up to the last moment there had been doubts that it would be able to do so. I indeed believe that some of the most ardent demagogues did several times feel tempted to do without it but did not dare; for they remained crushed beneath the weight of their own dogma of the sovereignty of the people.

I should be able to call to mind the look of that Assembly at its opening, but I find that my recollection is very blurred. It is a mistake to suppose that events stay in the memory because of their importance or greatness alone. It is more often the little things that happen that make a deep impression on the mind and stay in the memory. I can remember only our shouting, "Long live the Republic!" fifteen times in the course of the session in competition with one another. There are plenty of analogies for such behaviour in the history of other assemblies; one constantly finds one party exaggerating sentiments it does feel in order to embarrass its opponents, while the latter feigns sentiments it does not feel in order to avoid the trap. Thus an impetus common to both drives one beyond the truth and the other in the opposite direction to it. This time, however, I think the cry was sincere on both sides, but it stood for different or even contradictory thoughts. Everybody wanted to preserve the Republic, but some wanted to use it for attack, and others to defend themselves. The newspapers of the time talked about the enthusiasm of the Assembly and the enthusiasm of the people. Whereas actually there was a lot of noise but no enthusiasm. Thoughts of the morrow preoccupied everybody so much that nobody could allow any sentiment whatsoever to divert him far from that preoccupation.

A decree of the Provisional Government laid down the rule that we should all wear the dress of members of the Convention, in particular the white waistcoat with turned-down collar always worn by actors playing Robespierre. At first I supposed this fine idea had been Ledru-Rollin's or Louis Blanc's, but I found afterwards that it was the result of Armand Marrast's flowery literary imagination. Of course nobody obeyed the decree, not even its author, except for Caussidière who did disguise himself in the prescribed manner. It was this that made me notice him, for I did not know either him or most of the rest of those who came to call themselves Montagnards, again conforming with memories of '93. His body was very large and fat, and his expressive head was triangular and sunk deep between his shoulders; his eyes were cunning and mischievous, but the rest of his features had a good-natured look. In short, it was a pretty shapeless lump of stuff, but within it was a mind subtle enough to know how to turn vulgarity and ignorance to advantage.

The next day and the day after that the members of the Provisional Government each in turn gave us an account of what they had done since the 24th February. Each had much good to say of himself, and even a certain amount of good about his colleagues, although it would be hard to find a body of men who nourished more sincere hatreds of one another than these. Apart from the political hatreds and jealousies separating them, I thought they showed that particular irritation towards each other that one meets in passengers who have had to endure a long stormy crossing together without learning to get on with or understand one another. Almost all the parliamentary figures among whom I had lived reappeared at that first session. Except for M. Thiers who failed to get elected, the Duke of Broglie who had not stood, and MM. Guizot and Duchâtel who had fled, I think all the famous orators and most of the known speakers of the old political world were there; but these men felt themselves out of their element, isolated and suspect; they were frightened themselves, and they frightened others, two contraries often found together in politics. At that moment they had none of the influence that talent and experience were soon to restore to them. All the other members of the Assembly were complete novices, just as if we had stepped straight out of the Ancien Régime; for our centralization had always kept public life limited to the boundaries of the two Chambers, and people who had not been either peers or deputies scarcely knew what an Assembly was, or how one should behave or talk there; they were profoundly ignorant of its daily habits and most ordinary customs; at decisive moments they were inattentive, but they listened very attentively to things of no importance. I recall that on the second day all these new arrivals crowded around the rostrum and insisted on perfect silence, in order to hear the minutes of the previous sitting read, imagining this formality to be a matter of grave importance. I am sure that nine hundred English or American peasants chosen at random would have had much more the look of a great political body.

Again imitating the Convention, those professing the most radical and revolutionary opinions took their seats on the highest benches; they were very uncomfortable up there, but it gave them the right to call themselves Montagnards, and, as men ever love to feed on agreeable fantasies, they flattered themselves that they resembled the famous scoundrels whose name they had taken.

These Montagnards soon separated into two very distinct groups: the revolutionaries of the old school and the socialists; nevertheless the shades between them were never very clearly defined, and men passed from one to the other by imperceptible gradations. Almost all those who could properly be called Montagnards had some socialist ideas in their heads, and the socialists were very ready to fall in with their revolutionary proceedings. The differences between them were, however, sufficiently deep to prevent their always marching in step, and it was this that saved us. The socialists were the more dangerous, for they were more in harmony with the true character of the February Revolution and with the only real passions engendered by it; but they were men more of theory than of action, and to be able to overthrow society at their pleasure, they needed the practical energy and skill in handling insurrections that only their colleagues possessed in an adequate degree.

From my seat I could easily hear what was being said on the benches of the Mountain and, especially, see what was being done. Consequently I had occasion to study the men in that part of the Chamber with rather exceptional care. For me it was like the discovery of a new world. One consoles oneself for not knowing foreign lands by supposing that one knows one's own country at least, and one is wrong; for there are always areas of one's own land that one has not visited, and races of men who are new to one. I experienced this fully then. I felt that I was seeing these Montagnards for the first time, so greatly did their way of speaking and mores surprise me. They spoke a jargon that was not quite the language of the people, nor was it that of the literate, but that had the defects of both; it was full of coarse words and ambitious expressions. A constant jet of insulting or jocular interruptions poured down from the benches of the Mountain; they were continually making jokes or sententious comments; and they shifted from a very ribald tone of voice to one of great haughtiness. Obviously these people belonged neither in a tavern nor in a drawing room; I think they must have polished their mores in the cafés and fed their minds on no literature but the newspapers. In any case this was the first time since the beginning of the revolution that this type of man had come into prominence in any of our Assemblies; until then it had been represented only by isolated and unnoticed individuals, who were more anxious to conceal than to flaunt themselves.

There were two other peculiarities in the Constituent Assembly which struck me as just as novel, although in quite different ways. It contained infinitely more large landowners and also gentlemen than did any of the Chambers elected when it was a necessary condition for electors and elected to have money. Also there was a more numerous and more powerful religious group than there had been under the Restoration; I counted three bishops, several vicars general and one Dominican, whereas under Louis XVIII and Charles X only one abbé had ever succeeded in getting elected.

The abolition of any property qualification, which meant that some of the electors were dependent on the rich, and the visible dangers threatening property, which made people choose those who had the most interest in defending it, were the main reasons for the presence of the great number of landowners. The election of the ecclesiastics was due to similar reasons, and also to one different reason that is even more worth consideration, that is, the very widespread and quite unexpected return of a great part of the nation to a concern with religious matters.

When the Revolution of '92 struck the upper classes, it cured them of their lack of religion; it vividly taught them, if not the truth, at least the social usefulness of belief. This lesson was lost on the middle classes, who inherited the upper classes' political position and became their jealous rivals; indeed the middle classes became even more unbelieving as the upper classes seemed to become devout once more. On a small scale the Revolution of 1848 had just done for the bourgeoisie what '92 had done for the nobility: the same setback, same fears, same return; the same picture but on a smaller scale and with colours less vivid and, of course, less durable.[3] The clergy had made this return easier by separating itself from all the old political parties and returning to the ancient and true spirit of all Catholic clergy, which is that it should belong to the church alone. Consequently it readily professed republican opinions but at the same time gave to long-established interests the guarantee of its traditions, mores and hierarchy. It was accepted and made much of by all. The priests elected to the Assembly were always held in very high esteem there, and they deserved it for their good sense, moderation and modesty. Some of them did try to

[3] For further information on the religious revival of 1792, see J. Godechot, *La Contre-Révolution.* Paris, 1961; F. Baldensperger, *Le mouvement des idées dans l'émigration française, 1789–1815.* Paris, 1924. For that of 1848, see W. Gurian, *Die politischen und sozialen Ideen des französichen Katholizismus 1789–1914,* M. Gladbach, 1928; A. Dansette, *Histoire religieuse de la France contemporaine* (revised edition), Paris, 1965. The 1948 edition of this work has been translated into English and was published in 1961. (Ed.)

speak from the rostrum, but they could never learn the language of politics; they had forgotten it too long ago; all their speeches imperceptibly turned into sermons.

Universal suffrage had shaken the land from top to bottom without bringing into prominence any new man deserving of attention. I have always thought that, no matter what procedure is followed in a general election, most of the exceptional men in the country will surely succeed in getting elected. The electoral system chosen influences only the type of ordinary individuals included in an assembly, who are bound to be at the base of any political body. The classes from which these members are drawn and their attitudes vary widely according to the electoral system used. The appearance of the Constituent Assembly confirmed me in this opinion. I knew almost all the men who played leading parts in it, but the crowd of other members was like nothing I had seen previously.[4]

Taken all in all, in my considered judgement this Assembly was an improvement on any I had seen before. There were more men who were sincere, disinterested, honest and, especially, courageous than in any other Chamber to which I had belonged.

The Constituent Assembly had been elected to face civil war; that was its main merit; as long as it was necessary to fight, it was in effect splendid; it only became a wretched sight after victory, when it felt itself disintegrating as a result and under the weight of that victory.

I chose a place to the left of the hall from which I could easily hear the orators and also get to the rostrum if I wanted to speak myself. A good number of my old friends joined me there; Lanjuinais, Dufaure, Corcelle, Beaumont and several others sat nearby.

I should like to say a few words about the hall itself, although it is familiar to all. This is necessary to make my account intelligible, and although the wood-and-plaster structure will probably last longer than the Republic cradled there, I do not think it will last very long, and when it has gone, several things that happened there will be hard to understand.

[4] *The following words are marked for omission in the manuscript:* They were animated by a new spirit, and their character and mores were new.

The hall was oblong and very large. The President's platform and the rostrum were at one end; there were nine tiers of benches along the other three sides. In the middle, in front of the rostrum, was a great empty space, like the arena in an amphitheatre except that it was oblong, not round. Consequently most of the listeners could only catch a glimpse of the speaker from the side, and only those who could see him straight in front were very far away. This was an arrangement strangely calculated to encourage inattention and disorder. Those sitting to the side, seeing little of the speaker but much of the members opposite, were busier threatening and apostrophizing each other than listening; and those at the end were no more attentive, for though they could see, they could not hear the speaker very well.

Big windows along the top of the hall opened directly out of doors, letting in air and light. The walls were decorated with nothing beyond a few flags, for luckily time had been too short to add those dull allegories on cardboard or canvas with which the French love to cover their public buildings, although those who can understand them find them stupid, and they are incomprehensible to the people. The whole thing looked vast, cold, solemn and almost sad. Seating had been prepared for nine hundred members, a larger Assembly than any there had been in France for sixty years.

I felt at once that the atmosphere of this Assembly suited me, and in spite of the seriousness of the situation, I had a sense of happiness I had never known before. For this was the first time since I entered public life that I felt myself moving with the current of a majority in the only direction that my tastes, reason and conscience could approve, and that was a new and delightful sensation for me. I discovered that this majority would rebuff the socialists and the Montagnards but sincerely desired to support and organize the Republic. I agreed with them about the two main points; I had no monarchical convictions and no affection or regret for any prince; and I had no cause to defend except freedom and human dignity. To protect the ancient laws of society against the innovators by using the new strength the republican principle could give to government; to make the clear will of the people of France triumph over the passions and desires of the Paris working men, and in this way to conquer demagogy by democracy, such was my only design. Never has an aim seemed to me higher or clearer. I am not sure that the dangers to be faced before it could be attained did not make it even more attractive to me, for I have a natural inclination for adventure. I detest the sight of very great and imminent danger. But I have always found that a touch of danger lends spice to most of life's actions.

CHAPTER SIX

My relations with Lamartine – His Subterfuges

This was the time when Lamartine was at the zenith of his fame. He seemed a saviour to all who had been harmed or frightened by the revolution, and they were the great majority of the nation. Paris and eleven departments had just elected him to the National Assembly. I do not think anybody else has ever inspired such transports of enthusiasm; one must have seen love goaded by fear to understand the silly extremes of affection of which men are capable. Every deputy arriving in Paris, determined to restrain the excesses of the revolution and to fight against the demagogic party, regarded him from the start as the only leader and waited for him to put himself unhesitatingly at the head of the fight against the socialists and demagogues. They soon discovered that they were mistaken and that Lamartine did not see the part he ought to play in such simple terms. One must recognize that his position was very complicated and difficult. It was forgotten at the time, but he himself could not forget, that he had done more than anybody else for the success of the February Revolution. Terror momentarily obliterated this memory from the public mind, but as public order returned, the fact would, of course, soon be remembered. It was easy to foresee that as soon as the current that had brought things to their present state had been stopped, a current in the reverse direction would carry the nation the opposite way faster and farther than Lamartine could or would go. The Montagnards' success would entail his immediate ruin, but their complete defeat would render him useless, and sooner or later it could and should make rule slip from his hands. He therefore saw almost as many disadvantages and dangers for himself in victory as in defeat.

I in fact believe that, had Lamartine from the first put himself resolutely at the head of the immense party that wanted to slow down and control the revolution, and had he succeeded in leading it to victory, he would very soon have been buried under his own triumph; he could not have halted his army in time, and it would soon have left him behind and appointed other leaders.

I do not think it was possible for him, whatever line of conduct he adopted, to keep power long; I think the only chance left to him was to lose it gloriously in saving the country. Of course Lamartine was not the man to sacrifice himself in that way, or in any other. I do not think I ever met in the world of ambitious egoists in which I lived any mind so untroubled by thought of the public good as his. I have seen a great many men unsettle the country to raise themselves, for that perversity is fashionable. But he, I think, was the only one who always seemed ready to turn the world upside down for the fun of it. Furthermore I have never known a less sincere mind, or one that more completely despised truth. When I say that he despised it, I am wrong; he never honoured it enough to be concerned with it in any way at all. Talking or writing, he departed from truth and returned to it without taking any notice, being solely concerned with the particular effect he wanted to produce at that moment.

I had not seen Lamartine since the 24th February. Then I did see him on the day after the Assembly had first met in the new hall where I had just chosen my place. But I did not talk to him. He was surrounded by some of his new friends. As soon as he saw me, he pretended to have something to do at the far end of the hall and got away from me precipitately. Afterwards he sent me word by Champeaux (who was attached to him half as friend and half as servant) that I must not take his avoiding me ill, as his position forced him to behave like that towards men of the old Parliament; that of course there was a place marked out for me among the future leaders of the Republic, but that we must wait for the first momentary difficulties to be surmounted before we could come to a direct understanding. Champeaux also said that he had been instructed to ask my opinion about the present state of affairs; I gave it gladly, but to no purpose whatsoever. Thus an indirect link was established between Lamartine and me with Champeaux as intermediary. The latter often came to see me to tell me, on his patron's behalf, about preparations afoot; and I sometimes went to see him in a little attic flat in a house in the rue Saint Honoré, where he used to receive dubious visitors, although he had official quarters in the Ministry of Foreign Affairs.

Usually I found him surrounded by petitioners, for in France every government has its political beggars; even revolutions directed against corruption increase their numbers, because all revolutions ruin a certain number of men, and with us a ruined man never turns anywhere but to the state to remake his fortunes. There was every type in this crowd of beggars, all attracted by the reflection of Lamartine's power which very ephemerally illuminated Champeaux. I remember particularly a certain cook, not, I should suppose, a great ornament to his profession, who was absolutely set on entering the service of Lamartine, the President, as he called him, of the Republic. "But he is not that yet," Champeaux protested. "Even if, as you say, he is not president yet," the other answered, "he will be. And he ought to be thinking about his kitchen already." To get rid of this stubborn ambitious scullion, Champeaux promised to mention him to Lamartine when he became President of the Republic, and the poor man went away well content, dreaming no doubt of the imaginary splendours of his ovens.

At that time I kept in pretty close touch with Champeaux, although he was exceedingly vain, garrulous and boring, because in talking to him I was better able to keep up to date with Lamartine's thoughts and plans. Lamartine's intelligence was filtered through Champeaux' stupidity like the sun through a smoked glass; the brilliance was lost, but one could see the detail more plainly. I easily discerned that everybody in that world was, like the cook, feeding on illusions, and that Lamartine himself in the depths of his heart was already enjoying the taste of the supreme power that nonetheless was just then slipping through his fingers. He was following the tortuous path that was so soon to lead to his ruin, striving to dominate the Mountain without overthrowing it and to damp down without quenching the revolutionary fires, so that the country would bless him for providing security, but would not feel safe enough to forget about him. His greatest fear was that control of the Assembly might fall again into the hands of the old parliamentary leaders. I think this was the thing he cared most about then. That became very plain in the great debate over the constitution of the executive power. There has never been a better example of the sort of pedantic hypocrisy that makes parties hide their real interests behind general theories: that is, of course, usual behaviour, but this time it was much more blatant, because immediate necessity forced each party to take shelter behind theories that were as far from its principles as possible, or indeed utterly opposed to them. The old royalist party maintained that the Assembly ought to govern itself and choose the ministers, which bordered on demagogy; the demagogues urged that executive power be entrusted to a permanent commission, which would rule and appoint all government officials, a system close to monarchical ideas. All this verbiage meant merely that one side wanted to keep Ledru-Rollin out of power, and the other wanted him in.

At that time, the nation saw Ledru-Rollin as the bloody image of the Terror. They regarded him as the evil and Lamartine as the good genius, mistakenly in both cases. Ledru was nothing but a great sensual sanguine boy, with no principles and hardly any ideas; he had no true courage of mind or heart, but he was also free of malice, for by nature he wished all the world well and was incapable of cutting an enemy's throat, except perhaps as an historical reminiscence or to please his friends.

The result of the debate was long in doubt: Barrot turned it against us by making a very fine speech in our favour. I have seen many such unexpected incidents in parliamentary warfare, and the parties constantly make the same mistake because they think only of the pleasure their great orator's words give them and never consider how dangerously they excite their opponents.

When Lamartine, who until then had remained silent and, I think, undecided, heard the former leader of the left speaking again for the first time since February with brilliance and success, he suddenly made his decision and asked permission to speak. "You understand," Champeaux told me the next day, "that it was all-important to stop the Assembly from adopting a resolution proposed by Barrot."

Lamartine spoke, therefore, and, as usual, spoke brilliantly.

The majority, who had already started down the path cleared by Barrot, wheeled around as they heard him (for this Assembly was more susceptible than any other I have known to the deceits of eloquence; it was naïve and innocent enough to seek reasons for its decisions in the speeches of orators). So Lamartine made his point, and ruined his career. For that day gave birth to a distrust which quickly increased and threw him from the peak of his popularity faster than he had climbed there. Suspicion took definite shape the very next day, when he was seen patronizing Ledru-Rollin and forcing the hands of his own friends in order to have Ledru appointed his colleague on the executive commission. This sight filled the Assembly and the nation with indescribable disappointment, terror and anger. I for my part fully shared the two latter feelings; I clearly saw that Lamartine was turning away from the main road leading us out of anarchy, and I could not guess to what abyss we might be led along the tortuous paths he was now taking. For how could one guess whither leaping imagination unrestrained by reason or conscience might take us? I had no more confidence in Lamartine's common sense than in his disinterestedness, and indeed thought him capable of anything except a cowardly act or vulgar phrase.

I confess that I did somewhat modify my opinion of his conduct in the light of the events of June. For it was then proved that our opponents were more numerous, better organized and, especially, more determined than I had supposed.

For two months Lamartine had seen nothing but Paris, where he had been living so to speak in the heart of the revolutionary party, so he naturally exaggerated the power of Paris and the apathy of France. But, while he thus failed to see the truth, perhaps I carried the opposite impression too far. The road to follow seemed to me so well marked and clear that I could not conceive of anybody's missing it by mistake. I thought it obvious that we should hurry to take advantage of the moral strength of an Assembly just elected by the people in order boldly to take over the government, and, by a great effort, establish it on a solid basis. I thought any delay was bound to weaken our forces and increase those of our adversaries.

In fact, it was in the six weeks that passed between the opening of the session and the events of June that the Paris workers became determined to resist, took courage, organized themselves, provided themselves with ammunition as well as arms, and made final preparations for the fight. Nevertheless it is possible that Lamartine's subterfuges and semi-connivance with the enemy, although they ruined him, saved us. Their effect was to keep the leaders of the Mountain occupied and to divide them. The old-school Montagnards, who were kept in the government, became separated from the socialists, who were excluded. If, before our victory, they had all been united by a common interest and goaded by a common despair, as did happen afterwards, it is doubtful whether that victory would have been won. When I think how near to destruction we came, although we had only the revolutionary army without its leaders against us, I wonder how the struggle would have ended if the leaders had come forward and the insurrection had counted on the support of a third of the National Assembly.

Lamartine saw these dangers more closely and clearly than I did. And I think now, that fear of engendering a mortal conflict influenced his action as much as ambition did. Even at the time I ought to have been able to see that this was so from listening to Madame de Lamartine and her excessive fears for her husband's safety and for that of the National Assembly.

"Be careful," she said every time she saw me, "not to push things to extremes. You do not know the strength of the revolutionary party. If we start a fight with it, we shall all perish."

I have often regretted that I did not cultivate Madame de

Lamartine's acquaintance more, for I have always appreciated her genuine virtue. But she had pretty well every defect that can be associated with virtue and, without altering its character, make it less agreeable. She had an imperious temper, great pride, and a mind that, although upright, was inflexible and sometimes harsh, so that it was impossible not to respect her but equally impossible to like her.

CHAPTER SEVEN

The 15th May

The revolutionary party had not dared to oppose the meeting of the Assembly, but it did not want to be dominated by it. On the contrary, it intended to keep it under its thumb and to gain by constraint what the Assembly refused to grant from sympathy. The clubs were already echoing with threats and insults against the deputies. And since in their political passions the French are equally bent on reasoning and on being unreasonable, these popular assemblies were uninterruptedly employed in manufacturing principles that could later justify acts of violence. It was maintained that the people, always superior to their representatives, never completely hand over their will to their representatives, a true principle from which they derived the utterly false conclusion that the Parisian workers were the people of France. Since our first sitting, a vague, widespread agitation in the city had never calmed down. Every day, crowds collected in the streets and squares; they spread as aimlessly as waves in a swell. The neighbourhood of the Assembly was always cluttered with these dangerous idlers. There are so many heads to a demagogic party, and chance plays so large and intention so small a part in its actions that it is almost impossible to say at the time what it wants, or afterwards what it wanted. I did, however, think then, and I think now, that the main demagogic leaders did not plan to destroy the Assembly but intended to go on dominating and using it. The attack made against it on the 15th May was intended more to frighten than to overthrow it: at least it was one of those equivocal undertakings, so common in times of popular agitation, whose plan and aim is carefully left vague and undefined by its promoters themselves, so that it can be either controlled as a pacific demonstration or pressed on to a revolution, as the chances of the day suggest.

Some attempt of the sort had been expected for a week. But Assemblies, like individuals, get used to living in a state of continual alarms, so that in the end they cannot discern, amid all the signs of imminent peril, the one that shows it is actually upon them. It was only known that there was a great popular agitation in favour of Poland, and one was worried about it, but in a vague way. Of course members of the government must have known more and been more worried than we, but they concealed both their information and their fears, and I was not sufficiently close to them to know their secret thoughts.

Consequently I came to the Assembly on the 15th May without any anticipation of what would happen. The sitting began like any other; and, what was very odd, twenty thousand men had surrounded the Chamber before any sound from outside had indicated their presence. Wolowski was at the rostrum; he was mumbling between his teeth some platitude or other about Poland when the people suddenly demonstrated how close they were by a terrible shout which, bursting through all the windows at the top of the Chamber, left open on account of the heat, fell upon us as if it came from the sky. I would never have imagined it possible for human voices, by combining, to produce such a terrific noise, and the sight of the crowd itself, when it invaded the Assembly, did not strike me as so frightening as that first roar before it came into view. Several deputies, yielding to a first impulse of curiosity or fear, rose; others shouted loudly, "Keep your seats." Everybody sat down again, stayed in their places and kept silent. Wolowski started again on his speech and kept on with it for some time. I think it was the first time in his life that people listened to him in silence; but even then it was not he to whom people were listening but to the continually louder soughing of the crowd drawing in closer.

Suddenly Degousée, one of our questors, marched formally up onto the rostrum, silently pushing Wolowski aside, and said:

"Contrary to the wishes of the questors, General Courtais has ordered the Gardes Mobiles[1] guarding the door of the Assembly, to sheath their bayonets."

Having said these few words, he was silent. Degousée was an excellent fellow, but he had the most hangdog look and sepulchral voice that you could find. So the announcement, the man and the voice combined to make a strange impression. The Assembly was roused but calmed down at once; it was too late to do anything; the Chamber was forced.

Lamartine, who had left when the noise began, came back to the door looking disconcerted; he crossed the central aisle and got back to his seat with long strides, as if pursued by some enemy we could not see. However a few men of the people made their appearance almost at once behind him; they halted on the threshold, surprised at the sight of this vast assembly seated. At the same moment, as on the 24th February, the doors of the galleries burst open with a crash; a flood of people poured into them, filled them, and soon overfilled them. Pressed forward by the crowd following them, which pushed them on without seeing them, the first arrivals climbed over the balustrades of the galleries and tried to find an exit into the hall itself, which was only ten feet below them; they let themselves down at the sides of the walls and jumped the last five or six feet into the middle of the Assembly. There was a dull thud as each of these bodies struck the floor, and, with all the noise going on, I at first mistook that for the sound of distant guns. While one group of the people fell into the hall, another, composed mainly of the leaders of all the clubs,

[1] There is no equivalent English term for this militia, properly called the *Garde Nationale Mobile*, which was formed by a decree of 25 February 1848. It was composed of volunteers aged mainly between sixteen and twenty. These volunteers were armed and equipped by the State who also paid them a daily wage of one franc, fifty centimes. This militia rendered a signal service to its employer during the June days of 1848. However, its numbers were reduced by half in January 1849; it was then split up and sent in small groups to the provinces and was subsequently disbanded. (Ed.)

invaded us through every door. These latter carried various emblems of the Terror, and they waved a lot of flags, some of them with a red cap on top.

In a moment the crowd had filled the great empty space in the middle of the Assembly and, finding itself short of room, began climbing the narrow aisles between our benches. The overcrowding was worse than ever in these narrow spaces, but the movement did not stop. In all this tumult and commotion the dust and the heat became so stifling that, had only the public interest been in question, I might have gone out to get some fresh air, but honour kept us nailed to our benches.

Some of our invaders were armed, and others appeared to have hidden weapons, but not one seemed to have a fixed resolve to strike us. There was astonishment and ill will rather than enmity in their expressions; in many cases, the satisfaction of a vulgar curiosity seemed to be the dominant feeling; for even in our most bloody insurrections there are always a lot of people, half rascals, half boobies, who fancy they are at the theatre. Furthermore, there seemed to be no obedience to a common leader; it was a rabble, not a troop. I did see some drunks among them, but most of them seemed to be prey to a feverish excitement due to the shouting outside and the stifling, crushing discomfort and heat inside; they were dripping with sweat, although the nature and state of their clothing should have made the heat not particularly disagreeable, for sometimes a good deal of naked skin was showing. In the confused noise rising from this multitude one could sometimes hear very threatening proposals. I saw some men shaking their fists and calling us their agents. They often repeated that word. For some days the ultra-democratic papers had been calling the representatives nothing but agents of the people, and the idea pleased these scoundrels. A moment later I had a chance to see how clearly and vividly the people notice things and find the right phrase. A man in a blouse beside me was saying to his companion: "Look at that vulture there. I should love to twist his neck." Following the movement of his hand and eyes I saw that he meant Lacordaire sitting in his Dominican habit high up on the benches of the left. The suggestion struck me as very wicked, but the comparison admirable; the priest's long, bony neck sticking out of his white cowl, his shaven head with just a ring of black hair, his narrow face, aquiline nose and fixed, glittering eyes really did make him strikingly like that bird of prey.

Throughout this disorder the Assembly remained passive and motionless on its benches, neither resisting nor giving way, silent and firm. Some members of the Mountain fraternized with the people, but furtively and in whispers. Raspail had got possession of the rostrum and was getting ready to read the petition from the clubs; a young deputy, Adelsward, got up and said: "By what right does citizen Raspail speak here?" A furious howl arose; some of the common people rushed at Adelsward but were stopped and held back. With great difficulty Raspail obtained a moment of silence from his friends and read the petition, or rather the command of the clubs, which instructed us to pronounce *immediately* in favour of Poland.

"Hurry up, we are waiting for your answer," was shouted from all sides. The Assembly continued to give no sign of life; in any case the frightful tumult of the impatient, disorderly mob made it impossible to reply. Buchez, the President, whom some regard as a rascal and others a saint, but who on that day was undoubtedly a great fool, rang his bell as hard as he could in an attempt to obtain silence, as if in the present circumstances the silence of the multitude was not more to be feared than its shouts.

It was at that moment that I saw a man go up onto the rostrum, and, although I have never seen him again, the memory of him has filled me with disgust and horror ever since. He had sunken, withered cheeks, white lips, and a sickly, malign, dirty look like a pallid, mouldy corpse; he was wearing no visible linen; an old black frockcoat covered his lean, emaciated limbs tightly; he looked as if he had lived in a sewer and only just come out. I was told that this was Blanqui.[2]

Blanqui said a word about Poland, then, turning abruptly to domestic affairs, he demanded revenge for what he called

[2] For further information on Blanqui, see M. Dommanget, *Les idées politiques d'Auguste Blanqui*, Paris, 1957. (Ed.)

the massacre at Rouen; in threatening terms he reminded us
of the misery in which the people had been left and complained
of the wrongs they were beginning to suffer at the hands of
the Assembly. Having roused his audience in this manner, he
returned to Poland and, like Raspail, demanded an immediate
vote.

Still the Assembly remained motionless and the people restless, shouting a thousand contradictory things, and still the
President rang his bell. Ledru-Rollin tried to persuade the crowd
to withdraw, but no one could do anything with it any longer.
Ledru, almost hooted down, left the rostrum.

The tumult was renewed and grew worse; it, so to speak,
engendered itself, for the people were no longer masters of
themselves enough to understand that they must restrain themselves for a moment in order to attain the object of their
passion. A long time went by; finally Barbès climbed, or rather
leaped onto the rostrum. He was one of those men in whose
nature the demagogue, the madman and the knight are so
mixed that one can never say where one begins and the other
ends; a type who would never come into prominence except
in a society as sick and distracted as ours. However, I think
that in him the madman predominated, and his folly turned
to fury when he heard the people's voice. Popular passions
made his soul boil as naturally as water over a fire. Ever since
the crowd had burst in on us, I had had my eye on him,
considering him the man most to be feared among our adversaries, because he was the most insane, disinterested and
resolute of them all. I had seen him get up onto the platform
where the President was seated and stay there motionless for
a long time, looking in agitation at the Assembly. I had noticed,
and pointed out to my neighbours, how his features changed, how
livid and pale he was, and how convulsively he was constantly
twisting his moustache between his fingers. He seemed the
very image of indecision, but leaning already towards extreme
courses. This time Barbès had made up his mind; he wanted
in some fashion to sum up the people's passions and to ensure
their victory by stating their aim in precise terms.

"I demand," he said in abrupt, panting phrases, "that immediately, at this present sitting, the Assembly should vote for sending an army to Poland; impose a tax of a milliard on the rich; send the troops out of Paris, and forbid the beating to arms; if not, the representatives shall be declared traitors to their country."

I think we should have been lost if Barbès had succeeded in bringing that motion to a vote; if the Assembly had passed it, it would have been dishonoured and rendered powerless, but if, as seemed more probable, we had rejected it, we ran the risk of having our throats cut. But even Barbès could not obtain a moment of silence in which we could have come to a decision. The colossal row that greeted his last words never died down; on the contrary it was renewed with a thousand variations. Barbès wore himself out in efforts to control it, but to no effect, although he was powerfully supported by the President's bell, which rang like a knell the whole time.

This extraordinary sitting had lasted since two o'clock. The Assembly held out, its ears pricked to catch any sound from outside, waiting for help to come. But Paris seemed a dead city. Listen as we would, we heard no sound from there.

This passive resistance annoyed the people and drove them to despair; it was like some cold, smooth surface over which its fury slid with nothing to catch onto; it writhed and struggled in vain, getting no result from its efforts. A thousand different or contradictory slogans filled the air: "Let us be off," shouted some. "The organization of work! . . . A ministry of Labour! . . . A tax on the rich! . . . We want Louis Blanc!" shouted others. It ended with fights at the foot of the rostrum to decide who should get up onto it. Five or six orators filled it at once and sometimes spoke at the same moment. As always happens in riots, the ludicrous was mingled with the terrible. The heat was so overpowering that many of the first intruders left the hall; they were at once replaced by others waiting at the door for their turn to enter. One of these was a fireman in uniform whom I saw going along the aisle in front of my bench. "We can't make them vote," someone shouted to him. "Wait, wait," he said. "I'll go there. I'll tell them what's what." Thereupon he pulled his helmet over his eyes with a look of determination, fastened the strap under his chin, forced his way through the crowd, knocking over everything in his way, and got up onto the rostrum. He imagined that he would feel as much at ease there as on a roof; but words failed him as soon as he got there, and he stopped short. The people shouted, "Speak up, fireman!" But he did not say a word, and in the end he was chased off the rostrum. Just then some of the common people took Louis Blanc up in their arms and carried him in triumph through the hall. They held him over their heads by his little legs; I saw him vainly trying to escape, twisting and turning in every direction, but never succeeding in slipping through their hands, and talking the whole time in a choking, strident voice. He reminded me of a snake having its tail pinched. At last they put him down on a bench below mine. I heard him shout: "My friends, the right you have won . . ." but the rest of his words were lost in the din. I was told that Sobrier had been carried round in the same way a little farther off.

A thoroughly tragic event nearly put a stop to this saturnalia; suddenly the galleries at the end of the hall cracked and bent more than a foot under the weight on them; the crowd that was overloading them was in danger of being hurled into the Chamber, and it rushed away in terror. The alarm this caused put a moment's stop to the row, and it was then that I first heard in the distance the call to arms in Paris. The crowd heard it too and let out a prolonged yell of rage and terror. "Why are they beating to arms?" exclaimed Barbès, beside himself, again appearing on the rostrum. "Who is beating to arms? Let those who have given the order be outlawed!" From the people rose cries of, "We are betrayed! To arms! To the Hôtel de Ville!"

The President was driven from the chair or, if the account he gave afterwards is to be believed, he willingly let himself be removed. A leader of a club called Huber got onto the platform and hoisted there a flag with a red cap on top. It seems that this man had had a long epileptic fit brought on by the excitement and the heat and he had only just wakened

out of this nightmare when he came forward; his clothes were
still in disorder, and he looked frightened and haggard. Twice
he shouted: "In the name of the people betrayed by its representatives, I declare the National Assembly dissolved!" His voice,
as loud as a trumpet, came down on us, filling the hall and
dominating every other noise.

The Assembly, having no officers, dispersed. Barbès and the
boldest of the club supporters went out to go to the Hôtel de
Ville. This conclusion was far from pleasing everybody. I heard
some of the common people near me saying sorrowfully: "No,
no; that is not what we want." Many sincere Republicans were
in despair. In the midst of the confusion Trélat came up to
me; he was a revolutionary of the sentimental, dreamy type,
who had continually plotted in favour of a republic under the
Monarchy; he was also a distinguished doctor in charge of one
of the largest hospitals for the insane in Paris, although he was
a bit touched himself. He took my hands effusively and with
tears in his eyes said:

"Ah, sir, what a misfortune. And how strange to think that
it is madmen, real madmen, who have brought this about!
I have treated or prescribed for them all. Blanqui is a madman.
Sobrier is mad. Huber is the maddest of all. They are all mad,
sir. And they ought to be in my Salpêtrière, and not here."

He would certainly have added himself to the list if he had
known himself as well as he knew his friends. I have always
thought that in revolutions, especially democratic revolutions,
madmen (not those metaphorically called such, but real madmen) have played a very considerable political part. At least it
is certain that at such times a state of semi-madness is not out
of place and often leads to success.

The Assembly had dispersed, but there was good reason to
believe that it did not consider itself dissolved.

It did not even consider itself defeated. Most of the members
who left the hall did so with the firm intention of meeting
again soon elsewhere; they were saying that among themselves,
and I am convinced that they were firmly resolved on it. For
my part I decided to stay, half because of the invincible curi-

osity that keeps me in places where strange things are going on, and half because of the feeling I had then, as on the 24th February, that the strength of an Assembly depends partly on the hall it occupies. So I stayed, and I was present at the grotesque disorders, without any interest or meaning, that followed. The crowd, amid the shouting and confusion, set about forming a provisional government. It was a parody of the 24th February, just as the 24th February had been a parody of other revolutionary scenes. That had been going on for a good while when I thought I heard an odd noise from outside the palace. I have a very sensitive ear, and it did not take me long to recognize the sound of an advancing drum beating the charge; for in our days of civil discord, everyone has learned the language of these martial instruments. I ran at once towards the door by which the new arrivals would enter.

It really was a drum, and some forty Gardes Mobiles marched behind it. These young people made their way into the crowd resolutely enough, but not so that one could at first see what they had come to do; they quickly disappeared and remained apparently submerged, but a short distance behind them marched a compact column of national guards, and they rushed into the hall with the meaningful shouts of "Long live the National Assembly!" I put my deputy's card in my hat and went in with them. First of all, five or six orators speaking all at once were turned out of the rostrum and somewhat unceremoniously deposited on the little flight of steps leading up to it. At this sight the insurgents at first wanted to resist, but then a panic terror seized them. Climbing over the empty benches, tumbling over one another in the gangways, they made for the outer lobbies and jumped from all the windows into the courtyards. In a few minutes there was no one but national guards, in the hall, and the only cries were, "Long live the National Assembly!" loud enough to shake the walls.

The Assembly itself was not there; but little by little the dispersed members hurried back from the neighbourhood. We shook hands with the national guards, embraced each other, and got back to our places. The national guards shouted: "Long

live the National Assembly!" And the deputies: "Long live the
National Guard!" and "Long live the Republic!"[3]

As soon as the hall was recaptured, General Courtais, the
originator of our perils, had the incomparable impudence to put
in an appearance; the national guards greeted him with shouts
of fury; he was seized and dragged to the foot of the rostrum,
looking, as he went past me, as pale as death between the
flashing swords; I thought they were going to cut his throat,
and I shouted as loud as I could: "Tear off his epaulettes, but
do not kill him!" and that was done.

Then Lamartine appeared. I have never known how he passed
the time during the three hours' invasion. I did catch a glimpse
of him during the first hour; at that moment he was on a bench
below mine, and he was combing his hair, which was stuck
together with sweat, with a little comb he took out of his pocket;
the crowd formed once more, and I did not see him again. It
would seem that he had gone into the inner rooms of the palace,
whither the crowd had also penetrated; that he wanted to harangue the crowd and was very badly received. The next day
I was told some odd details about that scene, and I would set

[3] *Against the passage printed below, Tocqueville wrote as follows in the
margin of his notebook:* Page to be cut out completely; it is not worth
saying and interrupts the narrative.
In the first scramble which followed the entry of the National Guard I
had a little adventure which I should like to relate as a warning to judges
of the mistakes to which their profession is liable. That morning I had
brought a swordstick to the Assembly and had left it standing inside the
door. I was going to fetch it again when I heard the beating of the charge,
and I stopped looking for it. A moment later the flooding crowd carried
me to the side of a young man with a naked sword in one hand and my
stick in the other, and he was shouting for all he was worth: "Long live
the National Assembly!" "One minute," I said, "that stick is mine."—"It
is mine," he answered.—"It certainly is mine," I said, "and it has a sword
in it." "I can well believe that," he answered, "for it was I who had it
fixed two days ago. But who are you?" I told him my name. He immediately
took off his hat, and respectfully handed me the swordstick by its knob.
"Sir," he said, "that stick is mine, but I shall be glad to lend it to you
today, as you may need it more than I. I shall have the honour of coming
to your house to fetch it." The next day I did find my stick in a corner of
of the Assembly. It was so exactly like my thief's that I could not tell them
apart when I put them side by side, and, having confused them, I never
knew whether it was mine or his that I returned to him when he came as
he promised to fetch it.

them down here, had I not resolved to restrict myself to what I saw myself. I was told that after that he went to the nearby site on which the future Foreign Office was being built; undoubtedly he would have done better to put himself at the head of the National Guard and come to our deliverance. I think he was seized by one of those attacks of faintheartedness to which even the bravest (and he was of that number) are subject, when their imagination is active and vivid.

When he came back into the hall, he had regained his energy and his eloquence; he told us that his place was not in the Assembly but in the street; that he was going to march to the Hôtel de Ville and suppress the insurrection there. That was the last occasion on which I heard him applauded with enthusiasm. It is true that not he alone was being cheered, but the victory also; the cheers and claps were echoes of the tumultuous excitement felt by all. Lamartine went out. The drums that had beaten the charge half an hour before, now beat the march. The members of the National Guard and Garde Mobile, who were still mixed up in the crowd with us, formed ranks and marched after him. The Assembly, still very incomplete, resumed its sitting.

I went home to take a hasty meal and then went back to the Assembly, which had declared its session permanent. We soon learned that the members of the new Provisional Government had been arrested. Barbès was impeached and so was that old fool Courtais, who deserved no more than a thrashing. Many wished to include Louis Blanc on the list. He courageously undertook to defend himself. He had just escaped from the fury of the national guards who held the door, and his clothes were still torn, dusty and disordered. This time he did not have the stool brought up on which he usually mounted to bring his head above the level of the rostrum balustrade (he was almost a dwarf); he even forgot about the effect he was trying to produce, concentrating entirely on what he had to say. In spite of that, or rather because of it, for the moment he made his point. That was the only occasion on which I felt that he had talent, for I do not call the facile manufacture of brilliant hollow phrases

—which are like beautifully chased dishes with nothing on them
—"talent."

For the rest, the day's excitement had left me so tired that
I have only a dull, blurred memory of the night sitting; so, as
it is my personal recollections that I want to record, I will say
no more about it; the *Moniteur* can supply the sequence of
events better than I.

CHAPTER EIGHT

The Festival of Concord and the eve of the June Days

The revolutionaries of 1848, being unwilling or unable to imitate the bloody follies of their predecessors, consoled themselves
with imitations of their ridiculous ones. So they took it into their
heads to give the people a series of grand allegorical festivals.

Despite the frightful state of its finances, the Provisional Government had decided to set aside a sum of one or two million
francs to celebrate the Festival of Concord on the Champ de
Mars.

According to the programme, published in advance and then
followed faithfully, the Champ de Mars was to be filled with
representations of all manner of allegorical personages, virtues,
political institutions and even public services. France, Germany
and Italy hand in hand; Equality, Liberty and Fraternity also
hand in hand; Agriculture, Trade, the Army, the Navy, and
above all a colossal figure of the Republic. A car was to be
drawn by sixteen plough horses; this car, according to the programme, was to be of simple, rustic shape and to carry three
trees, an oak, a laurel and a fig, symbolizing strength, honour and
plenty, and it was also to carry a plough surrounded by ears
of corn and flowers. Labourers and young girls dressed in white
would stand round the plough singing patriotic songs. We were
also promised oxen with gilded horns, but they did not give us
those.

The National Assembly had not the slightest desire to see all
these fine things. There was moreover the fear that such an im-

mense concourse as was bound to assemble on this occasion,[1] might lead to some dangerous disorder.

The Assembly therefore put off the date of the Festival as long as possible; but the preparations were finished and, there being no means of retreat, the date was fixed for the 21st May.

On that day I came early to the Assembly, which was to go on foot as a body to the Champ de Mars and take the place reserved for it on a platform at the Military School. I put pistols in my pocket, and, chatting with my colleagues, found that most of them were also secretly armed. Edmond Lafayette showed me a peculiar sort of weapon; it was a ball of lead sewn into a short leather thong which could easily be tied to the wrist: one might call it a sort of pocket club. Lafayette told me that this little club was much worn by members of the National Assembly, especially after the 15th May. This was how we set out for the Festival of Concord.

Sinister rumours foretold great danger for the Assembly as it went through the crowd on the Champ de Mars to reach its reserved platform at the Military School. In truth it would have been very easy to stage a *coup-de-main* during the long, practically unguarded progress on foot. But green memories of the victory on the 15th May were its real safeguard, and that was enough.[2] Besides the French never do two things at once, for although they quickly change the object of their attention, they are always completely concentrated on the matter of the moment, and I don't think there is any example of an insurrection in the middle of a festival, or even of a ceremony. On that day the people seemed ready enough to join in this pretence of happiness, and, forgetting their miseries and hatreds for the moment, they were excited without being turbulent. The programme had announced that "fraternal confusion" would prevail. The confusion was extreme, but without disorder, for we are strange people: we can't do without the police when we are properly organized, but when we are in the middle of a revolution, they seem useless. The moderate and sincere republicans

1 *Variant:* To flock to this great nonsense.
2 *The following passage is marked for omission in the manuscript:* It is very seldom, whatever opportunity may offer, that any authority is challenged the day after it has won a victory.

were enraptured by this popular rejoicing, and they became a bit sentimental.

Carnot, with the sort of silliness that honest democrats invariably mix with their virtue, said to me: "Believe me, my dear colleague, one must always trust the people."

I remember answering rather brusquely: "Ah! Why did you not tell me that just before the 15th May?"

The Executive Commission occupied one part, and the National Assembly the other, of a long platform erected beside the Military School. First the various emblems of all the nations filed past us, and this took up an enormous amount of time because of the "fraternal confusion"; then the car came, and finally the young girls dressed in white. There were at least three hundred of them, wearing their virginal robes in such a manly way that one might have taken them for boys dressed up as girls. They had each been given a large bouquet to throw gallantly to us as they passed. But as they had brawny arms more accustomed, I suppose, to wielding a washerwoman's beetle than to strewing flowers, their bouquets hit us like hard-driven hail.

One tall young woman stepped aside from her companions and, standing in front of Lamartine, recited an ode in his honour. Gradually, as her recitation went on, she got so excited that her expression became alarming, and her face went into terrible contortions. I have never seen enthusiasm look so like epilepsy. Nonetheless, when she had finished, the people wanted Lamartine to kiss her; she presented two fat cheeks dripping with sweat to him, and he kissed them with the tip of his lips and none too graciously.

The review was the only serious part of the festival. Never in my life have I seen so many armed men in one place, and I think few people can have seen more; apart from the innumerable sightseers filling the Champ de Mars, a whole nation in arms was there; the *Moniteur* gave a figure of three hundred thousand for the national guards and soldiers of the line assembled there, and though that figure seems to me exaggerated, I do not think one could bring it down to less than two hundred thousand.

The sight of those two hundred thousand bayonets will never leave my memory. As those who bore them were tightly packed to fit into the slopes of the Champ de Mars, and since from our position not far above it we could get only a horizontal view of them, they seemed like some smooth, slightly undulating surface flashing in the sun, making the Champ de Mars look like a lake of liquid steel.

Each corps marched past us in turn, and as it did so we noticed that there were many more muskets than uniforms.

Only the rich sections sent out any large number of the National Guard wearing military uniform. They were the first to file past, and they shouted, "Long live the National Assembly!" with enthusiasm. Among the legions from the suburbs, which by themselves stretched out into whole armies, one saw little but jackets and blouses, although that did not prevent them marching with very warlike expressions. Most of them, as they came by us, shouted, "Long live the democratic Republic!" or sang the "Marseillaise" or the Girondins' song. Next came the legions from the outskirts composed of ill-equipped and ill-armed peasants, dressed in blouses like the workmen from the suburbs, but imbued with a very different spirit, as could easily be seen from their gestures and their shouts. The various exclamations which we could hear from the battalions of the Garde Mobile left us full of doubts and anxiety about the intentions of these young men, or rather children, who, more than anybody else at that time, held our destinies in their hands.

The regiments of the line, who closed the review, marched past in silence.

My heart was filled with sadness as I watched this prolonged spectacle. Never at any time had so many arms been put at once into the hands of the people. It can be imagined that I did not share the silly confidence and foolish delight of my friend Carnot; on the contrary, I foresaw that all these bayonets glinting in the sun would soon be lifted against each other, and I felt that these were the two armies of the civil war that we were just beginning. On that day I still often heard the cry, "Long live Lamartine!" but his great popularity was already passing. One could almost say that it had already passed, but in all crowds there are always a great number of belated individuals touched by the enthusiasms of yesterday, just as provincials begin to adopt Paris fashions on the very day the Parisians are giving them up.

Lamartine himself did not delay in withdrawing from this last glimmer of his setting sun; he left long before the ceremony had come to an end. He looked worried and tired. Many other members of the Assembly, equally worn out, followed his example, and the review ended in front of almost empty benches. It had started early in the morning and did not end till night was drawing in.

It is fair to say that the whole interval between the 21st May and the days of June was filled with anxious anticipation of those days. Daily there were fresh rumours, and the army and National Guard were called out. Workmen and middle-class people no longer lived in their houses, but in the public squares, and under arms. Each ardently hoped to escape the necessity for a conflict, and each vaguely felt that that necessity was becoming more inevitable every moment. The National Assembly was so constantly obsessed with this thought that one felt one could read the words "civil war" written on each of the four walls of the hall.

On all sides great efforts of prudence and patience were being made to avoid, or at least delay, the crisis. Those members who in the depths of their hearts were most opposed to the revolution carefully refrained from expressing either their antipathies or their sympathies; the former parliamentary orators kept quiet, lest the sound of their voices cause offence; they left the rostrum free for the newcomers, but these rarely occupied it, for the great debates had come to an end. As happens with all Assemblies, the thing that really worried people in the depths of their souls was never mentioned, but daily there was evidence that it was not forgotten; all sorts of means of succouring the misery of the people were proposed and discussed. We were even ready to examine the different socialist systems, and each man tried in good faith to find something that was applicable to, or at least compatible with, the ancient laws of society.

During this time the National Workshops continued to fill, and their population was already more than a hundred thousand. One felt that we could not live if they were kept on, but we feared destruction if we tried to break them up. The burning question of the National Workshops was mentioned daily, but in a superficial, timid way; we constantly touched on it, but never grasped it firmly.

On the other hand it was clear that the different parties outside the Assembly, although they were afraid of the struggle, were actively preparing for it. The wealthy legions of the National Guard gave banquets for the army and the Garde Mobile at which they mutually urged each other to unite for the common defence.

On their side, the workers in the suburbs were secretly amassing the bullets, that were later to enable them to sustain so long a struggle. As for muskets, the Provisional Government had been at pains to furnish those in profusion; it would be fair to say that there was not a single workman who didn't have at least one and often several.

The danger was as apparent from afar as from near. In the provinces, indignation and irritation against Paris rose; for the first time in sixty years people dared to entertain the idea of resisting the capital; men armed themselves and encouraged each other to come to the help of the Assembly; thousands of addresses were sent congratulating it on the victory of the 15th May. Ruined trade, war everywhere, and the fear of socialism made the Republic more and more hated. This hatred overflowed especially in the secrecy of the ballot. There were new elections in twenty-one departments, and, in general, the voters chose men who seemed to them to stand for monarchy in one form or another. M. Molé was elected at Bordeaux and M. Thiers at Rouen.

It was then that suddenly for the first time, the name of Louis Napoleon came to the fore. That prince was elected simultaneously in Paris and in several of the departments; some Republicans, some Legitimists, and some demagogues gave him their votes; for at that time the whole nation was like a flock of frightened sheep running hither and thither, following no path. I never thought, when I heard of Louis Napoleon's election, that exactly a year later I should be his minister. I confess that I viewed the return of the former parliamentary leaders with much apprehension and regret, not because I did not do justice to their talents and their *savoir-faire*, but because I was afraid that their presence would drive moderate Republicans who were drawing close to us towards the Mountain. Moreover, knowing them so well, I realized that as soon as they had got back into public life, they would immediately want to take command, and that it would not suit their book to save the country unless they ruled it. Consequently their return seemed to me premature and dangerous. Our role and theirs should be to help the reasonable Republicans to govern the country, without attempting to rule it ourselves indirectly and, above all, without appearing to try to.

Personally I had no doubt that we were on the eve of a terrible struggle; nevertheless I did not fully understand all the dangers of that time until a conversation I had with the famous Madame Sand. I met her at the house of an English friend of mine, Milnes,[3] a Member of Parliament, who was then in Paris. Milnes was a man of parts who did and, what is rarer, said many foolish things. I have seen a great many men in my time with two contradictory profiles: man of sense on one side, fool on the other. Never have I seen Milnes not infatuated about somebody or something.[4] This time he was dazzled by Madame Sand and, despite the seriousness of the situation,

[3] Richard Monckton Milnes (1809–85), politician and man of letters. He held a unique place in English society as a patron of writers of all kinds. The luncheon to which Tocqueville was invited and which he found so strange was by no means out of the ordinary for Milnes. He was noted in London for his breakfast parties to which were invited people of widely differing interests, talents and social position. For further details about Monckton Milnes' life and activities, see T. W. Reid, *The Life, Letters, and Friendships of Richard Monckton Milnes*, 2 vols., London, 1891, and J. Pope-Henessy, *Richard Monckton Milnes*, vol. I *The Years of Promise: 1809–1851*, vol. II *The Flight of Youth: 1851–1885*, London, 1949 and 1951.

[4] He hurried towards anything bright with a stupid greed that reminded me of those fishes one attracts by lighting a straw fire, which they invariably mistake for the sun. *Tocqueville has written in the margin against this passage:* To be cut out, I think; I am not sure that someone else has not said this already.

wanted to give a literary luncheon for her. I was there, and
crowded memories of the June days that followed almost at once,
far from obliterating that day from my recollection, have reminded me of it.

The company was anything but homogeneous. Besides Madame
Sand, there was a young English lady whose name I have
forgotten, but whose agreeable and modest appearance struck
me and who must have found the company she was in rather
odd; then there were some fairly obscure writers and Mérimée.
Some of the guests did not know each other, and others knew
one another too well. That was the case, if I am not mistaken,
between Madame Sand and Mérimée. A short time before there
had been a very tender but very ephemeral relationship between them. One was even told that they had followed Aris-
totle's rules in the conduct of their romance, with the whole
action obedient to the unities of time and place. Our host
from across the channel did not know that story and had very
clumsily brought them together without warning. So they met
unexpectedly for the first time after their adventure, and as
Madame Sand was very offended with Mérimée for having triumphed so fast and made so little use of his success, there was
great embarrassment on both sides; but they soon pulled themselves together, and for the rest of the day there was nothing
to notice.

Milnes put me beside Madame Sand; I had never spoken to her,
and I don't think I had even seen her before (for I have
not lived much in the world of literary adventurers which she
inhabited). When one of my friends asked her what she thought
of my book about America, she replied: "Sir, I make it a habit
only to read the books that are presented to me by the
authors." I had a strong prejudice against Madame Sand, for I
detest women who write, especially those who systematically
disguise the weaknesses of their sex, instead of interesting us
by displaying them in their true colours. In spite of that, she
charmed me. I found her features rather massive, but her expression wonderful; all her intelligence seemed to have retreated
into her eyes, abandoning the rest of her face to raw matter.
I was most struck at finding her with something of that natural-

ness of manner characteristic of great spirits. She really did have a genuine simplicity of manner and language, which was perhaps mingled with a certain affectation of simplicity in her clothes. I confess that with more adornment she would have struck me as still more simple. We spoke for a whole hour about public affairs, for at that time one could not talk about anything else. Besides, Madame Sand was then in a way a politician; I was much struck by what she told me on that subject; it was the first time that I had found myself in direct and familiar conversation with somebody able and willing to tell me part of what was taking place in our adversaries' camp. Political parties never know each other; they come close, jostle and grip one another, but they never see. Madame Sand gave me a detailed and very vivacious picture of the state of the Parisian workers: their organization, numbers, arms, preparations, thoughts, passions and terrible resolves. I thought the picture overloaded, but it was not so, as subsequent events clearly proved. She seemed to be herself greatly frightened by the popular triumph, and there was a touch of solemnity in her pity for our anticipated fate.

"Try to persuade your friends, sir," she said to me, "not to drive the people into the streets by rousing or offending them, just as on my side I want to instill patience into our people; for if it comes to a fight, believe me, you will all perish."

With those consoling words we parted, and I have not seen her since.

CHAPTER NINE

The June Days

Now at last I have come to that insurrection in June which was the greatest and the strangest that had ever taken place in our history, or perhaps in that of any other nation: the greatest because for four days more than a hundred thousand men took part in it, and there were five generals killed; the strangest, because the insurgents were fighting without a battle cry, leaders, or flag, and yet they showed wonderful powers of co-ordination and a military expertise that astonished the most experienced officers.

Another point that distinguished it from all other events of the same type during the last sixty years was that its object was not to change the form of the government, but to alter the organization of society. In truth it was not a political struggle (in the sense in which we have used the word "political" up to now), but a class struggle, a sort of "Servile War." It stood in the same relation to the facts of the February Revolution as the theory of socialism stood to its ideas; or rather it sprang naturally from those ideas, as a son from his mother; and one should not see it only as a brutal and blind, but as a powerful effort of the workers to escape from the necessities of their condition, which had been depicted to them as an illegitimate depression, and by the sword to open up a road towards that imaginary well-being that had been shown to them in the distance as a right. It was this mixture of greedy desires and false theories that engendered the insurrection and made it so formidable. These poor people had been assured that the goods of the wealthy were in some way the result of a theft committed against themselves. They had been assured that inequalities of fortune were as much opposed to morality and the interests of society as to nature. This obscure and mistaken conception of right, combined with brute force, imparted to it an energy, tenacity and strength it would never have had on its own.

One should note, too, that this terrible insurrection was not the work of a certain number of conspirators, but was the revolt of one whole section of the population against another. The women took as much part in it as the men. While the men fought, the women got the ammunition ready and brought it up. And when in the end they had to surrender, the women were the last to yield.

It is fair to say that these women carried the preoccupations of a housewife into battle: they counted on victory to bring easy circumstances for their husbands and help them to bring up their children. They loved this war much as they might have enjoyed a lottery.

The scientific strategy of this multitude can be sufficiently explained by the warlike nature of the French, their long experience of insurrections, and, especially, the military education that, each in turn, most of the common people have received. Half the Parisian workers have served in our armies, and they always gladly take to arms again. Plenty of old soldiers usually take part in riots. On the 24th February, Lamoricière, surrounded by enemies, twice owed his life to insurgents who had fought under his command in Africa, for whom memories of that war counted more than the fury of the civil strife.

As we know, it was the closing of the National Workshops that was the occasion of the rising. Not daring to disband this redoubtable militia at one stroke, an attempt was made to disperse it by sending some of the workmen in question away into the country: they refused to go. On the 22nd June they paraded in troops through Paris, monotonously chanting in chorus: "We won't go, we won't go." Deputations came from them and made arrogant demands to the members of the Commission of the Executive Power, and, these being refused, withdrew announcing that the next day they would have recourse to arms.

Thus everything gave warning that the long expected crisis had arrived.

Of course, when this news reached the Assembly, it caused deep disquiet. Nevertheless the Assembly did not interrupt its order of the day but continued to discuss a trade law and even, despite the emotion, listened to the discussion; it is true that the law was highly important and that a very eminent orator was speaking.

The government was proposing to acquire all the railways on terms. Montalembert opposed this; his case was good and his speech even better; I don't think I have ever heard him speak better before or since; of course I agreed with him on this occasion, but I think that even his adversaries would have admitted that he surpassed himself. He made a vigorous attack, but without being as snarling and offensive as usual. A touch of fear tempered his natural insolence and set a limit to his paradoxes and belligerence, for like many another man fluent with his tongue, he had more boldness of language than staunchness of heart.

The sitting came to an end without any reference to what was going on outside, and the Assembly adjourned.

On the 23rd, as I was going to the Assembly before the usual hour, I saw a large number of omnibuses gathered round the Madeleine, and I realized that barricades were beginning to be raised in the streets. This was confirmed when I got to the palace. People were, however, still in doubt as to whether this meant a serious resort to arms. I decided to go and find out for myself how things were. So, with Corcelle, I went to the neighbourhood of the Hôtel de Ville. In all the little streets around that building I found the people busy constructing barricades. They went about the work with the methodical skill of engineers, not taking up more paving stones than were needed to provide squared stones for a solid and even fairly tidy wall, and they usually left a narrow opening by the houses to allow people to circulate. Being impatient to collect information about the state of the town as quickly as possible, Corcelle and I decided to separate; he went one way and I the other; his excursion nearly turned out badly for him. He told me afterwards that, having first passed several half-constructed barricades without obstruction, he was halted at the last one; the workers building it, seeing a fine gentleman in a black suit with clean white linen quietly walking around the dirty streets by the Hôtel de Ville and stopping in front of them with a placid air of curiosity, decided to make some use of this suspicious onlooker. They asked him in the name of fraternity to help them in their work. Corcelle was as brave as Caesar, but in the circumstances he rightly thought it best to yield without a fuss. So there he was levering up the pavement and putting the stones one on top of another as tidily as he could. His natural clumsiness and his wandering thoughts luckily came to his aid, and he was soon dismissed as a useless labourer.

I had no similar adventure. I passed through the Saint Martin and Saint Denis districts without coming across any barricades, but the excitement in that part was extraordinary. On my way back in the rue des Jeûneurs, I met a member of the National Guard covered with blood and bits of brain; he was very pale and was on the way home. I asked him what was happening; he told me that his battalion had just been facing very murderous fire at point-blank range at the Saint Denis gate; one of his comrades, whose name he told me, had been killed by his side, and it was that unlucky man's blood and brains with which he was spattered.

I returned to the Assembly, astonished not to have met a single soldier anywhere I had gone; it was not until I was in front of the Palais Bourbon that I at last saw great columns of infantry marching, followed by guns.

Lamoricière, in full-dress uniform and on horseback, was at their head. I have never seen a face shining with such warlike passion and, I could almost say, with joy. It was not, I think, just the natural fire of his mettle that carried him forward, but also partly a longing to be avenged for the dangers and insults he had suffered in February.

"What are you doing?" I asked him. "There has already been a battle at the Saint Denis gate, and the neighbourhood of the Hôtel de Ville is cluttered with barricades."

"Patience," he replied, "we are going there. Do you think we would be so stupid, on such a day as this, as to let our soldiers be scattered in the little streets of the suburbs? No, no! We will let the insurgents concentrate in the districts from which we cannot keep them, and then we shall go and destroy them there. They won't escape us this time."

As I was going back into the Assembly, a terrific storm came on, inundating the town. I had a faint hope that the bad weather might extricate us from trouble for that day; and indeed it would have been enough to make any ordinary riot abortive: the people of Paris need fine weather to fight in and are more afraid of the rain than of grapeshot.

I soon gave that hope up. More disturbing news was continually arriving. The Assembly, which had wished to carry on with its normal work, found it hard to do so; agitated but yet not cowed by the excitement outside, it suspended the order of the day, returned to it, and then finally suspended it, concentrating its attention on the civil war exclusively.[1] Various members went to the rostrum to recount what they had seen in Paris. Others urged courses of action to follow. Falloux, in the name of the Committee of Public Assistance, had just proposed a decree dissolving the National Workshops; he was applauded. Time was wasted in futile conversations and futile speeches. Nothing precise was known; there was a continual demand for the presence of the Executive Commission to inform us about the state of Paris, but they did not come. There is nothing more wretched than an Assembly in a moment of crisis when the government is not there; it is like a man still full of passion and desire but impotent and tossing childishly about in physical frustration. At last two members of the Executive Commission did appear. They announced that the situation was dangerous, but they still hoped that the insurrection would have been smothered before nightfall. The Assembly declared itself in permanent session, and adjourned until the evening.

When the sitting resumed, we learned that Lamartine had been received with fire at every barricade he had approached;

[1] *Marginal note (Tocqueville)*: For all this I am reduced to rely on my memory alone, not having a copy of the *Moniteur* of the 24th: must read that in Paris.

two of his colleagues, Bixio and Dornès, had been mortally wounded attempting to harangue the insurgents. Bedeau got a bullet through his thigh at the turning into the Faubourg Saint Jacques; many distinguished officers were already killed or put out of action. One member, Considérant, spoke of making a concession to the workers; the Assembly, which was in a tumult of agitation but not weak, rose at these words: there were angry shouts of "Order! Order!" on all sides. "It is not permissible to talk like that until after victory." The rest of the evening and part of the night were spent in vain talk, listening and waiting. Towards midnight Cavaignac appeared. Since that afternoon, all military powers had been concentrated in his hands by the Executive Commission. In a jerky, abrupt voice and using simple, exact words, Cavaignac recounted the main events of the day. He announced that he had given orders for all the regiments along the line of the railway to converge on Paris, and that all the national guards in the outskirts had been called up; he ended by saying that the insurgents had been beaten back to the barriers, and he hoped soon to be master of the town. The Assembly, worn out by fatigue, left its officials in permanent session and adjourned till eight o'clock the next day.

When, leaving the Assembly, I found myself at one in the morning on the Pont Royal, Paris was wrapped in darkness, calm as a sleeping city, and I found it hard to convince myself that all I had seen and heard since the morning had actually existed and was not a figment of my imagination. The squares and streets that I crossed were absolutely deserted; not a sound, not a cry; one would have supposed that an industrious population, tired with the day's work, was resting before resuming its peaceful labours the next day. The serenity of that night in the end overmastered me too; I finished by persuading myself that we had won already, and, when I got home, I went to sleep at once.

I woke up very early in the morning; the sun had been over the horizon for some time, for we were near the longest day of the year. As I opened my eyes I could hear a sharp metallic sound that shook the windows and was lost in the silence of Paris.

"What is that?" I asked.

"It is the gun," my wife answered. "I have been hearing it for an hour now; but I did not think I should wake you, as you will certainly need all your strength today."

I dressed hastily and went out. Drums everywhere were beating the call to arms. In stark reality the day of the great battle had come. The national guards left their houses armed; all those I saw seemed full of energy, for the sound of guns that called the brave ones out made the others stay at home. But they were feeling desperate; they thought themselves either badly led or betrayed by the Executive Commission, and they uttered fearful curses against it. Such extreme distrust of their leaders by the armed forces seemed to me a serious symptom. As I went on and was turning into the rue Saint Honoré, I came on a crowd of workers anxiously listening to the gunfire. They wore blouses, which, as we all know, are their fighting as well as their working clothes; they were not actually carrying arms, but one could see from the look of them that they were pretty near to taking them up. With hardly restrained delight they noted that the sound of the firing seemed to be getting closer, which meant that the rebels were gaining ground. I had guessed before this that the whole of the working class backed the revolt, either actively or in its heart; this proved it to me. In fact the spirit of insurrection circulated from end to end of that vast class and in all its parts, like blood in the body; it filled places where there was no fighting as much as those that formed the battlefield; and it had penetrated into our houses, around us, above us, below us. Even the places where we thought we were the masters were creeping with domestic enemies; it was as if an atmosphere of civil war enveloped the whole of Paris, and, no matter where one withdrew, one had to live in it. In this context I am going to violate my self-imposed law and tell a story vouched for by somebody else. It was my colleague Blanqui[2]

[2] Adolphe Blanqui (1798–1854), brother of the revolutionary, was an economist and occupied the chair of political economy at the Conservatoire of Arts and Crafts. A partisan of free trade, he was of much less radical persuasions than his brother. He is principally remembered for his *Histoire de l'économie politique en Europe*, Paris, 1837. Elected deputy for Bordeaux in 1846, he joined the ranks of the conservative majority. He became a member of the Académie des Sciences morales et politiques in 1838. (Ed.)

who told it to me a few days later, and, although it is very trivial, it wonderfully illustrates the character of that time. Blanqui had brought up from the country and taken into his house as a servant the son of a poor man whose distress had touched him. On the evening of the day when the insurrection started, he heard this child say as he was clearing away after the family dinner: "Next Sunday (it was on a Thursday) it is we who will be eating the chicken's wings." To which a little girl who was working in the house answered: "And it is we who will wear the lovely silk dresses." What better illustration of the spirit of the time could one find than this childish story of naïve cupidity? The crowning touch is that Blanqui was very careful not to show that he had heard these monkeys: they made him very frightened. It was only after the victory that he dared to take this ambitious youngster and the vainglorious little girl back to their hovels.

At last I got to the Assembly; crowds of deputies were coming up, although it was before the time fixed for the sitting. The gunfire had called them together. The palace looked like a battleground; battalions were encamped around it, and guns were levelled down all the avenues approaching it.

I found the Assembly very determined but very uneasy, and it must be admitted that there was reason for that. Reports were contradictory, but it was easy to see that we had to deal with the greatest, best armed and most furious insurrection ever known in Paris. The National Workshops and several revolutionary bands that had just been disbanded provided ready trained and war-tested soldiers as well as leaders. The insurrection was spreading the whole time, and it was difficult to believe that it would not be victorious, remembering that all the great insurrections of the last sixty years had succeeded. To face all these enemies we had only the battalions of the bourgeoisie, regiments that had been disarmed in February, and twenty thousand untrained boys of the Garde Mobile, who were all sons, brothers or relations of the insurgents and whose loyalties remained very doubtful.

But it was our leaders that frightened us most. The members of the Executive Commission filled us with profound distrust. On that point I found the Assembly shared the feelings I had encountered among the National Guard. We distrusted the loyalty of some, the ability of all. Moreover the Commission was too numerous and too divided to act in complete accord, and it contained too many speakers and writers to act effectively in such a crisis, even if they had been agreed.

Nonetheless we did triumph over this formidable insurrection; furthermore, it was exactly the element that made it so terrible that saved us, and there has never been a better application of the famous phrase[3]: "We should have perished, had we not been so near to perishing." If the rebellion had been less radical and seemed less fierce, probably most of the bourgeoisie would have stayed at home; France would not have rushed to our aid; perhaps even the National Assembly would have yielded; at the least a minority of its members would have advised that, and its strength as a body would have been much diminished. But the insurrection was of such a nature that any dealings with it were at once out of the question, leaving no alternative from the start but victory or destruction.

The same consideration prevented any man of standing from putting himself at its head. It is usual for insurrections, and I am speaking of ones that succeed, to start without a leader; but they always end by finding one. This one came to an end without ever finding one; it embraced all the popular classes, but it never went beyond those limits. Even the Montagnards in the Assembly did not dare to pronounce in favour of it; they had not yet given up hope of attaining their ends by a different path; moreover they were afraid that a victory of the workers would shortly prove fatal to them. The greedy, blind, vulgar passions that had induced the people to take up arms frightened them: in fact those passions were almost as alarming for those who sympathized with them, without entirely abandoning themselves to them, as to those who rejected and fought against them.

The only men who could have put themselves at the head of the insurgents in June had, like fools, allowed themselves to be captured prematurely on the 15th May, and they only heard the sound of battle through the walls of their prison at Vincennes.

[3] *The following words are marked for omission in the manuscript:* Of the Prince of Condé during the wars of religion.

Preoccupied as I was with public affairs, I was still worried about my young nephews. They had been sent back to the little seminary, and I calculated that the insurrection must be pressing in very close to where they were living, if it had not actually reached them. As their parents were not in Paris, I decided to go and fetch them; so once more I made the long journey from the Palais Bourbon to the rue Notre Dame des Champs. I came across some barricades that had been put up during the night by lost children of the insurrection, but they had been either abandoned or recaptured at daybreak.

All these districts resounded with a diabolical music, a mixture of drums and trumpets, whose offensive, discordant, savage sounds were new to me. This was indeed the first time I heard it, and I have never heard it since: it was the general call to arms, which it had been agreed was to be beaten in the event of extreme danger, to call everybody to arms at once.

Everywhere national guards were coming out of houses; and everywhere groups of workers in blouses were listening with sinister expressions to the general call to arms and to the gunfire. The fighting had not reached the rue Notre Dame des Champs, though it was very close. Taking my nephews with me, I returned to the Chamber.

When I was getting near and was already in the midst of the troops guarding it, an old woman with a vegetable barrow stubbornly barred my way. I ended by telling her rather sharply to make room. Instead of doing so, she left her barrow and rushed at me with such sudden frenzy that I had trouble defending myself. I shuddered at the frightful and hideous expression on her face, which reflected demagogic passions and the fury of civil war. At moments of violent crisis even actions that have nothing to do with politics take on a strange character of chaotic anger: if one pays attention and notices such things, they provide a very reliable index of the general state of mind. It is as though these great public emotions create a burning atmosphere in which private feelings seethe and boil.

I found a thousand sinister rumours agitating the Assembly. The insurrection was gaining ground everywhere; its hearth and so to speak body was behind the Hôtel de Ville: thence it stretched its long arms far out into the suburbs of Paris and threatened to surround us ourselves soon. The gunfire was coming appreciably closer. A thousand false rumours were added to this correct news. Some said that our troops were beginning to run out of ammunition; others that some of our men had laid down their arms or gone over to the insurgents.

M. Thiers asked Barrot, Dufaure, Rémusat, Lanjuinais and me to go to a private room with him. There he said:

"I know something about insurrections, and, believe me, this is the worst I have yet seen. In an hour the insurgents could be here, and we should be massacred one by one. Don't you think it would be best to come to an understanding to propose to the Assembly, when we think it necessary and before it is too late, to call back the troops to guard it, so that thus protected we could leave Paris in a body and transfer the seat of the Republic to some other place, whither we could summon the army and all the national guards in France to our aid?"

He said all this in very excited tones, and showing perhaps more emotion than one should in moments of great danger. I could see the ghost of February was haunting him. Dufaure, whose imagination was less vivid and who moreover had difficulty making up his mind to act in concert with people he did not like, even to save himself, phlegmatically and somewhat sarcastically pointed out that the time had not yet come to discuss such a plan; that we could talk about it later; that our chances did not seem to him so desperate that one must think of such an extreme course, for it was a source of weakness even to think of it. He was certainly right, and his words broke up the conference. I immediately wrote a few lines to my wife telling her that the danger was increasing from moment to moment, and that the whole of Paris might fall into the hands of the revolt; that in that case we ourselves would be forced to leave the city to carry on the civil war elsewhere. I advised her to go immediately to Saint Germain by the railway, which was still open, and to await news from me there; I entrusted the letter to my nephews to take to her and went back to the Chamber.

A decree was under discussion to declare Paris in a state

of siege, terminate the powers of the Executive Commission and replace it by a military dictatorship under General Cavaignac.

The Assembly knew that this was exactly what it wanted to do. It was an easy thing to do, it was urgent, and yet it was not getting done. The current of the general desire was continually being interrupted and turned aside by some little incident or trivial motion; for Assemblies are very subject to nightmares of this sort in which some unknown, invisible force seems always to be interposed at the last moment between thought and act, preventing the one from ever becoming the other. Who would ever have supposed that it would be Bastide who made the Assembly decide? But it was.

I have heard him say quite rightly, speaking of himself, that he could never find more than the first fifteen words of a speech. But sometimes men who cannot speak can, as I have noticed on several occasions, have a greater effect, in the right circumstances, than the finest speakers. They bring only one idea, the idea of the moment, engraved in a single phrase, and then somehow they place it on the rostrum like an inscription in big letters[4] which all can read and immediately recognize in their own thoughts. So there was Bastide's long, honest, melancholy face in the rostrum, and he spoke sadly as follows:

"Citizens, in the name of the country I implore you to vote as quickly as possible. We have been told that in an hour perhaps the Hôtel de Ville will have been captured."

These few words put an end to argument; the decree was voted in the twinkling of an eye.

I objected to the clause putting Paris in a state of siege; I did so by instinct, rather than on reflection. I have such a natural distrust and dread of military tyranny that these feelings rose tumultuously in my heart when I heard talk of a state of siege and dominated even thoughts of our peril. In that I made a mistake, which luckily was not imitated by many.

The friends of the Executive Commission have said very bitterly that their adversaries and the partisans of General Cavaignac deliberately spread sinister rumours to hasten the vote. If

[4] *Variant:* They draft their thoughts in a monumental style.

they did use this trick, I gladly forgive them, for the measures they thus caused to be taken were indispensable to the country's safety.

Before adopting the decree just mentioned, the Assembly passed by acclamation another declaring that the families of those who fell in the struggle should receive a pension from the Treasury and their children should be adopted by the Republic.

It was resolved that sixty members of the Chamber, selected by the committees, should disperse through Paris, informing the national guards of the various decrees just passed by the Assembly and thereby restoring their confidence, for it was said that they were hesitant and discouraged.

In the committee to which I belonged, instead of immediately nominating the commissioners, an endless discussion started about the futility or danger of the resolution just taken[5]; much time was lost in this way. In the end I stopped this ridiculous blabber with one sentence: "Gentlemen," I said, "the Assembly may have been mistaken, but allow me to observe that, such a resolution having been publicly taken, it would be a disgrace for it to retreat, and a disgrace for us not to obey."

They voted instantly, and I was, as I expected, unanimously appointed a commissioner. I was given Cormenin and Crémieux as colleagues, and Goudchaux was added. The last was less well known at that time, although he was in his way the most original of the three. He was at once a radical and a banker,

---

[5] *The following passage has been marked for omission in the manuscript:* I walked up and down all this time rather impatiently, thinking that a word would be enough to stop this ridiculous blabber, but, in accordance with our parliamentary usages, to say that word would invite nomination as a commissioner, and I confess that I had little taste for that. I thought it a little hard to prepare my own grave in the middle of a harangue in full swing as Bixio and Dornès had done. "Let those people," I said to myself, looking at Cormenin and Crémieux who were members of the same committee as I, "who have brought all this on and are responsible for it, claim missions of this sort; nothing better; but for me who was driven off these premises by them six months ago, it would be incredibly stupid to solicit such a job."

It is true that we had been brought to a point where it was not just a question of "them" but of "us"; we were like honest travellers kidnapped by pirates, who must help them to save the ship, so as not to be drowned themselves. I kept turning that over in my mind, but finally I lost patience and stopped the discussion then and there with a word.

a rare combination; seeing business at close quarters had succeeded in putting a veneer of reasonable ideas over the mad theories filling the depths of his soul, but those theories always came to the top in the end. He did not look like a Jew, though he was one on both his mother's and his father's side, for he had round cheeks, thick red lips, and a plump, short body that made him look like the cook in a good family. It was impossible to be more vain, irascible, quarrelsome and petulant or more easily moved than he. He was unable to discuss difficulties in the Budget without bursting into tears; yet he was one of the most valiant little men one could meet.

Because of the tempestuous argument in our committee, the other deputations had already left, and with them the guides and escorts that should have gone with us. Nevertheless we put on our sashes and went out, making our way alone and a little hazardously towards the interior of Paris, along the right bank of the Seine. The insurrection by that time had made such progress that we saw batteries of guns drawn up and firing between the Pont des Arts and the Pont Neuf. The national guards who saw us from the top of the embankment as we passed looked anxiously at us and respectfully took off their hats, exclaiming in an emotionally charged undertone: "Long live the National Assembly!" Never have loud acclaims greeting a king come more clearly from the depths of the heart or borne witness to a more unfeigned sympathy. When we passed through the wicket gates and were on the Carrousel, I saw that Cormenin and Crémieux were gradually diverging to the right, that is to say towards the Tuileries, and I heard one of them (I don't remember which) say:

"Where could we go? And what good can we do without guides? Wouldn't it be best to limit ourselves to going through the Tuileries gardens? Several battalions of the reserve are stationed there; we will announce the Assembly's decrees to them!"

"Certainly," the other replied. "I even think that we will thus fulfil the Assembly's instructions better than our colleagues; for what can one say to men already in action? It is the reserves that we should prepare to take their turn in the line."

I have always found it interesting to follow the involuntary effects of fear in the minds of men of intelligence. Fools show their fear grossly in all its nakedness, but the others know how to cover it with a veil of such fine and delicately woven, small, convincing deceits that there is a pleasure in contemplating this ingenious labour of the intelligence.

Of course I, who was in a pretty nasty temper when we started, had no taste for a stroll in the Tuileries gardens. The wine once drawn, as we say, I thought we must drink it. So I spoke to Goudchaux, pointing out the way our colleagues were taking.

"I see it well enough," he replied angrily. "I am leaving them and will announce the Assembly's decrees without them."

Together we took the road leading to the opposite wicket gate. Cormenin and Crémieux soon joined us again—somewhat shamefaced. Thus we reached the rue Saint Honoré, and the appearance of that street was perhaps the thing that struck me most during the days of June. That noisy fashionable street was at the moment more deserted than I have ever seen it at four o'clock on a winter's morning. As far as the eye could see there was not a living soul; the shops, doors and windows were hermetically sealed. Nothing showed, nothing stirred; there was not the sound of a wheel or the clatter of a horse's hoof or a man's footstep; only the roar of the guns seemed to echo in an abandoned city. But the houses were not empty, for as we went along, through the casements we could see women and children glued to the windowpanes, looking at us with frightened expressions.

Near the Palais Royal we at last met large groups of national guards, and our mission began. Crémieux became all on fire when he realized that it was only a matter of talking; he told these men what had just happened in the National Assembly, and made a little bravura oration, which was loudly applauded. We found an escort there, and we went on farther. We wandered for a long time through the little streets of these districts until we came to the great barricade in the rue Rambuteau, which had not yet been captured and which stopped us. Thence we came back through . . .[6] In all these little streets we saw smears of blood from the recent fighting, and fighting broke out again there from time to time. For this was a war of ambushes, with no fixed theatre of operations, and it was continually doubling back on its tracks. When you least expected it, you would be shot at from a garret window; and when you got into the house, you would find the gun all right, but not the sniper: he would have slipped out of the back door while you were breaking down the front. Accordingly, the national guards had instructions to order all shutters to be opened, and to fire on all who appeared at the windows; and they took this order so literally that several people who put their noses out of doors from curiosity at seeing our sashes nearly got killed. We had to make at least thirty speeches in the course of the journey, which lasted two or three hours: I refer to Crémieux and myself, for Goudchaux could speak only about finance, and Cormenin was of course known to be as dumb as a fish. To tell the truth nearly all the burden fell on Crémieux. He filled me, I will not say with admiration but with surprise. Janvier once described Crémieux as an "eloquent louse." If only he could have seen him on that day, tired, untidy, his face covered by a mask of dust and sticky sweat, puffing, shouting, but always finding new clichés, or rather new words and turns of phrase to express what he had said before, sometimes using gestures to repeat what he had just said, and sometimes saying what he had first expressed in gestures; always eloquent, always heated, and always cheered. I don't think anyone has ever met, or perhaps even conceived of, a man so ugly and so eloquent.

I noticed that the national guards when told that Paris was in a state of siege were pleased, but when we added that the Executive Commission had been dismissed, they burst out cheering. Never has a people been so relieved to be rid of its freedom and its government. And that was what Lamartine's popularity had come to in less than two months.

When we had finished speaking, the men crowded around us; they asked if we were sure that the Executive Commission

---

[6] *The name of the street is left blank in the manuscript.* (Ed.)

had surrendered its functions; they had to be shown the decree to satisfy them.

What I especially noticed was the staunch attitude of these men; we had come to put courage into them, and it was they who were encouraging us. "Hold firm in the National Assembly," they shouted, "and we will hold firm here. Courage. No dealings with the rebels. We will put a stop to this riot; all will end well." The National Guard had never appeared so resolute, and I think it would be a mistake to expect it to be the same another time, for its courage was the courage of necessity and despair and depended on circumstances hardly likely to recur.

On that day Paris was like some city of antiquity whose citizens defend their walls like heroes, because they know defeat means slavery. As we were going back to the Assembly, Goudchaux left us. "Now that we have accomplished our mission," he told me, grinding his teeth and speaking with a half-Alsatian, half-Gascon accent, "I should like to go and fight a little." He announced this in such martial tones, which contrasted oddly with his pacific appearance, that I could not restrain a smile.

He did go and fight so bravely, I am told, that he could have had his little paunch riddled with two or three bullets had fate so willed. I returned from that round convinced that we would come out victorious, and what I saw as I drew near the Assembly confirmed that conviction.

Down all the roads not held by the insurgents, thousands of men were pouring in from all parts of France to aid us. Thanks to the railways, those from fifty leagues[7] off were already arriving, although the fighting had begun only in the evening of the previous day. The next day and the days following, they were to arrive from one and two hundred leagues away. These men were drawn without distinction from all classes of society; among them there were great numbers of peasants, bourgeois, large landowners and nobles, all jumbled up together in the same ranks. They were unsystematically and inadequately armed, but they all rushed into Paris with unequalled ardour:

[7] A league was roughly equivalent to three English miles. (Ed.)

this was a sight as strange and unparalleled in our revolutionary annals as the insurrection itself had been. Thenceforth it was clear that we would win in the end for the insurgents had no fresh forces, and we the whole of France as reserves.

On the Place Louis XV I met my cousin, Lepelletier d'Aunay, who had been Vice-President of the Chamber of Deputies during the last years of the Monarchy, surrounded by the armed inhabitants of his district. He was not in uniform and carried no musket but wore only a little ceremonial silver-hilted sword suspended from a white linen bandolier.

I was moved to tears at seeing this venerable white-haired man thus equipped.

"Won't you come and dine with me this evening?" I asked.

"No, no," he answered. "What would these good people who are with me, and who know that I have more to lose than they by the success of the insurrection, say if they saw me taking my ease and leaving them here? No, I will share their meal, and I will sleep here in their bivouac. The one thing I would ask of you is, if possible, to speed up the dispatch of our promised bread ration a little, for we have had nothing to eat since this morning."

I went back to the Assembly at about three o'clock, I think, and did not go out again.

The rest of that day was entirely taken up by accounts of the fighting, something new happening or news arriving every moment. There was the announcement of the arrival of volunteers from a department; prisoners were being brought in; flags captured on the barricades were presented. Acts of courage and heroic words were recounted; we were constantly hearing of the wounding or death of somebody of distinction. As to the final issue of that day, nothing had yet occurred to enable us to guess.

The President called the Assembly together only at long intervals for short periods; and he was right to do so, for Assemblies are like children in that idleness never fails to make them do or say a lot of silly things. Each time the sitting was resumed, he himself told us all that had been learned for certain, during the adjournment. This President, as we know, was Sénard, a well-known lawyer from Rouen, and a courageous man; however, the daily comedy of the bar had from his youth led him to contract such an inveterate habit of acting that he had lost the faculty of truthfully expressing his real impressions, if by chance he had any. Inevitably he would add some turgid phrases of his own to the acts of courage he was narrating, and when he expressed the emotion which he, I think, really felt, in sepulchral tones, with a trembling voice and a sort of tragedian's hiccup, he even then seemed to be acting. Never were the ridiculous and the sublime so close, for the deeds were sublime and the narrator ridiculous.

We did not disperse until very late in the night to get a little rest. Fighting had stopped but was due to start again the next day. The insurrection was everywhere contained, but nowhere tamed.

CHAPTER TEN

The end of the June Days[1]

At that time the house in which we lived in the rue de la Madeleine had a doorkeeper with a thoroughly bad reputation in the district; he was a slightly daft, drunken, good-for-nothing old soldier who spent the time he could spare from beating his wife, at the public house. One might say that this man was a socialist by birth, or rather by temperament.

The first successes of the revolution had gone to his head, and on the morning of the day in question he had been round the local pubs announcing, among other mischievous proposals, that he would kill me that evening when I came home, if I ever did come home; he even brandished a long knife intended for the purpose. A poor woman who had heard him hurried in great distress to inform Madame de Tocqueville; the latter, before leaving Paris, sent me a note recounting the rumour and asking me not to go home that evening but to spend the night at my father's house, which was nearby, he being out of Paris. I fully intended to do so, but when I left the Assembly toward midnight, I had not the strength of mind to follow the plan. I was exhausted and did not know whether I would find a bed ready anywhere except at home. Besides I thought it improbable that a murder announced in advance would be committed, and I was suffering from the listlessness that prolonged emotion induces. So I went and knocked at my door, having taken no further precaution than

[1] *Marginal note* (*Tocqueville*): Shorten a good deal by cuts towards the middle.

to load the pistols that in those unhappy days it was quite normal
to carry. It was that man who opened the door and, as he was
meticulously shutting the bolts after me, I asked him if all the
other tenants were in. He laconically informed me that they
had all left Paris that morning and that we two were alone in
the house; I should have preferred somebody else for a tête-à-
tête, but it was too late to draw back; so I looked him in the
whites of the eyes and ordered him to go in front of me, lighting
the way. He stopped at a door leading into the courtyard
and told me he could hear a peculiar noise coming from one of
the coach houses, asking me to go and investigate it with him;
as he said this, he turned towards the coach house. All this
struck me as very suspicious, but I thought, having gone so far, it
was safer to go on. So I followed him, but I kept an eye on all
his movements and had made up my mind to kill him like a dog
at the first sign of any evil plan. We did hear the very peculiar
noise of which he had spoken. It sounded like water flowing
underground or the distant rumble of a carriage, although it
clearly came from quite close by; I never did discover what it
was, but then I did not spend long looking. I soon went back
into the house, making my companion lead the way to my
landing, watching him the whole time. I told him to open the
door and, when he had done so, took the torch from him and
went in. It wasn't until he saw me turning away that he made
up his mind to take off his hat and bow. Did that man intend
to kill me and give up the plan only when, seeing me on my
guard with both hands in my pockets, he guessed that I might
be better armed than he? At the time I thought he never
seriously contemplated the crime, and I think so still. In times of
revolution people boast almost as much about the crimes they
intend to commit as they do in normal times about their good intentions. I have always thought that this poor wretch would
have become dangerous only if the fight seemed to be going
against us, whereas in fact, although still doubtful, the balance
inclined our way, and that was enough to make me safe.

At daybreak I heard someone coming into my room and awoke
with a start. It was my manservant who had let himself in with
his key to my apartment. That fine fellow had left the bivouac

(I had given him the National Guard uniform for which he had asked and a good musket) and looked in to see if I was back and if I needed his services. He assuredly was no socialist, either in theory or by temperament. He was not even touched by that most usual sickness of our time, a restless mind, and even at another period it would have been hard to find a man more satisfied with his station and contented with his lot. Always very pleased with himself and tolerably pleased with others, he generally desired nothing beyond his reach, and he usually did reach, or think he had reached, what he wanted. So he unconsciously followed the precepts inculcated by philosophers, but seldom observed by them, and enjoyed as a gift of nature that happy balance between powers and wants, that alone brings the happiness promised by the philosopher.

"Well, Eugène," I asked him when he came in that morning, "how are things going?"

"Very well, sir. Perfectly well."

"How do you mean 'very well,' when I can still hear gunfire?"

"Yes, they are still fighting," he answered, "but everyone is saying that it will end very well."

Having said that, he took off his uniform, cleaned my boots and brushed my clothes, and then, putting on his uniform again, said:

"If you do not need anything else, sir, with your permission, I will go back to the battle."

For four days and four nights he pursued this double calling as simply as I write it down. In those troubled days of savagery and hatred, it gave me a sense of repose to see that young man's peaceful, satisfied face.

Before going to the Assembly, where I did not think any important decisions would have to be taken, I decided to make my way to the places where the fighting continued and I could hear gunfire. Not that I wanted "to go and fight a little" like Goudchaux, but I wanted to judge for myself how things were, for, in my complete ignorance of warfare, I could not understand what made the fight go on so long. Besides, I must confess that sheer curiosity sometimes got the better of all the other feelings in my head. I traversed a great part of the suburbs without

seeing any traces of the battle, but after the Saint Denis gate
there were plenty of them; the insurrection, as it retreated, had
left behind broken windows, doors forced in, houses pitted
with cannon fire or bullets, trees thrown down, paving stones
piled up, and dirty straw stained with blood as melancholy re-
minders.

I eventually reached the Château d'Eau, where I found a
large body of troops from different branches of the army con-
gregated. At the foot of the fountain was a cannon trained down
the rue Samson. At first I thought the insurgents were answering
our fire from a gun of their own, but I finally saw my mistake; it
was the echo of our own firing that made the frightful noise.
I have never heard anything like it; one would have thought
one was in the midst of some great battle. But in fact the
insurgents answered only with infrequent but deadly musket
fire. It was an odd battle. As one knows, the rue Samson is
not very long; the Saint Martin canal cuts across the bottom of
it, and behind the canal is a large house facing the street.

The street was absolutely deserted; there was no barricade in
sight, and the gun seemed as if it was firing at a target; only
occasionally did a wisp of smoke coming out of one of the
windows in the street indicate the presence of an invisible enemy. Our snipers, posted along the walls, aimed at the windows
from which they saw the shots come. Behind the fountains,
Lamoricière, astride a large horse and in range of the guns,
gave his orders amid a rain of bullets. I found him more excited
and more talkative than I would have supposed a general in command should be at such a moment; he spoke and shouted in
a hoarse voice, and his gestures were wild. The clarity of his
thought and language made it obvious that, despite the apparent confusion, he had not lost his coolness: but orders so given
might make others lose theirs, and I would have admired his
courage more had it been calmer.

I found it very odd, this fight with no visible enemy in front
and firing apparently directed only against walls. I had never
imagined war was like that. As the boulevard seemed clear beyond the Château d'Eau, I could not see why our columns did
not advance, or why we did not capture the large house facing

the street at a rush, instead of remaining so long subject to the murderous fire from it. Yet nothing could have been easier to explain: the boulevard that I supposed free from the Château d'Eau onwards was not so; there was a bend in it, and after that point it bristled with barricades the whole way to the Bastille. Before attacking the barricades, we wanted to control the streets that would be behind us, and in particular to get control of the house facing the rue Samson, which dominated the boulevard and would have harassed our communications badly; finally, we could not take that house by assault because the canal stood in the way, but I could not see that from the boulevard. So we tried to destroy it, or at least make it untenable, by cannon fire. That took a very long time to achieve, and, whereas in the morning I had been wondering why the fight went on for so long, I now began to wonder if it would ever end at this rate. For what I then witnessed around the Château d'Eau was taking place in different forms in a hundred different parts of Paris at that same moment.

As the insurgents had no guns, this battlefield must have been less terrible to contemplate than one ploughed up by cannon balls. The men struck down before my eyes seemed transfixed by an invisible shaft; they staggered and fell with no more to be seen at first than a little hole in their clothes; in all the casualties I saw, it was not so much the physical pain as the moral agony that struck me. It was indeed a strange and a terrifying thing to see the quick change of expression, the fire of life in the eyes quenched in the sudden terror of death.

Somewhat later on I saw Lamoricière's horse sink to the ground shot through; it was the third horse he had had killed under him since the day before yesterday. He jumped lightly to the ground and went on giving his impassioned orders on foot.

I noticed that the soldiers of the line were the least eager of our troops. Memories of February appeared to weaken and benumb them, and they seemed a little afraid that the next day somebody might tell them they had done the wrong thing. Without any doubt the keenest were those very Gardes Mobiles whose fidelity we had questioned so seriously and, I still say,

even after the event, so rightly, for it would have taken very
little to make them decide against us instead of for us. True,
once involved, they performed prodigies of valour. They were all
those children of Paris who give our armies their most undisci-
plined and rash soldiers, for they rush towards danger. They
went to war as to a festival. But it was easy to see that they
loved war in itself much more than the cause for which they
fought. Besides, all these troops were very raw and subject to
panic: I can judge from experience there, having nearly been a
victim. A large high house was being built at the corner of the
rue Samson just by the Château d'Eau; some insurgents, who
must have passed through the courtyards at the back, got installed there before anybody suspected it; they fired a sudden
volley from the top of the building on our troops crowded in
the boulevard, who were far from expecting the enemy to be
posted in that position, or anywhere close. The sound of their
muskets echoed loudly from the opposite walls, giving the impression of an attack from that quarter too. Immediately our
column fell into utter confusion; in an instant, artillery, cavalry
and infantry were mixed up, and the soldiers fired in all directions, not knowing what they were doing, and fell back sixty
paces in a tumult. This disorderly, impetuous flight threw me
against the wall of the house opposite the rue du Faubourg du
Temple, where I was knocked over by the cavalry and so hard
pressed that I lost my hat and nearly left my body there too.
That was certainly the greatest danger I was in during the days
of June. This made me reflect that everything in the heroic game
of war is not heroic; I have no doubt that accidents of that
sort happen often and to the best troops, but nobody boasts
about them, and the bulletins do not mention them.

But what was sublime at that moment was Lamoricière; until then he had kept his sword sheathed; now he drew it and
rushed among his soldiers with the most splendid rage in all his
looks and actions; he halted them with his commands, seized
them with his hands, even struck them with the pommel of his
sword, turned them, rallied them, and putting himself at their
head forced them to pass at a trot through the fire in the rue
du Faubourg du Temple in order to capture the house from

which the firing came; this was achieved in an instant, and without a blow struck; the enemy had vanished.

The fight then resumed its sad pace and so continued for some time until the insurgents' fire was finally quenched and the street occupied. There was a moment's pause before the next operation began. Lamoricière went to his headquarters, a public house in the boulevard near the Saint Martin gate; and I was able to consult him at last about the state of affairs.

"How long do you think all this will last?" I asked him.

"How can I tell?" he answered. "That depends on the enemy, not on us."

He then showed me on the map all the streets that had been taken and occupied and all those that remained to be captured, and he added:

"If the insurgents want to hold out on the ground they hold, as bravely as they did on what we have already captured, we might have a week more ahead of us, and our losses would be enormous for we lose more than they do; in such a case it is the first whose moral stamina fails that will be defeated."

I then reproached him for exposing himself so rashly and, as I supposed, uselessly.

"What do you want me to do?" he asked. "Tell Cavaignac to send me generals who know how to support me and want to do so, and I will keep more in the background; but when you have only yourself to rely on, you must constantly run risks yourself."

At that moment M. Thiers came up and threw his arms round Lamoricière's neck, telling him he was a hero. I could not help smiling at that sight, for they did not love each other at all, but danger is like wine in making all men sentimental.

I left Lamoricière in M. Thiers' arms and went back to the Assembly. It was getting late, and I know no greater fool than he who gets his head broken at the wars from sheer curiosity.

The rest of the day passed like the one before; the same anxiety in the Assembly, the same feverish inaction, and the same staunchness.

Crowds of volunteers continued to pour into Paris; constantly some sad event or the death of some illustrious man was an-

nounced. Such news saddened but also inspired and fortified
the Assembly. Members timidly advancing proposals tending
towards a compromise with the insurgents were received with
angry shouts. Towards evening I wanted to go personally to the
Hôtel de Ville to get more certain news of the day's events. At
first it had been the violence of the insurrection that disturbed me, but now it was its duration. For who could fore-
tell the effect in certain parts of France, particularly in such
great industrial towns as Lyon, of a fight so long undecided and
Paris in such prolonged suspense. As I was passing along the
Quai de la Ferraille, I met some national guards from my
neighbourhood carrying several of their comrades and two
wounded officers on stretchers. Talking to them I noticed how
terribly quickly even in this civilized century of ours the most
pacific people will, so to speak, get in tune with the spirit of
civil war, and how in those unhappy times a taste for violence
and a contempt for human life suddenly spread. The men I was
talking to were sober, peaceful artisans whose gentle and slightly
soft mores were even farther removed from cruelty than from
heroism. But they were dreaming of nothing but destruction and
massacre. They complained that they were not allowed to use
bombs or to sap and mine the streets held by the insurgents, and
they did not want to give quarter to anybody any more.[2] I did
what I could to calm these furious sheep down. I assured them
that the next day more drastic measures would be taken. In fact
that morning Lamoricière had told me that he had sent for shells
to fire behind the barricades, and I knew that a regiment of
sappers was expected from Douai to tunnel through the walls
and blow the beseiged houses up with petards. I added that one
should never shoot a prisoner, but that they shoot on the spot
any man who made as if to defend himself. I left these folk of
mine a little calmer. But as I went my way I could not help
reflecting about myself, feeling astonished at the nature of the

[2] *The following passage is marked for omission in the manuscript:* Already
that morning I almost saw a poor devil shot on the boulevards: he had
been arrested without arms in his hands, but his mouth and hands were
blackened with something that they took to be, and that probably was,
gunpowder.

arguments I had just been using and the speed at which, within two days, I had become familiar with ideas of relentless destruction and severity, ideas that were far from my natural bent. Going back through the little streets, which I had seen two days before being closed with such solid, tidy barricades, I noticed that gunfire had seriously disturbed these fine works, but one could still see the remains of them.

It was Marrast, the Mayor of Paris, who received me. He told me that the Hôtel de Ville was secure for the moment, but that perhaps in the night the insurgents might try to recapture the streets won from them. He seemed less reassuring than his bulletins. He took me to a room where Bedeau, who had been dangerously wounded on the first day, was lodged. This post at the Hôtel de Ville was indeed lethal for the generals commanding there. Bedeau nearly perished there. And Duvivier and Négrier, who succeeded him, were killed. Bedeau thought himself only slightly wounded, and all his attention was concentrated on the state of the battle; such mental excitement seemed a bad sign to me, and I was worried.

The night was well advanced when I left the Hôtel de Ville to go back to the Assembly. They offered me an escort, which I refused, thinking it unnecessary; but I regretted it more than once on the journey. To prevent the insurgent districts from getting reinforcements, ammunition or information from the other parts of the town where so many were ready to join their side, a very sensible decision had been made that morning to prohibit completely circulation in all streets. Everyone who left his house without a pass or an escort was stopped. So I was stopped very often and had to show my medal. Ten times, at least, inexperienced sentries speaking every imaginable dialect held me covered, for Paris was full of countrymen from all over France, many of whom were there for the first time.

By the time I got there, the sitting was long finished, but there was great perturbation nonetheless; a rumour had spread that the workers of Gros-Caillou were going to take advantage of the night to seize the palace. So the Assembly, which in three days' fighting had pressed the struggle back into the heart of the enemy-occupied districts, was frightened for the safety of its home. No rumour ever had less foundation, but one could not find a better illustration of the nature of this war, where the enemy might always be one's neighbour, and where one could never be sure that one's own house would not be sacked while one was victorious far away. To protect the palace from such a sudden assault, barricades were erected that night to close all the possible approach roads. When I realized that it was only a false rumour, I went home to bed.

I will say nothing more about the fighting in June. My memories of the last two days have merged with those of the first and are lost. It is well known that the Faubourg Saint Antoine, the last citadel of the civil war, did not lay down its arms until Monday, that is to say, the fourth day after the beginning of the struggle. It was not until the morning of that day that the volunteers from La Manche were able to reach Paris. They made excellent speed, but they had more than eighty leagues to go over country without railways. They numbered fifteen hundred. I was touched to recognize among them landowners, lawyers, doctors and farmers, my friends and neighbours. Almost every member of the old nobility of the district had taken up arms and formed part of the column.

The same was true almost everywhere in France. The most stick-in-the-mud little squire from the backwaters and the elegant, useless sons of the great houses all remembered that they had once formed part of a warlike ruling class, and all displayed dispatch and energy, such vigour there is in these old aristocratic bodies. Even when they seem reduced to dust, they keep some trace of their former selves; and they rise again out of the shadow of death several times before they finally sink into eternal rest.

It was during these June days that death came to the man who had best preserved the spirit of the ancient stock, M. de Chateaubriand, with whom I was linked by many family ties and childhood memories. For some time he had been in a sort of speechless stupor, which at times made one think that his brain had gone. In that state, however, he heard a rumour of the February Revolution, and wanted to know what was happening. He was told that the Monarchy of Louis-Philippe had been overthrown; he said, "That is well done!" and was silent again. Four months later, the tumult of the June days reached his ears, and again he asked what the noise was about. He was told there was fighting in Paris and that it was gunfire. Then he made vain efforts to get up, saying: "I want to go there," and then he was silent, this time forever, for he died the next day.

Such were the days of June; necessary, fateful days. They did not quench the fire of revolution in France, but they brought to an end, at least for a time, what one might call the proper work of the February Revolution. They delivered the nation from oppression by the Paris workmen and restored it to control of its own fate.

Socialist theories in the shape of greedy, envious desires[3] continued to spread among the people, sowing the seeds of future revolutions, but the socialist party itself remained beaten and impotent. The Montagnards, who did not belong to that party, soon felt that they had been struck down beyond recall by the same blow that felled it. Even the moderate Republicans were not slow to see that the victory which had saved them had left them on a slope that might send them sliding beyond a republic, and they immediately made an effort to pull back, but in vain. I, detesting the Montagnards and not attached to the Republic but adoring liberty, felt on the aftermath of those days great apprehension for the Republic. I had realized at once that the fight in June was a necessary crisis, but that after it the nation's character would be in some way changed. The former love of independence would be followed by a dread of, and perhaps a distaste for, free institutions; after such an abuse of freedom, the reaction was inevitable. This retrograde movement did begin after the 27th June; at first it was very slow and almost invisible to the naked eye, then fast, then impetuous and irresistible. Where will it stop? I do not know. I think we shall find it difficult not to go back far beyond the point we had reached in February, and I foresee that all of us,

[3] *Variant:* Helped by the wretched existence of the poor and by their envious greed.

Socialists, Montagnards, Republicans and Liberals, will all fall into the same discredit until the memories peculiar to the Revolution of 1848 have moved into the background and grown dim and the general spirit of the age has regained its sway.

The Drafting Committee for the Constitution[2]
(Sorrento – March 1851)

My subject changes now, and I gladly leave scenes of civil war to return to my parliamentary life. I want to talk about what happened in the Committee for the Constitution, of which I was a member. We need to go back a little, as the appointment of this Committee and its meetings started before the days of June; but I did not want to mention it sooner for fear of interrupting the sequence of events leading directly and swiftly to those days. On the 17th May the task of appointing the Committee for the Constitution began; it was a long business because it had been decided that the members should be chosen by the whole Assembly and by an absolute majority of votes. I was elected on the first vote[3] together with Cormenin, Marrast, Lamennais, Vivien and Dufaure. I don't know how many votes were taken before the full eighteen members were appointed.

Although the Committee was appointed before the victory in June, almost all of its members belonged to one or another of

[1] *Marginal note (Tocqueville):* Try to look at the official record again. I no longer have any recollections of the details of the lengthy arguments about the preamble.
[2] *Marginal note (Tocqueville):* There is a great gap in this chapter: I do not mention the discussions and resolutions concerning *general principles.*
    Several of these discussions went quite deep, and most of the resolutions were reasonably wise and even courageous. Most of the revolutionary and socialist enthusiasms of the time were combated in them. On these general questions there was some preparedness and alertness.
[3] *Note by Tocqueville:* I had 496 votes.

the various moderate par*'es in the Assembly. There were only two members from the Mountain: Lamennais and Considérant. And even they were hardly more than fantastic dreamers, Considérant especially. For Considérant, if he was sincere, should have been put in a mental home, but I'm afraid he deserved something worse than that.

Taking the Committee as a whole, it was easy to see that nothing very remarkable was to be expected from it.

Some of the members had passed their lives in direct or indirect control of the administration under the former government. They had never seen, studied, or understood any system other than monarchy. Moreover most of them had applied principles rather than studied them, and their thoughts scarcely rose above the routine of business. Now that they were called upon to give reality to theories that they had always despised or combated, and that had forced them to submission without convincing them, it was very difficult for them to introduce any ideas but monarchical ones into their work; or, if they did venture republican ideas, they were sometimes timid and sometimes enthusiastic, but always rather haphazard, like novices.

As for the Republicans, properly so called on the Committee, they had few ideas of any sort beyond what they had read or written in the newspapers, many of them being journalists. It is well known that Marrast had edited the *National* for ten years; at that time Dornès was editor-in-chief; Vaulabelle, who had a serious but coarse and somewhat cynical turn of mind, habitually wrote for that paper. A month later he was vastly, and rightly, astonished to find himself Minister of Education and Public Worship.

All this bore little resemblance to those men, so sure of their aim and so well acquainted with the best means to reach it, who drafted the American Constitution sixty years ago with Washington in the chair.

Moreover, even if the Committee had been capable of doing good work, lack of time and preoccupation with what was going on outside would have prevented it.

No nation feels less attachment to its government than the French, and none is less able to do without it. When the nation sees that it has to walk alone, it suffers from a sort of giddiness, which makes it think that it is going to fall into an abyss at any moment. At the moment of which I am speaking, the nation had a sort of frenzied desire to see the work of constitution making finished and to see authority established, perhaps not firmly but in a permanent and orderly fashion. The Assembly shared this longing and was constantly goading us, though there was hardly any need to do so, for memories of the 15th May and apprehension of the days of June, combined with the sight of a divided, weak and incapable government in charge of affairs, were enough to drive us on. But the thing that most effectively deprived the Committee of its freedom of mind was, one must admit, fear of outside events and the excitement of the moment. It is difficult to appreciate how much this pressure of revolutionary ideas affected even those minds least subject to such influence, and how it almost unconsciously drove them farther than they meant to go, and sometimes even in a different direction. There is no doubt that, had the Committee met on the 27th June instead of the 16th May, its work would have turned out to be entirely different.

The discussion opened on the 22nd May. The first question was to decide the method of tackling this immense task. Lamennais[4] advocated starting with the state of the communes. He had already put this idea forward in a proposal for a constitution, which he had just published in order to assure himself of the credit for his discoveries. Then he moved from the question of priorities to discuss the basic issue and began talking about administrative centralization, for he never kept his ideas separate: his mind was always preoccupied with one single system, and all his ideas were so closely linked together that, when one came out, it was pretty well inevitable that all the others would follow. Accordingly he argued passionately that a republic whose citizens did not have the sense and daily experience to run their own affairs was a monster not fit to live.

At that the Committee took fire; Barrot, who has always had a vivid enough, though perhaps a confused, conception of the

4 For further information on Lamennais see F. Duine, *Lamennais*, Paris, 1922. (Ed.)

advantages of local liberties, strongly supported Lamennais; I did the same. It was Marrast and Vivien who attacked us. Vivien was in his element defending centralization, for he was a bureaucrat by profession and by inclination. He had everything it takes to make a good academic lawyer or commentator, but none of the qualities needed in a lawgiver or a statesman. At this point the danger that he saw threatening the institutions that were so dear to him inflamed him; he was so carried away that he claimed that the Republic, far from restricting centralization, should intensify it. One would have said that that side of the February Revolution suited him.

As for Marrast, he was one of the usual run of French revolutionaries who always mean by "freedom of the people" despotism exercised in the people's name. So the sudden agreement between Vivien and Marrast came as no surprise to me. I was used to the sight, having long ago observed that the only way of getting a Conservative and a Radical to agree was to attack the authority of the central government, not in practice but in principle. That was sure to throw them at once into each other's arms.

So when people say that we have nothing that is safe from revolutions, I tell them that they are wrong, that centralization is one thing. In France there is only one thing that we cannot make: a free government; and only one that we cannot destroy: centralization. How could it perish? The government's enemies love it, and the rulers cherish it. It is true that rulers notice that it occasionally exposes them to sudden, irremediable disasters, but that does not make them disgusted with it. The pleasure of meddling with everything and holding everybody in the palm of their hands makes up for the danger. They prefer such an agreeable existence to a longer, steadier life, saying like the Regency roués, "A short life, but a merry one."

The question could not be decided that day; but the decision was settled in advance by a ruling that we should not deal with the communal system first.

The next day Lamennais sent in his resignation. In the circumstances in which we found ourselves, anything of that sort was bound to cause trouble. It could not fail to spread or to reinforce existing prejudices against us. So urgent and rather humble representations were made to Lamennais, asking him to change his mind. As I had agreed with him, I was sent to see him and urge him to come back. I did so, but to no avail. He had been overruled on a formal point only, but he concluded that he would not be the master, and in that case he would rather be nothing at all. He remained inflexible in spite of everything I could say on behalf of ideas that we both shared.

One should take particular notice of unfrocked priests if one wants to understand the indestructible and so to speak infinite power that clerical customs and ways of thought, once contracted, have over a man. It was no matter that Lamennais sported white stockings, yellow waistcoat, striped tie and green coat; in character and even in appearance he remained a priest. He moved forward with little, quick, discreet steps, never turning his head or looking at anybody, and glided through the crowd with an air of awkward modesty as if he had just come out of a sacristy; but with it all he had pride enough to walk over the heads of kings and hold his own with God.

Unable to overcome Lamennais' obstinacy, we passed on to other business; to avoid further waste of time in premature discussions, a sub-committee was appointed to plan the order in which items were to be put before the main committee. Unluckily that sub-committee was so composed that Cormenin, as chairman, was the master of it and in practice took the place of it. The permanent initiative thus passed to him, and his control as chairman of the debates had the most fatal influence on our subsequent labours, and so perhaps the faults in our work are mainly due to that.[5]

Like Lamennais, Cormenin had written and published a constitution to his taste, and, like Lamennais again, he meant us to adopt it. But he didn't know quite how to lead us round to that. Extreme vanity generally makes people either very bold speakers or very shy ones. Cormenin's vanity made him unable to open his mouth in front of an audience of three. He would have liked to imitate one of my neighbours in Normandy, who loved an

[5] See P. Bastid, *Un juriste pamphlétaire. Cormenin. Précurseur et Constituant de 1848*, Paris, 1948. (Ed.)

argument but to whom the gods had denied the gracious gift of arguing *viva voce,* so that, when I raised objections to his views, he would hurry home and immediately send me a letter containing what he should have said. For this reason Cormenin had no hope of convincing us, but he flattered himself that he could take us by surprise. He hoped to get us to accept his system little by little and so to speak unconsciously, by handing us a small piece of it every day. He did so well that it was never possible to stage a discussion about the Constitution as a whole, and even in arguing about parts of it, it was almost impossible to trace things back and find the basic idea. Sometimes we kicked back, but generally for the sake of peace we yielded to this constant, gentle pressure. The chairman's influence on a committee is immense, as all those familiar with these little meetings will agree. But of course if several of us had really definitely intended to escape from this tyranny, we could in the end have come to an understanding among ourselves and managed it. Both time and taste for lengthy argument were lacking, however. Anticipatory alarm at the vast complexity of the subject made us tired before we started: most of the members had not even attempted to study it,[6] or had picked up only some very confused ideas; and those who had clearer brains were ill at ease at having to expound their ideas. Moreover there was the fear that, if we went to the bottom of things, we would plunge into endless violent argument, and we preferred to keep a semblance of harmony by staying on the surface. We journeyed in this manner right to the end, explicitly adopting great principles for reasons of petty detail, and bit by bit building up the machinery of government without properly taking into account the relative strength of the various wheels and how they could work together.

In our moments of rest from this fine work, Marrast, who was a Republican of the same ilk as Barras[7] and always preferred

---

[6] *Variant:* Most of us had never given any thought to such a vast topic.
[7] Viscount Paul de Barras (1755–1829), a member of the Convention, played an important part in the Thermidor conspiracy which brought about the fall and execution of Robespierre. When a member of the Directory (1795–99), he was notorious for his venality and for his excessively luxurious and licentious mode of life. It is in these latter respects that Tocqueville is comparing Marrast to him. (Ed.)

luxury, good food, and women to democracy in rags, recounted little stories of gallantry, while Vaulabelle made dirty jokes. I very much hope, for the honour of the Committee, that the record of our proceedings will never be published, especially as the secretary responsible made a very bad job of it. With such exuberantly rich material, people would certainly be surprised at the debate's sterility. For my part I have never been so wretched in any other committee I have served on.

There was, however, one major argument. It turned on the question of a single Chamber. In truth this was the only time that the two parties silently dividing the Committee attacked and came to grips with one another. It was not so much a question of two Chambers as of the general character to be given to the new government; were we to persevere with a well thought-out and complicated system of counterbalance, giving the head of the Republic powers that were restricted and moderate and would be so used after prudent reflection? Or were we to take the opposite path, adopting the simpler theory that things should be entrusted to a single power, homogeneous in all its parts and uncontrolled, which in action would be impetuous and irresistible? That was the core of the argument. Many other clauses could have been the context for discussing this general question, but the choice between one or two Chambers raised it most acutely.

It was a long struggle, lasting over two sessions, but the result was never in doubt; public opinion in almost all the departments as well as in Paris had come out strongly in favour of a single Chamber. Barrot was the first to speak in favour of two Chambers; he took up my thesis and worked it out very ably but intemperately, for his mind had lost its balance during the February Revolution and not recovered it again. I supported Barrot, returning several times to the attack. I was a bit surprised to find Dufaure coming out against us, and doing so rather energetically. Lawyers can hardly escape one of two habits: either they get accustomed to pleading causes in which they do not believe, or they get very good at persuading themselves to believe what they want to plead. Dufaure was of the latter sort. Neither the swing of public opinion nor his own passions and interests would ever have persuaded him to adopt a cause he thought bad; but such motives were enough to make him wish to find it good, and often that was enough. His naturally vacillating, ingenious, subtle mind would gradually swerve in that direction, and he sometimes ended by adopting the cause with enthusiasm as well as conviction. Time and again I have been astonished to see him energetically defending theses I had seen him adopt after much hesitation.

The main reason that he pressed for a single legislative body this time (and I think it was the best reason that could be found) was that, with us, executive power in the hands of a single man elected by the people would certainly become preponderant if nothing more than a legislative power weakened by division into two branches were placed beside that man.

I remember my answer, which was that this might happen, but that one thing up to now had proved certain: namely that two great powers naturally jealous of each other placed in an eternal tête-à-tête (that was the phrase I used) without the possibility of referring to the arbitration of a third power would at once be on bad terms if not at war with each other, and that that would go on until one had destroyed the other. I added that if it was possible that a president elected by the people and possessed of the immense prerogatives that in France belong to the head of the public administration, could sometimes curb a divided legislature, a president conscious of such an origin and rights would never settle down as a simple functionary subject to the capricious and tyrannical will of a single Assembly.

Both sides were right. The problem, put in that way, was insoluble, as I will have occasion to mention later; but that was the way the nation posed the problem.[8]

[8] *The following passage is marked for omission in the manuscript:* However one looks at it, a Republic is an impossibility if one leaves the president the powers that formerly belonged to the king and has him elected by the people. As I shall explain later, either the sphere of his powers must be infinitely restricted, or he must be elected by the Assembly; but the nation would not put up with either of these alternatives.

See also: Tocqueville, *Oeuvres Complètes* (ed. Beaumont) vol. I, p. 574 ff. *Rapport fait à l'Assemblée Législative au nom de la Commission chargée d'examiner les propositions relatives à la Revision de la Constitution.* (Ed.)

Dupin completed our discomfiture; he defended a single Chamber with astonishing energy. One would have thought he had never held another opinion. I expected as much. I knew that at heart he was selfish and cowardly, although subject to occasional fits of courage and integrity. For ten years I had watched him prowling round every party without joining any and pouncing on all the vanquished: half ape and half jackal, biting, grimacing and leaping around, he was always ready to fall on any luckless man who slipped. He behaved like himself on the Committee for the Constitution, or rather he surpassed himself. I did not notice any fits of integrity: he was uniformly commonplace from start to finish. Usually he kept quiet while the majority was making up its mind; but as soon as he saw them coming out for democratic opinions, he rushed to put himself at their head and went much farther than they. On one occasion he noticed halfway through that he was on the wrong road and the majority was not following in the expected direction: at once his ready, nimble wits told him to stop, and he turned and went back, still running, to the view from which he had been fleeing.

Almost all the parliamentarians were against two Chambers. Most of them sought more or less plausible pretexts for their votes. Some hoped to find the balance they saw was needed in a Council of State; others proposed that a single Assembly should be subject to formalities so slow-working that it would be protected against both its own enthusiasms and surprise. But in the end the true reason was given. On our committee we had a minister of the Gospel, M. Coquerel, who, seeing his colleagues of the Catholic clergy entering the Assembly, wanted to do so too. But in that he made a mistake: from having been a much-admired preacher, he suddenly became a very ludicrous political speaker. He could hardly open his mouth without uttering some pompous blunder. On this occasion he was naïve enough to admit that, although he still favoured two Chambers, he would nevertheless vote for one because public opinion was pushing him that way, and (to use his own phrase) he did not want to swim against the current. Such candour pained the others who were doing the same thing, but it rejoiced us greatly, that is, Barrot and me. But that was our sole gratification, for when it came to a vote, we numbered three.

This flat defeat discouraged me a little from the fight, but it knocked Barrot completely off his perch. He only returned at rare intervals, and then merely to express his impatience or disdain, rather than to give any advice.

We went on to discuss the executive branch. In spite of all I have said about the circumstances of the time and the composition of the Committee, it seems hard to believe that such an immense, difficult and novel subject did not provide material for one general debate, or even for any very searching discussion.

We were unanimously in favour of entrusting executive power to a single man. But how to elect that man; what prerogatives and what subordinates to give him; and what responsibilities to load on him? Obviously none of those questions could be dealt with in the abstract; each of them was of necessity linked to all the others and, especially, could be decided only with reference to the particular state of mores and customs in the country. Of course the problems were old, but the novelty of the circumstances made them new.

Cormenin, as was his way, opened the discussion by proposing a little clause already drafted, which provided that the head of the executive branch, or the president as he came to be called thenceforth, should be elected directly by the people by relative majority, with a fixed minimum of two million votes. I think that Marrast was alone in opposing this; he suggested that the head of the executive branch should be elected by the Assembly; good luck had gone to his head, and, strange though it seems now, he flattered himself that he would be the Assembly's choice. Nevertheless Cormenin's clause was passed without any trouble as far as I can remember. But I must confess that it was not self-evident that the people should appoint the president, and the clause authorizing direct election was as new as it was dangerous. In a country without monarchical traditions, in which the executive branch has always been weak and continues to be thoroughly restricted, nothing could be wiser than to entrust the choice of its representative to the nation. A president lacking the strength derived from such an origin would be the plaything of the Assemblies, but our situation was quite different. We were emerging from a monarchy, and even the Republicans' habits were monarchical. In any case, centralization made our position unique, for it meant that the whole administration of the country, from the greatest to the most trivial matters, would be in the president's hands; all the thousands of officials controlling the whole land could depend from no one but him; that was the position according to the laws in force and also according to prevailing opinion, both of which were left intact by the February Revolution; we had lost our taste for monarchy but had preserved the spirit of it. In such conditions who could be the president elected by the people, unless he were a pretender to the throne? The institution could serve the turn only of somebody wishing to transform presidential into royal power. I thought it clear then, and today it is obvious, that if one wanted to have the president elected by the people, without danger to the Republic, the sphere of his prerogatives must be strictly curtailed; and even then I am not sure that this would have been enough, for the sphere of the executive thus restricted by law would still have kept a wider dominion in the memories and habits of the people. If, on the other hand, the president was to be left with his powers, he should not be elected by the people.[9] Cormenin's clause was adopted at first, but afterwards very lively attacks were made on it; the attacks were, however, made for different reasons than those I have just explained. It was the aftermath of the 4th June. Prince Louis Napoleon, who had been in nobody's thoughts a few days before, had just been elected to the Assembly by Paris and three departments. It began to be feared that he would soon be placed at the head of the Republic if the choice of president were left to the people. The various pretenders and their friends got excited; the question was again put to the Committee, and the majority voted as before.

As I remember, the whole time the Committee was occupied

---

[9] *The following words are marked for omission in the manuscript:* These truths were not expounded; I believe that the members of the Committee caught hardly a glimpse of them.

with this matter, I was searching my mind to discover on which side the balance of power should habitually tend in a republic of the sort I saw was being created; sometimes I thought it must fall on the side of the single Assembly, sometimes on that of the elected president: this uncertainty was a great trouble to me. The truth was that this was something impossible to tell beforehand; the victory of one or the other of these great rivals would depend on the circumstances and dispositions of the moment. Nothing was certain except that they would wage war and thereby ruin the Republic.[10]

Not one of the ideas I have been expounding here was seriously considered by the Committee; one could even say that none of them was discussed. One day Barrot did touch on them in passing, but without stopping. His intelligence (which was slumbering but not weak, enabled him to see very far ahead when his attention was concentrated) caught a glimpse of them for a moment between sleep and waking, but he thought no more about it.

I myself pointed them out only with a certain hesitation and reserve. My rebuff over the two Chambers left me little heart for the fight. Besides, I was, I confess, much more concerned with putting a powerful leader quickly at the head of the Republic than with drafting a perfect republican constitution. At that time we were under the divided, vacillating rule of the Executive Committee, socialism was at our doors, and we were drawing near to the days of June, all of which should not be forgotten. Later on, after those days, I energetically supported in the Assembly election of the president by the people and to some extent helped to get this accepted. The main reason that I gave was that, having announced to the nation that this ardently desired right would be granted, it was no longer possible to refuse it: that much was true. Yet I regret having spoken on that occasion.

To return to the Committee: being unable or unwilling to oppose the adoption of the principle, I tried to reduce the danger in practice at least. I first proposed to restrict the sphere of executive action in several respects, but I saw clearly that

10 *Variant:* And cause yet more revolutions.

nothing serious could be attempted in that direction; I then fell back on the actual method of election and had the discussion on the part of Cormenin's clause that dealt with that reopened. Under that draft clause, as I have mentioned before, the president would be appointed directly by a *relative* majority, two million votes being fixed as the minimum for that majority. There were several very serious disadvantages in this.

If the president was directly elected by the people, their enthusiasm and infatuation were much to be feared; moreover the prestige and moral power of the man elected would be all the greater. If a relative majority were to be enough to make the election valid, it might happen that the president represented the ideas of only a minority of the nation. I suggested that the president should not be directly elected by the citizens, but that that duty be entrusted to delegates elected by the people.

In the second place, I suggested substituting an absolute for a relative majority: if there were no absolute majority on the first count, the Assembly should become responsible for the choice. These ideas, I think, were good, but they were not new. I had taken them from the Constitution of the United States. I don't think anybody would have noticed that, had I not mentioned it, so little prepared was that committee for the great part it had to play.

As I expected, the first part of my amendment was rejected; our great men decided that this system was not simple enough and had a slight taint of aristocracy about it; the second was allowed: it is part of the actual Constitution.

Beaumont proposed that the president should not be eligible for re-election. I supported him very energetically, and the proposal was passed. On this occasion we both made a big mistake which, I am much afraid, had untoward consequences; we had always been conscious of what a danger a re-eligible president could be to freedom and public morality, for it was inevitable that he would, before the end of his term, employ all the vast means of constraint and corruption that our laws and mores grant the head of the executive branch, to obtain his re-election. Our minds were not supple and quick enough to turn around and see that as soon as it was decided that the citizens themselves should choose the president, the ill was without remedy, and that any rash attempt to hinder the people in their choice would only increase it.

The vote on this matter, and the great influence I had on the result, is my most vexatious memory from that time. We were constantly running foul of centralization, and, instead of removing the obstacle, we ourselves stumbled. It was of the essence of the Republic that the head of the executive branch should be responsible, but responsible in what way and to whom? Could he be responsible for the thousands of administrative details with which our legal administration is overloaded, matters that were impossible for him to supervise personally and dangerous for him to attempt to? That would have been both unfair and ridiculous. But if he was not responsible for the administration properly so called, who should be? It was decided that the president's responsibility should be shared with the ministers, and that their counter-signature should be necessary, as under the Monarchy. Thus the president was responsible, but he was not entirely free in his actions, and he could not protect his subordinates.

We passed on to discussion of the constitution of the Council of State. Cormenin and Vivien took charge of this and were, so to speak, like people working to build their own houses. They did their best to make the Council of State a third force, but without success. It became indeed something more than an administrative council, but infinitely less than a legislative assembly.

The only part of our work that was handled with superior intelligence and, as I think, wisely contrived was the part dealing with justice. On that ground the Committee found its feet again, for most of the members had been or were still lawyers. Thanks to them we were able to preserve the principle of the judges' freedom from dismissal; as in 1830 this held firm against the current that carried everything else along. But the principle was attacked by the Republicans of yesterday, in my view very stupidly, for it does more to protect the citizens' freedom than to strengthen the rulers' power. The Court of Appeal and, most important, the court to judge political crimes were constituted at once just as they are today (1851). Beaumont drafted most of the clauses concerning these two great Courts. What we did there is a great improvement on all the attempts at the same task during the last sixty years. Probably it is the only part of the Constitution of 1848 that will survive.[11]

A motion of Vivien's was accepted making it impossible to amend the Constitution except by another Constituent Assembly, which was fair; but it was added that this amendment could take place only if an express vote of the National Assembly demanded it three times consecutively by a four-fifths majority, which made any regular amendment practically impossible. I abstained from voting on this. I have long thought that, instead of trying to make our forms of government eternal, we should pay attention to making methodical change an easy matter. All things considered, I find that less dangerous than the opposite alternative. I thought one should treat the French people like those lunatics whom one is careful not to bind lest they become infuriated by the constraint.

I have noted down several curious opinions that were expressed. Martin, not content to be a "Republican of yesterday," once ludicrously proclaimed from the rostrum that he was a "Republican by birth." And yet this same Martin proposed to give the president the right to dissolve the Assembly, without seeing that such a right would make it easy for the president to take over the Republic. Marrast wanted to have a committee of the Council of State given the duty of working out "new ideas," and it was to be called the "Committee of Progress." Barrot proposed that the jury should decide all civil suits, as if such a revolutionary change in the judicial system could be hastily improvised. Finally, Dufaure proposed to forbid replacements and oblige everybody to do their military service in person, a measure that would have ruined all liberal education, unless, of course, the period of service had been drastically reduced, which would have ruined the organization of the army.

Thus it was that, pressed for time and ill prepared to deal

[11] See *Les Constitutions et les principales Lois politiques de la France depuis 1789* par Duguit et Monnier, Paris, 1932. (Ed.)

with such great matters, we drew near to the appointed end
of our task. One kept saying, let us provisionally accept the draft
of these clauses; we will come back to it later, and this sketch
will help us polish the final version and adjust the different
parts to one another. But we did not come back, and the sketch
was the picture.

We appointed Marrast recording secretary. And his way of
performing this important task clearly exposed the idle, blundering impudence characteristic of him. First he spent several days
doing nothing, although the Assembly was constantly asking to
see the result of our deliberations, and the whole of France
was waiting in suspense. Then he polished off the task in one
night, the night before he had to show it to the Assembly. In
the morning he showed it to one or two colleagues whom he
chanced to meet; then he boldly got into the rostrum and read
in the Committee's name a report of which hardly any of the
members had seen the first word. That was on the 19th June.
There were 139 clauses in the draft Constitution, and it had
been prepared in less than a month. One could not have
gone faster, but one could have done better. We had adopted
many of the little clauses Cormenin brought in in batches, but
we had rejected even more of them, and that had caused their
author an irritation all the more bitter because he could not
give it expression. He wanted consolation from the public. He
published, or he had published (I am not sure which) in all
the newspapers an article giving an account of what happened
inside the Committee, attributing everything good to Cormenin
and everything bad to his adversaries. Of course we took strong
exception to such a publication, and it was decided that we
should let Cormenin know our feelings about his behaviour.
But nobody wanted to be our spokesman. Among our number
was a workman (for workmen were put on everything then)
called Corbon who had quite a straightforward mind and firm
character. He was willing to undertake the task. So the next
day, just as the Committee's meeting was to open, Corbon rose
to speak and with laconic and slightly brutal directness told
Cormenin what we felt. The latter became disconcerted and
cast his eyes round the table looking for someone to come to

his aid. Nobody moved. He then said hesitatingly, "Am I to conclude from what has just passed, that the Committee wishes me to leave it?" We did not say a word. He took his hat and went out. Never was so great an insult swallowed so smoothly without a wry face. I think that, although he was prodigiously vain, he was not very sensitive about secret insults, and, provided his self-esteem were tickled in public, he would not have made too much fuss about a few strokes of the cane in private.

Many have believed that Cormenin, who was a viscount suddenly turned Radical but remaining a devout Catholic, never stopped play-acting and betraying his true views; I would not dare to assert that this was so, although I have noticed a strange lack of connection between what he said in talking and what he wrote, and, to tell the truth, I have always thought him more sincere in his horror of revolutions than in the ideas he picked up from them. But it was the gaps in his understanding that always struck me most. Never has a writer engaged in public work kept the habits and disadvantages of that trade more completely. When he had established a certain relation between the different provisions of a law and made an ingenious and striking draft, he thought he had done the whole job: form, links and symmetry absorbed him. But what he sought above all was the new. Institutions tried out elsewhere or at other times seemed as loathsome to him as clichés, and in his eyes the first merit of a law was in no way to resemble what had gone before it. It is known that the law regulating the appointment of the Constituent Assembly was his work. At the time of the general election I met him, and he said rather complacently, "Has the world ever before seen anything like what is happening today? What country has gone so far as to give votes to servants, the poor and soldiers? Admit that no one had even imagined that until now." And he added, rubbing his hands: "It will be very curious to see what all this produces." He talked about it as if it were a chemistry experiment.

PART THREE

---◆---

MY TERM OF OFFICE

3 June to 29 October 1849

This part was begun at Versailles on 16 September 1851 during the prorogation of the National Assembly.

To come at once to this part of my recollections I skip over the period between the uprising in June 1848 and 3 June 1849.[1]

I will come back to that later, if I have time. I thought it more important to record my five months in the government while my memories are still fresh.

[1] For this intervening period see Tocqueville's note printed in Appendix IV, pp. 276–81. (Ed.)

CHAPTER ONE

My return to France – Formation of the cabinet

While I was thus watching on the private stage of Germany one of the acts of the great drama of the European revolution, unexpected and alarming news called my attention back to France and our own affairs.[2] I learned of the almost unbelievable check to our army before the walls of Rome, the abusive debates arising therefrom in the Constituent Assembly, the agitation in the country due to these two causes, and finally the general election results, which, against the expectations of both parties, brought a hundred and fifty Montagnards into the new Assembly. However, the demagogic breeze that suddenly blew up over part of France had not prevailed in the department of La Manche. On the contrary, all those former members for the department who had broken away from the Conservative Party had been voted out. Of the thirteen representatives in question, only four had survived. I had received more votes than any of the others, although I had been away and silent, and though I had openly voted for Cavaignac the previous December. Nevertheless everybody supported me, less on account of my political opinions than because of the great personal consideration I enjoyed outside of politics. That was certainly an honourable position, but one hard to maintain in the midst of parties, and one that would become very precarious if ever the parties turned to violence and consequently became exclusive.

[2] Concerning Tocqueville's relation to Germany and German problems, see W. Ohaus, *Volk und Völker im Urteil von Alexis de Tocqueville*, Berlin, 1938, p. 60 ff. (Ed.)

I started off as soon as I got this news. At Bonn a sudden indisposition compelled Madame de Tocqueville to stay behind; she pressed me to leave her and go on with my journey, which I did, but reluctantly. For I left her alone in a country still torn by civil war, and beyond that, in moments of difficulty and danger, I find support in her courage and great good sense.

I arrived in Paris, if I remember correctly, on 25 May 1849, four days before the opening of the Legislative and during the last convulsions of the Constituent Assembly. A few weeks had been enough to make the political scene completely unrecognizable, less because of changes in external conditions than because of the prodigious revolution that had taken place in men's minds within a few days.

The party that held power before I left still held it, and the actual results of the elections should, it would seem, confirm its position. This party, composed of such a variety of smaller parties all wanting to halt the revolution or drive it back, had won an enormous majority in the electoral colleges; it would make up more than two thirds of the new Assembly. Nevertheless, I found it a prey to such profound terror that one can compare it only to its feelings after February, for it is a true saying that in politics one must use the same type of reasoning as in war and never forget that the effect of events depends less on themselves than on the impression they give.

The Conservatives, who for six months had seen all the by-elections going in their favour, and who filled and dominated almost all the local councils, had come to put unlimited confidence in the system of universal franchise, which had formerly filled them with unlimited mistrust. So, in the election that had just taken place, they had expected not only to defeat, but to annihilate their adversaries, and they were as downcast at falling short of the triumph of which they had dreamed as they would have been if they had really been defeated. On the other side, the Montagnards, who had thought themselves lost, were as drunk with joy and mad audacity as if the elections had assured them of a majority in the new Chamber. Why was it that the event deceived both parties in their hopes and fears? It is difficult to say with certainty, for great masses of men move for reasons almost as unknown to mortal men as the reasons that regulate the movements of the sea. In both cases the reasons are in a sense hidden and lost in the sheer immensity of the phenomenon.

We are, however, entitled to think that the Conservatives owed their rebuff chiefly to the mistakes they made themselves. Their intolerance, when they thought themselves sure to triumph, towards those who, without sharing all their ideas, had helped them to triumph over the Montagnards; the high-handed administration of the new Minister of the Interior, M. Faucher; and, most of all, the ill success of the Roman expedition prejudiced a part of the population, naturally inclined to vote for them, against them, and suddenly threw it into the arms of agitators.

So, as I was saying, one hundred and fifty Montagnards had just been elected. Some of the peasants and most of the soldiers had voted for them; it was the two main anchors of mercy that threatened to snap in the storm. The terror was universal: it retaught the various monarchical parties the virtues of tolerance and modesty, virtues they had cultivated after February, but that had been widely forgotten during the last six months. On all sides it was recognized that there was no longer a question of changing from a republic for the present and that all that remained to be done was to get the moderate Republicans to oppose the Mountain.

People now accused those same ministers they had once supported and incited, loudly shouting for changes in the Cabinet. The Cabinet itself recognized its insufficiency and asked to be replaced. At the time of my departure I had seen the Committee of the rue de Poitiers[3] refuse to put M. Dufaure's name

---

[3] The so-called *réunion de la rue de Poitiers* was composed of all those deputies who belonged to the "party of order." It was formed soon after the session of the Constituent Assembly had opened, but exercised little influence on the voting of these same deputies. The Committee that Tocqueville mentions here is of much greater significance. It was formed from members of the reunion to exercise a unifying and conciliating influence on conservatism in general. Committee members, although all conservative, were of very diverse political origin, from avowed Bonapartists and personal friends of the pretender, right through the political spectrum to

on its lists; I now found all eyes turned towards M. Dufaure
and his friends, as people adjured him most pathetically to
save society by taking power.

The very evening I got back I learned that some of my
friends were having dinner together at a little restaurant in the
Champs Elysées. I hastened to join them and found Dufaure,
Lanjuinais, Beaumont, Corcelle, Vivien, Lamoricière, Bedeau
and one or two more whose names are not so well known. In
a few words they put me in the picture. Barrot, entrusted by
the President with forming a cabinet, had for the last few
days worn himself out in vain efforts to do so. M. Thiers, M. Molé
and the more important of their friends had refused to join
the government. However, they fully intended, as we shall see,
to remain masters but not to become ministers. The uncertainty
of the future, the universal instability, the difficulties and perhaps the dangers of the moment kept them aloof. They were
eager for power all right, but not for responsibility. Barrot,
rebuffed there, had come to us.[4] But which of us to take? Which
ministries to give us? What colleagues should we have? What
common policy should we adopt? Practical difficulties had arisen
which up to then had seemed insurmountable. Several times
already Barrot had gone back to the natural leaders of the
majority and, rebuffed by them, returned to us.

Time was running out in this sterile labour; the dangers and
difficulties were growing greater; daily the news from Italy
became more alarming, and from one moment to the next the

Catholics and Legitimists. The Committee included men like Molé, Thiers,
Broglie, Berryer, Duvergier de Hauranne, Montalembert, Morny and
Persigny. Its efforts were always directed towards the unifying and therefore
strengthening of conservatism throughout the country. This was to be
achieved by conciliation and the patching up of old quarrels in the face
of the common danger—socialism. Thus, for example, at the moment of
the elections to the Legislative Assembly, compromising candidatures,
like that of Guizot, were carefully avoided, as being too likely to cause
offence to those electors who, although conservative, were by no means
of Orleanist persuasions. For further details on the action of the Committee,
see P. de la Gorce, *Histoire de la Seconde République Française*, Paris,
1925, vol. II, pp. 133–35. (Ed.)
[4] *The following words are marked for omission in the manuscript:* He
asked, or rather implored us to become his colleagues.

government might be impeached by the dying but infuriated Assembly.

I went home very preoccupied, of course, by what I had just heard. I was convinced that it depended on myself and my friends whether or not we became ministers. We were the obviously necessary men. I knew the leaders of the majority well enough to feel sure that they would never compromise themselves by taking responsibility for affairs under a government that seemed to them so ephemeral, for even if they had the disinterestedness, they lacked the necessary courage: their pride and their timidity made me sure of their abstention. So we had only to hold our ground, and one would have to come and fetch us. But ought I to want to be a minister? I asked myself that question very seriously. I think I can fairly say that I had not the slightest illusions about the real difficulties of the undertaking, and I saw the future with a clarity one rarely attains except in looking at the past.

Fighting in the streets was generally expected. I, too, thought it imminent; the wild audacity the elections had given to the party of the Mountain and the opportunity provided by the Rome affair seemed to me to make such an event inevitable. However I had little fear of the result. I was convinced that, although a majority of the soldiers had voted for the Mountain, the army would without hesitation fight against it. The soldier voting individually for a candidate by secret ballot and the soldier who acts as part of a body under pressure of military discipline are in practice two men. The thoughts of the one do not control the actions of the other. The Paris garrison was very numerous, well commanded, had great experience in street fighting, and the passions felt and the deeds done in the days of June were still fresh in its memory. So I felt certain of victory. But I was greatly troubled at the thought of the aftermath of victory; the apparent end of our troubles seemed to me their beginning. I judged that these difficulties were pretty well insoluble, and I think that in fact this was so.

Whichever way I looked, I could see nothing either solid or durable amid the general malaise affecting the nation; everybody wanted to get rid of the Constitution, some through socialism, others by monarchy.

Public opinion was summoning us, but it would have been very rash to count on that; it was fear that pushed the country in our direction. Memories, interests, instincts and passions could hardly fail to draw it back again quickly, as soon as the fear was gone. Our aim was, if possible, to establish the Republic, or at least to keep it going for a time, by governing in a methodical, moderate, conservative and completely constitutional manner. And that could not make us popular for long, for everybody wanted to be free of the Constitution. The Mountain Party wanted more than it, and the Monarchists wanted a great deal less.

In the Assembly it was much worse still. The interests and vanities of the party leaders intensified the effect of these same general causes in thousands of different ways. Those leaders might well consent to let us take over the government, but as for letting us govern, that could not be expected. Once the crisis was over, we could expect every sort of ambush from them.

As for the President, I did not yet know him, but it was clear that the only support we could count on to keep us in his confidence was the jealousy and hatred he felt towards our common adversaries. His sympathies were bound always to be elsewhere, for our points of view were not only different but naturally contrary. We wanted to make the Republic live; he wished to inherit from it. We offered him no more than ministers when he needed accomplices.

These difficulties were inherent in the situation and consequently permanent; but there were other ephemeral ones that were no easier to surmount: the revolutionary agitation reviving in part of the country; the spirit and habit of exclusive and high-handed behaviour which had spread and become rooted in the public administration; the Roman expedition which had been so ill conceived and badly conducted that it had become as hard to push it to a conclusion as to withdraw; and finally the inheritance of all the mistakes made by our predecessors.

Here were many reasons for hesitation, and yet basically I did not hesitate at all.

The idea of accepting a post when fear kept so many from doing so, and being able to rescue society from the wretched situation into which it had fallen, touched both my integrity and my pride. I was quite aware that I would only pass through the government and not remain in it; but I hoped to stay long enough to render some signal service to my country and to develop my own powers. That was attraction enough for me.

Accordingly, I made three resolutions on the spot:

The first was not to refuse office if a good opportunity offered.

The second, not to join the government unless my principal friends controlled the main offices, so that we would always remain masters of the Cabinet.

And third, to behave each day when a minister as if I would cease to be one on the morrow: that is to say, never to subordinate the need to be myself to that of being a minister.

The next five or six days were spent in unsuccessful efforts to form a government. There were so many tries, and they overlapped each other and were so filled with little incidents—great events of one day forgotten the next—that I find it hard to retrace them in memory, even though I was myself the main character in some of these incidents. The problem really was difficult to solve in the given conditions. The President wished to give the impression of changing his Cabinet, but he wanted to retain the men he considered his main friends. The leaders of the monarchical parties refused to take responsibility for the government themselves, but they were unwilling to have it entrusted to anybody over whom they had no hold. If we were to be allowed in, it would have to be in very small numbers and in offices of secondary importance. We were regarded as a medicine, necessary but unpleasant to take, and one that should be administered only in very small doses.

First Dufaure alone was asked to join and to make do with the Ministry of Public Works. He refused and asked for the Interior and two other offices for his friends. The Interior was very reluctantly offered, but the rest refused. I have reason to

think that he was on the point of accepting this proposal and
again leaving me in the lurch as he had done six months before;
this was not because he was deceitful or indifferent to his
friends, but the sight of that great office almost within his
grasp, and in such a way that he could honourably accept it,
had a strange fascination for him; that fascination did not exactly
lead him to betray his friends, but it distracted him and made
him ready to forget them. This time, however, he did stand
firm; and, not being able to get him by himself, they offered
to take me with him. I was particularly indicated because the
new Legislative Assembly had just appointed me one of its
vice-presidents.[5] But where should I be put? I thought myself
qualified only for the Ministry of Public Instruction. Unfortunately M. de Falloux held that office, and he was an indispensable man; it was important for the Legitimists to have him there
because he was one of their leaders, the religious party considered him a protector, and the President had come to regard
him as a friend. I was offered Agriculture and refused. Finally,
in despair, Barrot offered me the Ministry of Foreign Affairs. I
had been making great efforts to persuade M. de Rémusat to
accept that office, and what passed between him and me on that
occasion is so characteristic that I must record it. I attached great
weight to M. de Rémusat being with us in the Cabinet. He was
both a friend of M. Thiers and a man of honour, a rare combination; he alone could guarantee us, if not the support, at least the
neutrality of that statesman without infecting us with his spirit.
One evening Rémusat, overcome by the insistence of Barrot and
the rest of us, yielded. He made us a promise, but the next
morning he came to retract his word. I knew for certain that
he had seen M. Thiers in the interval, and he told me himself
that M. Thiers, who was loudly proclaiming the need for our
taking a share in public life, had dissuaded him from going in
with us.

"I saw clearly," he said, "that by joining you I should not
guarantee his support for you, but only take the risk of myself
being at war with him soon!"

[5] *Note by Tocqueville:* The 1st June: 336 votes out of 597.

So that was the sort of men we had to deal with![6]

I had never thought of the Ministry of Foreign Affairs, and my first impulse was to reject the offer. I felt myself ill suited to perform a task for which nothing had prepared me. Among my papers I have found a record of these hesitations in a sort of written conversation that took place at that time at a dinner with some of my friends.[7]

I decided at last to accept the Ministry of Foreign Affairs, but

[6] Rémusat's account (see his memoirs, vol. IV, pp. 408–12) differs from that of Tocqueville in that he attributes his conduct, not to vacillation, but to an extreme reluctance to serve under Louis Napoleon Bonaparte. However, his political friends, Thiers among them, urged him to take office; Rémusat allowed himself to be persuaded and accepted the portfolio of Foreign Affairs. The Cabinet was almost completed when Barrot, Rémusat and Thiers met the President to finalize the arrangement and to discuss the choice of persons for the various ministries. In this Cabinet, Dufaure was to be Minister of the Interior, but the President objected strongly to this choice. After urging in vain the necessity for Dufaure's inclusion in the Cabinet, the three men left, saying that the dropping of Dufaure rendered the whole arrangement null and void. As they left, Rémusat told Barrot that he now considered himself free from all engagements made and that in attempting to form another cabinet, Barrot should not consider him. On the following day, the President changed his mind and Dufaure was accepted, but Rémusat still maintained his position, refusing to become a member of the Cabinet. (Ed.)

[7] *Several lines have been left blank in the manuscript. Here is the text of that written conversation, found by M. André Jardin among the papers at Tocqueville:*

May 1849.

Written conversation between me and Rivet at table with our friends the day before accepting the Ministry.

We must shut the door of the Cabinet against Thiers and Molé or else we shall be betrayed. As things stand, Falloux will open it for them and betray you.

—What do you say to the combination in general and to my participation in particular?

—I think the combination is risky, and I feel great hesitation as far as you are concerned. Falloux and Changarnier together—that is too much! The Ministry of Foreign Affairs will be the target of the whole opposition, and you cannot play Bastide's part there.

—What do you think of a possible arrangement that could put Passy at Foreign Affairs and me in Falloux' place?

—I don't like to say anything, for you would be worth more than Passy at Foreign Affairs. But he is already conversant with the present state of those matters, whereas they would be new to you.

M. Jardin notes that the questions are in Tocqueville's handwriting and the answers in that of Rivet. (Ed.)

I made it a condition that Lanjuinais should enter the Council at the same time as myself. I had several very strong reasons for this. In the first place I thought it indispensable for us to have three ministers in the Cabinet in order to gain the preponderance necessary to do any good. I also thought that Lanjuinais would be very useful to me in keeping Dufaure to the line I wanted to follow, for I felt that I had not enough hold on Dufaure. Above all I wanted to have a friend close to me to whom I could open my heart about everything; that is a precious advantage at all times, and it is exceptionally valuable in times of suspicion and inconstancy such as ours, and when the task ahead was as dangerous as mine.

From all these different points of view Lanjuinais was wonderfully suited to me, although our natural dispositions were very different; his temper was as calm and peaceful as mine was restless and troubled. Methodical, slow, lazy and prudent, even meticulous, he was reluctant to begin any undertaking, but, once in, he never drew back but proved as resolute and stubborn as a Breton peasant to the very end. He was very reserved about expressing an opinion, but when he did so that opinion was very explicit and even rude in its frankness. One could not expect from his friendship enthusiasm, warmth or abandon; but one had no occasion to fear inadequacy, treachery or mental reservations. All in all, he was a very reliable colleague, and the most honest man I ever met in public life. Of us all he seemed best able to keep his love for the public good clear of personal considerations and interests.

No one had any objection to Lanjuinais, but the difficulty was to find an office for him. I requested that he have that of Agriculture and Trade, which since the 30th December had been held by Buffet, a friend of Falloux and indeed his fawning servant in the Cabinet; Falloux refused to let his colleague go. I was stubborn. For twenty-four hours the new Cabinet, which had almost taken shape, seemed dissolved. To break down my resolve, Falloux tried a direct approach; he came to my house, where I was ill in bed, and pressed and implored me to give up Lanjuinais and leave his friend Buffet at the Ministry of Agriculture. I had made my decision and closed my ears.

Falloux, annoyed but with perfect self-control, at last rose to go. I thought all was lost, but in fact all was won.

"You wish it," he said with that gracious aristocratic manner he used so naturally to cover all his feelings, even the bitterest ones. "You wish it. I must yield. It shall not be said that at a time of such critical difficulty any private consideration made me break up such a badly needed combination—I shall stay alone among you. However, I hope you will not forget that I shall be, not only your colleague, but your prisoner."

An hour later the Cabinet was formed; and Dufaure, telling me of this, instructed me to take immediate possession of the Ministry of Foreign Affairs. It was 2 June 1849.

Such was the birth of this government, formed so slowly and painfully and fated to last so short a time. During the prolonged birth pangs no man in France can have been more worried than Barrot. His sincere concern for the public good led him to desire a change of Cabinet; but his ambition was intimately and closely intertwined with his integrity to an almost unbelievable extent, and his amibition made him ardently wish to remain at the head of the new Cabinet. So he went back and forth from one group to another, beseeching or scolding each individual with much pathos, and often with much eloquence too. Sometimes it was the leaders of the majority whom he addressed, sometimes ourselves. And sometimes he even visited those Republicans of yesterday whom he considered more moderate than the others. He was, for that matter, equally inclined to carry the one or the other along with him, for, in politics, he was always as incapable of friendship as of hatred. His heart is an evaporating jar in which nothing remains. Seeing him running hither and thither like that, trying to collect a cabinet, I could not help thinking of a hen cackling and flapping after her brood, but not much concerned to know whether they were chickens or ducklings.

Composition of the Cabinet – Its conduct down to the attempted insurrection of the 13th June

The Cabinet was composed as follows:

Minister of Justice and
  President of the Council .... Barrot
Finance .... Passy
War .... Rulhière
Navy .... Tracy
Public Works .... Lacrosse
Public Instruction .... Falloux
Interior .... Dufaure
Agriculture .... Lanjuinais
Foreign Affairs .... myself

Dufaure, Lanjuinais and I were the only new ministers, all the rest having been in the previous Cabinet.

Passy's merits were real, but they were not attractive. His mind was rigid, clumsy, provocative and disparaging, with more ingenuity than justice in it; but he was more disposed to be just when action really was required than when he was talking, for he was fond of a paradox, but not so fond of acting on one. I never knew a greater talker, or a man who so easily consoled himself for annoying events by explaining the causes that had produced them and the consequences likely to follow[1]; when

[1] *Marginal note written in pencil—Variant:* Nor one who consoled himself so well for the reverses of the statesman by the achievements of the philosopher.

he had finished painting the gloomiest picture of the state of affairs, he would smile placidly and say, "So there is practically no way of saving us, and we must just wait for the total subversion of society." In other respects he was a knowledgeable and experienced Minister, with courage and integrity proof against any test and as incapable of vacillation as of treachery. His views and feelings, his long standing intimacy with Dufaure, and, above all, his lively animosity to Thiers made us sure of him.

Rulhière would have belonged to the Monarchist and ultra-Conservative party, if he had belonged to any party at all, and especially if Changarnier had not been in this world; but he was a soldier, and his one thought was to remain Minister of War. At first glance we noticed his extreme jealousy of the commander of the army in Paris, whose relations with the leaders of the majority and whose influence over the President obliged Rulhière to come over to our side and left him very dependent on us.

Tracy's naturally weak character was, as it were, confined within and supported by the very systematic and absolute theories he had derived from the ideological education his father had given him. But in the end, contact with daily life and the shock of revolutions had worn this crust away, leaving behind nothing but a wavering mind and a weak but always honest and well-meaning heart.

Lacrosse was a poor devil whose fortune and mores were in equal disarray. The turns of revolution had driven him from deep obscurity in the dynastic opposition to the direction of affairs, and he was not sorry to be a minister. He was glad to lean on us, but he also sought to ingratiate himself with the President of the Republic by all manner of trivial services and platitudinous compliments. It would, of course, have been difficult for him to push himself in any other way, for he was a rare nonentity who understood exactly nothing about anything. People blamed us for taking office with such incapable colleagues as Tracy and Lacrosse, and they were right; it was a main cause of our collapse. The reason was not simply that they were bad at their jobs, but that their notorious inadequacy left the question of successors for them open the whole time and so generated a sort of permanent Cabinet crisis.

As for Barrot, with his basic feelings and ideas, it was natural for him to stick close to us. All his old liberal ways, republican tastes and memories of opposition days in Parliament linked him to us. With other associates he might, however regretfully, have become our adversary, but once we had him among us, we were sure of him.

Of the whole ministry only Falloux was a stranger to us by reason of his point of departure, connections and inclinations. He alone represented the leaders of the majority, or rather was thought to do so, for actually in the Cabinet and everywhere else he represented only the Church, as I shall explain later. This isolated position combined with the secret aims of his policy induced him to seek support beyond us, in the Assembly and with the President; but he did this, like everything else, discreetly and shrewdly.[2]

There was one great weakness in a Cabinet so composed: it had to depend on a coalition majority, but was not itself a coalition ministry. But it did have the great strength of having ministers of like origin and instincts, linked by old ties of friendship, mutual confidence and common aim.

I shall, of course, be asked what that aim was and what we actually wanted. In a time of such shifts and troubles for the consciences of men, it would be rash for me to answer for my colleagues, but I do so gladly for myself. I did not then think, any more than I think now, that a Republican form of government was the one best suited to the needs of France, meaning by "Republican government" an elected executive branch. Where the habits, traditions and mores of a people have assured such a vast sphere of power for the executive, its instability will always, whenever troubled days come, lead to revolution, and even in peaceful times such instability will be uncomfortable. In any case for me a republic is an ill-balanced form of govern-

[2] *Marginal note* (*Tocqueville*): Perhaps all this should come in when I describe Falloux and his quarrels with Dufaure.

ment, promising more freedom and giving less than a constitutional monarchy. Nonetheless I sincerely desired to maintain the Republic; and, although there were, so to speak, no Republicans in France, I did not think maintaining it was an absolutely impracticable proposition.

I wished to maintain it because I saw nothing either ready or fit to put in its place. Most people in the country had a deep antipathy towards the old dynasty. All other political passions languished in the weariness brought on by revolutions with all their empty promises, but one alone did remain active: hatred of the old régime and distrust of the former privileged classes, who, in the people's eyes, stood for it. This feeling filtered through revolution unaltered and undissolved, like those miraculous springs that, so the ancients believed, passed through the salt sea without mixing or vanishing. As for the Orleans dynasty, recent experience did not encourage the desire for a quick return to it. Without question that dynasty would again have provoked the hostility of all the upper classes and the clergy, would again have driven a gap between itself and the people, leaving the care of and advantages from government exclusively to those same middle classes who had for eighteen years been showing me how inadequate they were to rule France well. Besides, of course, nothing was ready for their triumph.

Only Louis Napoleon was ready to take the Republic's place, because he already held power. But what could spring from his success except a bastard monarchy, despised by all the enlightened classes, hostile to liberty, and controlled by intriguers, adventurers and lackeys? None of that was worth a new revolution.

Undoubtedly the Republic was hard to maintain, for most of those who cared for it were incapable or unworthy of leading it, while those who could have established and led it, hated it. But it was also fairly difficult to destroy. The hatred felt towards it was of a soft variety, like all the passions then felt in the country. Besides, people criticized this government without love for any other. Three parties disputed the succession, and they were irreconcilable, being more hostile each to the other than any were towards the Republic. There was no such thing as a majority.

So I thought that the rule of the Republic, supported by the fact of power and opposed by nothing but minorities that would find it hard to unite, might be able to keep going amid the inertia of the masses, if it was conducted with moderation and wisdom. So I was determined to lend no hand to attempts against the Republic, but rather to defend it. Almost all the other members of the Cabinet thought the same. Dufaure had more faith than I in the excellence of republican institutions and in their future. Barrot was less disposed than I always to respect them. But we all wished at that moment to maintain them firmly. This common resolution was our bond and our flag.

As soon as the Ministry was formed, it went to the President of the Republic to hold a Council. This was the first time I had seen that man close, for in the Constituent Assembly I had seen him only from a distance. He received us politely. We could not expect more than that, for Dufaure had opposed him vigorously and spoken almost insultingly about his candidature only six months before, and I, as well as Lanjuinais, had openly voted for his competitor.

Louis Napoleon will play such a large part in the rest of this story that I think he deserves a separate portrait, while sketches are enough for the rest of my contemporaries. I think that of all his Ministers, and perhaps of all the men who refused to take part in his conspiracy against the Republic, I was the one most in his good graces, who saw him closest and could judge him best.

He was a great deal better than the impression of him one might fairly have formed from his earlier career and mad enterprises. That was my first impression as I got to know him. In this he disappointed his adversaries, but perhaps he disappointed his friends even more, if one can give that name to the politicians who supported his candidature. For most of them had chosen him, not for his worth, but for his presumed mediocrity. They thought he would be a tool for them to use at will and break any time they wanted. In this they were mightily deceived.

As a private individual, Louis Napoleon had some attractive qualities: a kindly, easy-going temperament; a humane character; a soul that was gentle and even rather tender, but without delicacy; great confidence in his relations with people; a perfect simplicity; an element of personal modesty mixed with immense pride in his ancestry; and a better memory for kindnesses than for resentment. He could feel affection, and he aroused it in those who came near him. He spoke little and poorly; he had not the art of making others talk and establishing intimacy with them, and no facility in expressing himself; he had the habits of a writer and something of an author's pride. His power of dissimulation, which, as one would expect from a man who had spent his life in conspiracies, was profound, and was peculiarly assisted by the immobility of his features and his want of expression; his eyes were lustreless and opaque like thick glass portholes that let light through but are not transparent. Careless of danger, his courage in moments of crisis was fine and cool, but, as is common enough, his plans were very vacillating. He was often noticed changing course, advancing, hesitating and drawing back, which greatly damaged his reputation. For the nation had chosen him to dare all and expected audacity, not prudence, from him. He was said to have been always much given to physical pleasures and not discriminating in his choice of them. This taste for vulgar enjoyments and comforts increased with the opportunities given by power. This was a daily drain on his energy, and it blunted and reduced his very ambition. His mind was incoherent and confused, being filled with great thoughts ill-clothed, some of them borrowed from Napoleon's example, some from socialist theories, and some from memories of England where he had lived for a time—those were very different and often contradictory sources. And they were the laborious result of solitary meditations far from men and affairs, for he was by nature a fantastic dreamer. But when forced to come down from these vast, vague regions and confine his attention within the limits of a definite matter, he could take a fair view of it, sometimes with subtlety and compass and occasionally even with a certain depth; but sure he never was, being always ready to put some fantastic idea beside a reasonable one.

One could not be in intimate contact with him for long without noticing a little vein of madness running through his good sense, which constantly brought the escapades of his youth to mind and served to explain them.

But yet, in the actual circumstances, he owed his success and strength more to his madness than to his sense, for the world's stage is a strange place. Sometimes the worst plays are the ones that come off best there. If Louis Napoleon had been a wise man, or a genius if you like, he would never have been President of the Republic.

He trusted his star, firmly believing himself the instrument of destiny and the necessary man. I have always thought that he was really convinced of his right, and I do not think Charles X was more infatuated with his legitimism than he. He was also quite incapable of giving any reason for his faith, for while he had a sort of abstract adoration for the people, he had very little taste for liberty. In political matters, the basic characteristic of his mind was hate and contempt for assemblies. The rule of constitutional monarchy he found even more insupportable than that of the Republic. The pride he derived from his name, which knew no limit, would willingly bow before the nation but revolted at the idea of submitting to the influence of a parliament.

Before he came to power, he had had a long time in which to strengthen the taste that mediocre princes always have for lackeys, by the habits of twenty years spent in conspiracies with low-class adventurers, ruined men or men of blemished reputations, and young debauchees, the only persons who all that time would consent to serve him as go-betweens or accomplices. In him, too, for all his good manners, traces of the adventurer and prince of gamblers showed through. He continued to take pleasure in inferior company when he was no longer obliged to live in it. I think his difficulty in expressing his thoughts except in writing drew him to people who had long been familiar with his ideas and his dreams, and that his inferiority in discussion made the company of men of parts uncomfortable to him.

Besides he desired above all devotion to himself and his cause (as if either he or his cause could inspire devotion); he felt hampered by merit when it was combined with any touch of independence. He wanted believers in his star and vulgar adorers of his fortune. So one could not reach him except through a group of intimate servants and personal friends, and I remember General Changarnier at that time using two rhyming words of abuse to describe the whole pack of sharpers and knaves. To conclude, nothing was worse than his familiars except his family, who were mostly good-for-nothings and hussies.

This was the man whom the need for a leader and the power of a memory had set at the head of France and with whom we were going to conduct the government.

There could hardly have been a more critical moment in which to take over the charge of affairs. Before the end of its turbulent existence the Constituent Assembly had passed a resolution (on 7 May 1849) forbidding the government to attack Rome. The first thing I learned on joining the Cabinet was that the order to attack Rome had been sent to our army three days before. This flagrant disobedience to a sovereign Assembly's injunctions, this war undertaken against a people in revolt because of that revolt and in defiance of the terms of the Constitution, which demanded respect for foreign nationalities, made the conflict we dreaded inevitable and brought it very close. What would be the issue of this new struggle? All the letters from prefects of departments that reached us, and all the police reports too, were calculated to throw us into a state of great alarm. At the end of Cavaignac's administration, I had seen how a government could be entertained by fantastic hopes through the self-interested flattery of its agents. This time I saw at much closer quarters how those same agents could work to increase their employers' terror. And the same cause was responsible for these contrary effects. For each agent, seeing that we were troubled, wanted to call attention to himself by discovering new plots and taking his turn to add fresh evidence of the conspiracy threatening us. The more they trusted in our success, the more willingly did they talk to us of our dangers. It is a characteristic peril of this sort of information that it becomes both rarer and less explicit as the danger increases and, therefore, news is needed more. At such moments the agents wonder how much longer the government hiring them will last and, beginning to be afraid of its successor, say scarcely anything or even become completely silent. This time they made a lot of noise. Listening to them it was impossible not to believe that we were on the slope of an abyss, yet I did not think anything of the sort. I was convinced at that time (and I have remained convinced of this ever since) that official letters and police reports, which may profitably be consulted when it is a question of discovering a plot, give one only very exaggerated, incomplete and invariably false impressions when one wants to judge or to anticipate the great movements of parties. In such a case it is the look of the whole country and knowledge of its needs, passions and ideas that will help our judgment; and this is all general data, which we can get for ourselves, but that the best accredited agents in the best position to see will never furnish.

These general considerations led me to believe that at the moment no revolution by force of arms was to be feared: but there was reason to fear a struggle; and civil war, always a cruel thing to anticipate, is much worse combined with the horrors of the plague. For cholera was then ravaging Paris. On that occasion death struck all classes of society. A good many members of the Constituent Assembly had already succumbed; and Bugeaud, whom Africa had spared, was dead.

Had I at all doubted how imminent the crisis was, the sight of the new Assembly would have persuaded me. Within its walls one felt one was breathing the air of civil war. Speeches were abrupt, gestures violent, the phrases used extravagant, and the insults outrageous and direct. We were temporarily meeting in the old Chamber of Deputies. This hall planned for 460 members now held 750 with difficulty. So one's body touched the neighbour one hated, for we were all crushed together in spite of the loathing that held us apart, and discomfort intensified anger. It was like fighting a duel in a barrel. How could the Montagnards contain themselves? Their numbers were enough to make them feel very strong in the nation and the army. Nevertheless they were too weak in Parliament to be able to hope to dominate it, or even to count there. A fine chance to resort to force was offered. The whole of Europe was still unsettled, and one great blow struck in Paris might throw everything back into revolution again. That was more than enough for men of such savage temper.

It was easy to see that the crisis would break out when it became known that the order to attack Rome had been given and acted on. And that did indeed happen.

The order given was kept secret. But on the 10th June, news of the first fighting spread.

On the 11th, the Mountain burst out in words of fury. From the rostrum Ledru-Rollin made an appeal to civil war, saying that the Constitution had been violated and that he and his friends were ready to defend it by all means, *even by arms.* He demanded the impeachment of the President of the Republic and of the former Cabinet.

On the 12th, the committee appointed by the Assembly to consider the question raised the day before rejected impeachment and called on the Assembly to pronounce on the fate of the President and Ministers at that sitting. The Mountain opposed immediate discussion and demanded that evidence be produced. What was their object in putting off the debate like that? It is hard to tell. Did they hope to use the interval to set men's minds on fire, or did they secretly intend to make time to calm them down? It is certain that their main leaders, who were more used to talking than fighting and who were more passionate than resolute, did on that day show, for all the intemperance of their language, a sort of hesitation not apparent the day before. Having half-drawn their sword, they seemed to want to sheathe it again,[3] but it was too late; the signal had been seen by their friends outside, and from thenceforth they no longer led but were led.

For those two days I was in a cruel position. As has been seen, I entirely disapproved of the way in which the Roman expedition had been undertaken and conducted. Before joining

[3] *Marginal note (Tocqueville):* I think that instinct more than calculation ruled their conduct; faced by civil war, they took a step back.

the Cabinet I had solemnly made clear to Barrot that I could accept responsibility only for the future, and that it was up to him to defend what he had done up to then in Italy. Only on that condition did I accept office. I therefore kept silent during the debate on the 11th, leaving Barrot to face the fight alone. But on the 12th, when I saw my colleagues threatened with impeachment, I felt I could not hold back any longer. The request for fresh evidence gave me my chance to intervene without saying anything about the fundamental issue. I did so vigorously but briefly.

On re-reading the *Moniteur,* I find that little speech rather insignificant and very badly turned. But the majority cheered me to the rafters; at a moment of crisis close on civil war, it is the substance of one's thought and the tone of one's voice that count more than the phrasing. I attacked Ledru-Rollin directly, passionately accusing him of looking for nothing but trouble and sowing lies to foment it. It was strong feeling that had driven me to speak, and my tone was resolute and aggressive; and although I spoke very badly, being still uncomfortable in my new role, I was highly appreciated.

Ledru answered by saying that the majority was backing the Cossacks. In reply he was told that he belonged to the party of plunderers and incendiaries. Thiers, adding a footnote to this, said there was an intimate relation between the man they had just heard and the insurgents of June. By a large majority the Assembly rejected the demand for impeachment and dispersed.

Though still outrageous, the leaders of the Mountain had not proved very resolute; so we were able to flatter ourselves that the decisive moment for the struggle had not yet arrived. But that was wrong. Reports received during the night told us of preparations to take up arms.[4]

And indeed the next day the language of the demagogic newspapers showed that their editors relied on a revolution, not the Courts, to justify them. They all made a direct or indirect appeal to civil war. The National Guard, the schools, and the whole population were invited by them to assemble unarmed at

---

[4] *Marginal note* (*Tocqueville*): Find out what happened between the leaders during the night.

a stated place, in order to proceed from there in a body to the doors of the Assembly. They wanted a 15th May to lead to a 23rd June. Seven or eight thousand people did assemble at about eleven o'clock at the Château d'Eau. Meanwhile we were holding a council at the President of the Republic's house. The latter was already in uniform, ready to mount his horse as soon as he was told that the battle had started. But it was only his clothes that he had changed. For the rest he was the same man as yesterday; the same slightly sad look, slow embarrassed speech, and lacklustre eyes. He had none of that warlike excitement and slightly feverish gaiety that the approach of danger often gives although perhaps such a reaction is no more than the mark of an unsettled mind.[5]

We summoned Changarnier, who explained his dispositions to us and promised victory. Dufaure passed on the information in his reports, which all gave warning of a formidable rising. He then went back to the Ministry of the Interior, which was the centre from which he operated, and about midday I went back to the Assembly.

It was rather a long time before the Assembly could meet, because the President, without consulting us when arranging the order of the day the preceding evening, had said there would not be a public meeting the next day, a strange blunder that in any other man would have looked like treason. While messengers were hurrying to inform the deputies at their homes, I went to the President of the Assembly's room to find most of the leaders of the majority already there. There was great excitement and anxiety in all their faces; they both feared the struggle and wanted it, and they were beginning to criticise the ministry severely for softness. Thiers, deep in one armchair with his legs on another, was rubbing his stomach (for he felt some signs of the prevailing illness) and was saying with arrogant ill temper in his shrillest falsetto voice that it was very odd that no one should think of declaring Paris in a state of siege. I quietly replied that we had thought of it, but the moment to

[5] *The following passage is marked for omission in the manuscript:* For my part I admit that I liked him better that way than if he had put on a heroic pose. On that day all his faults seemed to me to turn to his advantage.

do so had not yet come, because the Assembly was not yet sitting.

The deputies were pouring in from all sides, summoned less by the messages sent to their homes, which most had not received, than by the rumours current in the town. At two o'clock the sitting opened: the majority's benches were full, but the heights of the Mountain were bare. The doleful silence prevailing in that part of the Assembly was more frightening than the shouts usually issuing thence. It meant that debate had ended, and civil war was beginning.

At three o'clock Dufaure came and requested that Paris be proclaimed in a state of siege. Cavaignac supported him in one of those short speeches he sometimes made, in which his naturally plodding, muddled intelligence rose to the level of his soul and became sublime. In such circumstances he became for the moment the most truly eloquent man I have ever heard in our Assemblies: he left all the speakers far behind.

"You say," he said, addressing a certain Montagnard[6] who was coming down from the rostrum, "that I have fallen from power. I did come down, but the national will does not overthrow; it commands, and we obey. I repeat, and I hope the Republican Party will always fairly be able to say the same: I did come down, therein by my conduct honouring my republican convictions. You have said that we have been living under the Terror: history is there and will inform you. But what I on my own account want to say to you is that although you don't inspire terror in me, you do fill my heart with grief. Shall I tell you one thing more? You are Republicans of yesterday, whereas I did not work for the Republic before it was founded, and to my regret I have not suffered for it. But I have served it

[6] Pierre Leroux (1797–1871), publicist and social thinker. He adhered to the Saint-Simonian movement until it became schismatic, when he left it to form his own sect. Taking his ideas from Christian as well as from revolutionary tradition, he formulated a concept of progress based on the unity of the generations and maintained that politics should aim to have all members of society share in the fruits of its labour according to the needs, capability and work of each. He is also credited with having first coined the word "socialism" in its contemporary meaning. It is not therefore surprising to find him sitting as a Montagnard in each assembly of the Second Republic. (Ed.)

faithfully, and, what is more, I have governed it. And, understand me well, I will never serve anything else. Write that down, take it down in shorthand, so that it may remain engraved in the annals of our debates: I will not serve any other thing. Between you and me, I take it the question is, who will serve the Republic best.

"Well then, the cause of my sorrow is that you have served it so ill. I hope for my country's happiness that it is not fated to perish, but, should such a sorrow overtake us, remember well, remember that we shall blame your exaggerations and your furies for it."

Shortly after the state of siege had been proclaimed, we learned that the insurrection had been extinguished. Changarnier and the President, charging at the head of the cavalry, had cut in two and scattered the column heading for the Assembly. Some scarcely completed barricades had been destroyed with hardly a shot fired. The Montagnards, surrounded in the Conservatoire of Arts and Crafts where they had made their headquarters, were either under arrest or in flight. We were masters of Paris.

In several of the great cities there had been disturbances of the same nature only worse, but all without success. In Lyon a fierce fight went on for five hours, and for a moment victory seemed in doubt. Once victorious in Paris, however, we did not worry much about the provinces; we knew that in France, for order or against it, Paris lays down the law.

That was how the second June insurrection ended. In the amount of violence and in duration it was very different from the first, but the reasons for its failure were similar. On the first occasion, the people, led on more by appetite than opinion, had fought alone, unable to persuade their representatives to lead them. This time it was the representatives who could not induce the people to follow them into battle. In June 1848, the army had no leaders; in June 1849, the leaders had no army.

These Montagnards were a queer lot of people: their natural quarrelsomeness and conceit came out even in contexts least suited thereto. Considérant was one of those who, as journalist and speaker, had been most violent in advocating civil war and had heaped the most insults on us. He was the pupil and successor of Fourier,[7] writing a lot of socialist dreams, which at any other time would have been merely ridiculous but which were dangerous in ours. Considérant succeeded in escaping from the Conservatoire with Ledru-Rollin and in reaching the Belgian frontier. In the past I had had social relations with him, and he wrote to me from Brussels:

> My dear Tocqueville,
> (Here followed a request for a service to be done for him, and then he went on):
> Count on me when needed for any personal service. You are good for two or three months perhaps, and the pure *Whites* who will follow you may last for six months at the longest. Both of you, it is true, will have perfectly deserved what you will infallibly get a little sooner or a little later. But let us talk no more politics and respect the very legal, loyal and Odilon Barrotesque state of siege.

To this I replied:

> My dear Considérant,
> What you asked is done. I don't want to boast about such a small service, but, by the way, I am very glad to note that those odious

---

[7] Charles Fourier (1772–1837), economist and socialist thinker. Looking on industrial society with repugnance, he considered that society should be reorganized to fit the needs of the individual and to permit the free development of his faculties. To this end, he envisaged the organization of society into *phalanges,* autonomous, economically self-sufficient, co-operative groups of about 1600 persons, all living in one building (called a *phalanstère*). Each community would have sufficient land under cultivation for its needs. Members of the phalange joined voluntarily, and work was organized on a voluntary basis whereby all did the work for which they felt themselves most suited, which was, as a result, done well in an atmosphere of enthusiasm. Private property was not excluded by Fourier from this community, where both rich and poor could participate. All were to receive enough for their subsistence from the community's produce, and the remainder of the profits was to be apportioned out thus: five twelfths to labour, four twelfths to capital, and three twelfths to talent. Without any great influence in his own day, Fourier's ideas had a certain vogue in the United States between 1840 and 1850, when several attempts to set up phalanges were made, among them Brooke Farm (1841–47). Considérant was Fourier's most active disciple and propagandist and became the leader of the Fourierists on the death of the master. See H. Bourgin, *Fourier,* Paris, 1905. V. Considérant, *La Destinée Sociale,* 2 vols., second edition, Paris, 1847. See also M. Dommanget, *Victor Considérant, Sa Vie Son Oeuvre,* Paris, 1929. (Ed.)

oppressors of freedom called Ministers inspire enough confidence in their adversaries to allow the latter, after declaring them outlaws, to turn to them, trusting to get what is fair. That proves that there is some good in us, whatever anyone says. Are you quite sure that, if our parts were changed, I could behave in the same way? I do not mean behave so to you, but to one or other of your political friends whom I could name. I think not. And I solemnly declare that, if ever they are the masters and just leave me my head, I shall consider myself satisfied and ready to state that their virtue has surpassed my hopes.

CHAPTER THREE

Our domestic policy – Quarrels within the Cabinet –
Difficulties in its relations with the Majority and the
President

We had won, but, as I expected, our real difficulties were now
to appear. I had, moreover, always held to the maxim that it is
after some great success that the most dangerous threats of
ruin usually emerge; while the danger lasts, one has only one's
adversaries against one, and one triumphs over them, but after
victory one begins to have trouble with oneself, one's slackness,
one's pride, and the rash security born of success; and one
succumbs.

I was free from the last of these dangers, since I did not
imagine that we had surmounted our main obstacles. I knew
that those obstacles lay with the very men in whose company
we would have to rule the country. I knew, too, that the speedy
and complete defeat of the Mountain, far from protecting us
from their ill will, would immediately expose us to it. We would
have been much stronger if we had been less successful.

At that time the majority was composed mainly of three
parties (the President's party still had too few members and too
bad a reputation to count in Parliament). From sixty to eighty
members at the most tried sincerely as we did to establish a
moderate republic: that was our only solid support in this vast
Assembly. The rest of the majority was made up of Legitimists,
to the number of about one hundred and sixty, and of old
friends or supporters of the July Monarchy, mostly representing

the middle classes who had governed and, more particularly, exploited France for the last eighteen years. I felt at once that, of those two parties, the Legitimists were the easier to use in support of our plans. The Legitimists had been excluded from power under the last government, so they had neither places nor salaries to regret or reclaim. Moreover, being mostly large landowners, they had not the same need for public offices as the middle class had, or, at worst, habit had not taught them the delights thereof. Although their principles made them more irreconcilable towards the Republic than the others, they were better able to accept its continuance, for it had destroyed their destroyer and opened a way to power, thus both their ambition and their desire for vengeance owed something to the Republic; the only hostile emotion it roused in them was fear, and that was indeed great. The former Conservatives, who made up the bulk of the majority, were in a much greater hurry to escape from the Republic, but as the furious hatred they bore it was firmly bridled by fear of the risk they would run in endeavouring prematurely to abolish it, and as long habit had accustomed them to walk in the wake of power, it would have been easy for us to lead them if we had been able to obtain the support, or even the neutrality of their leaders, of whom, of course, the most important were M. Thiers and M. Molé.

Seeing this situation clearly, I appreciated that all subordinate objectives must give way to the main one, namely to prevent the overthrow of the Republic and in particular to stand in the way of a bastard monarchy under Louis Napoleon, which was then the most immediate danger.

First I considered how to insure against my friends' mistakes, for I have always thought there was profound sense in the old Norman proverb, "God preserve me from my friends; I will protect myself from my enemies."

The leader of our supporters in the National Assembly was General Lamoricière, and I dreaded his petulance and rash suggestions, but dreaded even more his idleness. I knew he was one of those men who would rather do good than harm, but who will do harm rather than nothing at all. I had it in mind to put him in an important embassy far away. Russia had spontaneously recognized the Republic; it was proper that we should renew the diplomatic relations with her that had almost been broken off under the last government. I thought of Lamoricière for this special distant post. And in any case he was just the man for such a post, in which only generals, and famous ones at that, ever have a chance of succeeding. I had some trouble persuading him, but the hardest to persuade was the President of the Republic. At first he resisted; on that occasion he told me, with a naïveté due less to frankness than to his difficulty in finding words (his words hardly ever expressed his thoughts, but sometimes permitted them to glimmer through) that at the great Courts he would like to have his *own ambassadors*. That was not my business, for I, who had to send instructions to those ambassadors, meant to serve none but France. I therefore insisted, but I should have failed without the help of Falloux, who was at that time the only man in the Cabinet the President trusted. I don't know what arguments Falloux used to persuade him. But Lamoricière went, and I will narrate later what he did there.

My fears about our friends' behaviour calmed by his departure, I put my mind to winning over or retaining our needed allies.[1] The task there was in every respect more difficult, for, outside my own department, I could act only with the Cabinet's agreement, and that Cabinet contained some of the most honest men I have ever met, but so inflexible and narrow in politics that I sometimes even regretted not having to do with clever rascals.

As for the Legitimists, my view was that we must leave them great influence in the field of public instruction. I admit that this was a great sacrifice,[2] but it was the only thing that would satisfy them and obtain their support in return when it was a question of restraining the President and preventing him from upsetting the Constitution. This plan was followed. Falloux was left free to act within his department, and the Cabinet let

[1] *Marginal note (Tocqueville):* Perhaps what I wrote before about secondary objectives should come in here.
[2] *The following words are marked for omission in the manuscript:* That plan had considerable disadvantages.

him put before the Assembly his project for public instruction, which has since become the law of [15 March 1850].[3] I also urged my colleagues individually as strongly as I could to cultivate good relations with Legitimists of importance. I took my own advice and soon was on better terms with them than was any other member of the Cabinet. In the end I even became the only intermediary between them and us.

It is true that my origin and the world in which I had been brought up gave me great advantages here, which the others did not have, for, although the French nobility may have ceased to be a class, it has remained a sort of freemasonry with all its members recognizing one another by I don't know what invisible signs, no matter what opinions may make them strangers or adversaries[4] one to another.

So it turned out that although I had crossed swords with Falloux more often than any other member before joining the Cabinet, I found it easy to make friends with him as soon as I was in it. And it was worth taking trouble to turn that man to account. In my whole political career I don't think I have met another man so unusual. He had both the qualities most necessary for leading a party: an ardent conviction, which continually drove him towards his objective undeterred by disappointments or dangers, and an intelligence not too severe but firm and subtle as well, which knew how to make many and various means serve a single end. He was honest in the sense that his concern was, as he alleged, for his cause and not for his private interest, but in other respects he was a great knave, practising a rare and very effective type of knavery, for he could succeed for a moment in mixing up true and false in his own mind before he served the mixture to others, and this is

---

[3] The date was left blank in the manuscript. (Ed.)
[4] *The following passage has been marked for omission in the manuscript:* The link that exists between all its members is invisible, but it is so close that I have found myself a hundred times more at ease dealing about some matter with aristocrats whose interests and opinions were entirely different from mine, than with the bourgeois whose ideas I shared and whose interests were similar to my own. In the first case I was in disagreement, but at least I knew what language to speak and felt instinctively what one could say and what was best left unsaid.

the sole secret of how to win the advantages of sincerity when lying, and how to lead one's associates or subordinates into an error that one believes beneficial.

However hard I tried, I never succeeded in establishing, I do not say good, but decent relations between Falloux and Dufaure; but of course those two men had exactly opposite qualities and defects. Dufaure, who at bottom remained a true bourgeois from the West, hating nobles and priests, could not get used to Falloux' principles, or even to his beautiful refined manners, however agreeable they were to me. I did by a great effort succeed in persuading him that Falloux must not be hampered in his own department, but as for letting him exert any influence over what was done at the Ministry of the Interior (even within the limits of what was legitimate and necessary), he would never listen to a word of it. In his native Anjou there was a prefect of whom Falloux felt he had reason to complain; he did not ask for him to be dismissed, or even passed over for promotion, he simply wanted him moved elsewhere; he felt his own position compromised until this change took place, and it was a change requested by the majority of the deputies from Maine-et-Loire. Unfortunately, this prefect was a declared friend of the Republic, and that was enough to fill Dufaure with distrust and convince him that Falloux' only object was to compromise him, by making use of him to strike down those Republicans whom he had not previously dared to attack. Consequently he refused; the other insisted; Dufaure turned stubborn. It was rather an amusing sight to see Falloux spinning around Dufaure, pirouetting with grace and skill, but never finding a single chance of penetrating his mind.

Dufaure let him have his say and then answered laconically, without looking at him or turning only a wry, wan glance towards him:

"I should like to know why you did not take advantage of your friend Faucher's term of office at the Ministry of the Interior to get rid of your prefect?"

Falloux restrained himself although he was, I think, naturally very incensed; he came and told me his troubles, and I could taste the bitterest gall trickling through the honey of his words.

I then intervened and tried to make Dufaure understand that this was one of those requests from a colleague that one cannot refuse, unless one intends to create a breach with him. I spent a month as daily go-between for those two, expending more energy and diplomacy on this matter than I gave, during that period, to the great affairs of Europe. Several times the Cabinet was on the point of splitting over the wretched business. In the end Dufaure did give way, but with such bad grace that nobody could feel grateful; so he gave up his prefect without winning Falloux over.[5]

But the most difficult aspect of the part we had to play was our relations with the former Conservatives who, as I have mentioned, formed the bulk of the majority.

The Conservatives had both general views that they wanted to force through and many private interests to be satisfied. They wanted order energetically re-established; in that respect we were their men, for we wanted the same as they, and we did it as well as they could desire and better than they could have done themselves. We had put Lyon and several departments near that city in a state of siege; used the state-of-siege powers to suspend six revolutionary newspapers in Paris; cashiered the three legions of the Parisian National Guard that had shown hesitation on the 13th June; arrested seven deputies caught *in flagrante delicto* and applied for warrants for the impeachment of thirty others. Similar measures were taken all over France. Circulars addressed to all officials demonstrated to them that they were dealing with a government that knew how to make itself obeyed and required that all should give way before the law.

Whenever the Montagnards still left in the Assembly attacked Dufaure for any of these acts, he answered with that virile,

[5] Neither Dufaure himself nor his un-co-operative behaviour is mentioned in Falloux' *Mémoires d'un royaliste*, 2 vols., Paris, 1888, vol. I, pp. 499–500. The prefect in Angers, named Bordillon, was a Republican, hostile to Falloux and, as such, an embarrassment to him. His removal to Grenoble and subsequent dismissal were brought about, not by the initiative of any minister, but by that of Louis Napoleon Bonaparte himself. Far from requiring or requesting Bordillon's removal, Falloux is at pains to show how disinterested he was in the affair. (Ed.)

strong, steely eloquence of which he was master, like a man who had burnt his boats.

The Conservatives were not content that the administration should simply be vigorous; they wanted to use our victory to impose repressive preventive laws. We ourselves felt the need to move in that direction although not wishing to go as far as they.

For my part, I believed that it was wise and necessary to make great concessions to the fears and legitimate resentments of the nation, and that, after such a violent revolution, the only way to save freedom was to restrict it. My colleagues agreed with me. Accordingly we introduced the following measures: a law to suspend the clubs, another to suppress the vagaries of the press with even more energy than had been used under the Monarchy; and a third to regularize the state of siege.

"Your law establishes a military dictatorship," they shouted at us.

"Yes," replied Dufaure, "it is a dictatorship, but a parliamentary one. No private rights can prevail over the inalienable right of society to save itself. There are certain imperious necessities that are the same for all governments, whether monarchies or republics. But whence do these necessities originate? To whom do we owe this cruel experience, which has given us eighteen months of violent disorders, constant plots and formidable insurrections? Yes, certainly what you say is true. It is deplorable that, after so many revolutions made in the name of liberty, we should once more be forced to shroud her statue and put terrible weapons into the hands of the public authorities! But whose fault is it, if not yours? And who serves the Republican government better, those who fan rebellion, or those who, like ourselves, strive to stamp it out?"

Such measures, laws and language pleased the Conservatives but did not satisfy them. To tell the truth, nothing short of the destruction of the Republic would have contented them. Instinct constantly pushed them in that direction, although prudence and reason kept them on the tracks.

But what they most desired was to oust their enemies from office and install their partisans and close friends in their places as quickly as possible. Again we had to face all those passions that had brought about the fall of the July Monarchy. The revolution had not destroyed them but only made them greedier; this was our great and permanent stumbling-block. Here, too, I judged that concessions could be made; many public appointments were still held by Republicans of indifferent capacities or bad reputation, who had been thrust into office by the turns of revolution. My advice was to be rid of them at once without waiting to be asked to dismiss them, so as to create confidence in our intentions and give us the right to defend all honest and capable Republicans; but I never could bring Dufaure round to this view.[6] "What is it we have undertaken to do?" I kept asking him. "Is it to save the Republic by means of the Republicans? No, for most of those who bear that name would assuredly kill us and it, and those who are worthy of the name number less than a hundred in the Assembly. We have undertaken to save the Republic with the help of parties who do not love it. Therefore we can rule only by making concessions— only one must never give away anything of substance. In this matter everything depends on measure. At this moment the best, and perhaps the only guarantee for the Republic is our continuance in office. Therefore we must take all honourable means to keep ourselves there."

To which he would answer that, by fighting with all his might, as he did daily against socialism and anarchy, he ought to satisfy the majority—just as if one could ever satisfy people by concerning oneself with their opinions without bothering about their vanity and their private interests. But even though he was refusing, he might have done so graciously, whereas the manner of his refusal caused even more offence than the

[6] *The following passage has been marked for omission in the manuscript:* He had been in charge of the Ministry of the Interior under Cavaignac. Many of the officials who should have been dismissed had been appointed or at least retained in office by him. His vanity was involved in defending them; and his distrust of their detractors would have been enough to make him resist; so he did resist. As a result he himself soon became the target of all their attacks. No one dared tackle him on the rostrum, for he was a tough champion there; but they constantly struck at him from a distance and in corners of the lobbies, and I soon saw a great storm piling up against him.

fact. I have never understood how it came about that a man who was such a master of words in the rostrum, so skilful in choosing the arguments and expressions most apt to please, so sure of finding just the nuance that would make his meaning go down best, was so ill at ease, gauche and clumsy in conversation. But I think his basic education is the key.

He was a man of much intelligence—or rather talent, for, if one uses words strictly, he had very little intelligence—but he had no knowledge of the world. He had had a hard-working, concentrated, almost anti-social youth. At forty he had married. But marriage merely gave his unsociable way of life a new form. He withdrew into his own house, no longer living in solitude but still in retreat. To tell the truth, even politics did not bring him out. He held himself aloof, not only from intrigues but from any contact with the parties; he hated the stir of Assemblies and stood in fear of the rostrum, although his only strength lay there. In his way he was ambitious, but with a measured and somewhat humble ambition, aspiring to manage rather than to dominate affairs.[7] His ways of treating people when he was a Minister were sometimes very odd. On one occasion General Castellane[8] (who was, it is true, a sad fool; but at that time his reputation was high) asked for an audience. He was received, and explained at length his claims and what he called his rights. Dufaure listened with patient attention; then he got up, bowed the general to the door, and left him standing there aghast, not having said a single word. When I reproached him for this behaviour, he answered:

"I would have had only disagreeable things to say to him. Wasn't the nicest thing to say nothing at all?"

It is not hard to believe that one seldom left such a man in anything but a bad temper.

---

[7] *Marginal note (Tocqueville)*: Good, but too long; take the last sentence in this piece and place it somewhere else.
[8] Boniface de Castellane (1788–1862), who continued his military career unbroken from the First Empire to the July Monarchy, was put on half pay by the Provisional Government of 1848, but was re-established in his command by Louis Napoleon Bonaparte in 1849. He was created a marshal of France in 1852. His *Journal 1804–1862* was published by his daughter, 5 vols., Paris, 1895–97. It contains some decidedly acid references to Dufaure, but does not mention this particular incident. (Ed.)

By ill luck he had as a sort of double a *chef de cabinet* who was as uncouth as himself, but stupid too; so when petitioners passed from the Minister's room into the secretary's, hoping for a little consolation, they encountered the same harshness combined with less sense.[9] It was as if, after struggling through a thickset hedge, one fell on a bundle of thorns. In spite of these disadvantages, Dufaure got the support of the Conservatives because in the rostrum he took such vengeance for the insults of the Montagnards; but he never won their leaders over.

Those leaders, as I had anticipated, wished neither to take charge of the government nor to let anyone else rule independently.[10] From the 13th June down to the final debates about Rome, that is to say almost the whole time that the Cabinet lasted, I don't think that a day passed without their attempting some ambush. It is true that they never fought us in the rostrum, but secretly they were continually inciting the majority against us, criticizing our appointments and our measures, putting unfavourable interpretations on our words, and, without any resolute wish to overthrow us, contriving that we should have no point of support, so that they could always send us to the ground with a gentle push. After all, Dufaure's distrust was not always without foundation. The leaders of the majority wanted to make use of us to get rigorous measures taken and repressive laws passed, so that government would be comfortable for our successors; and at that moment our Republican opinions made us more fit for the task than the Conservatives. They counted on being able to bow us out afterwards and bring their substitutes onto the stage. Not only were they unwilling for us to establish our influence within the Assembly, they also constantly worked to prevent our getting a hold over the President's mind. They were still under the illusion that Louis Napoleon would always be glad to stay under their protection. Accordingly they besieged him. Our agents informed us that most of them,

[9] Eugène Brissot de Warville was appointed *chef de cabinet* to the Minister of the Interior on 1 July 1849. (Ed.)

[10] *The following passage is marked for omission in the manuscript:* But they could not put up with ministers in office who were not their creatures and refused to be their tools.

especially M. Thiers and M. Molé, constantly saw him in private and pressed him with all their might to combine with them in overthrowing the Republic at their mutual expense and to their mutual profit.[11] From the 13th June onwards I lived in a state of continual alarm, daily fearing that they would take advantage of our victory to incite Louis Napoleon to some violent usurpation and that one fine morning, as I used to tell Barrot, the Empire would slip in between his legs.[12] I learned afterwards that our fears were even better founded than I realized. Since I left office, I have ascertained from a reliable source that, towards the month of July 1849, there was a plot to use force to alter the Constitution by a joint operation of the President and the Assembly. The leaders of the majority and Louis Napoleon had come to an agreement, and the stroke failed only because Berryer (either fearing that he had made a dupe's bargain, or seized by sudden panic at the moment of action, as was usual with him) refused his support and that of his party. The plan was not given up, however, but only postponed. And when I think that at the time I am writing this, that is to say only two years after the events described, most of these same men are waxing indignant at the mere idea of seeing the people violate the Constitution in doing for Louis Napoleon precisely what they themselves then proposed to him to do, I feel it would be hard to find a more outstanding example of human mutability and of the vanity of those great words "patriotism" and "right" with which their petty passions cloak themselves.

As has been seen, we were no more certain of the President than of the majority. Indeed, for us and for the Republic, Louis Napoleon was the greatest and most permanent of dangers.

I was convinced of this, and yet, after studying his character with great attention, I did not despair of persuading him, for a time at least, to accept us in a fairly solid way. I had soon

---

[11] *The following passage is marked for omission in the manuscript:* They formed as it were a secret Ministry by the side of the responsible Cabinet.
[12] *Marginal note (Tocqueville):* It is absolutely necessary to state somewhere that our fears were rendered more lively by the President's need for money; for lack of money, he was pushed into adventures for the sake of the comforts and material pleasures that, in other circumstances, might have restrained and soothed his ambition. Try and give a picture of a basket with holes in it and a man who butchers money.

discovered that although he allowed the majority leaders to
see him and listened to their advice, acting on it sometimes
and if necessary plotting with them, he nevertheless bore their
yoke very impatiently; to seem to be under their protection
was a humiliation from which he secretly longed to escape.
That gave us a point of contact with him and a hold on his
mind: for we, too, were firmly determined to stay free of these
prize manipulators and to keep executive power out of their
reach.

Besides I thought it not out of the question to enter partially
into Louis Napoleon's plans without abandoning our own. One
thing that always struck me in considering the situation of
this extraordinary man (extraordinary, not on account of genius,
but because circumstances had pushed his mediocrity to such
a height) was the need to keep his mind fed with some hope
or other if one wanted him to stay quiet. It seemed to me very
doubtful that such a man, after ruling France for four years,
could be sent back to private life; that he should agree to go,
quite fantastic; even to prevent him, while his mandate lasted,
from throwing himself into some dangerous undertaking, seemed
tremendously difficult, unless one could find some prospect to
charm, or at least to content his ambition. I therefore applied
my mind to that question from the beginning.

"I will never serve you," I told him, "in overthrowing the
Republic. But I will gladly strive to assure a great place for
you within it, and I think that ultimately all my friends will
join in helping there. The Constitution could be revised; Article
45, which forbids the re-election of the President, could be
changed. We would gladly help you to get that done."

Furthermore, as the prospects for revision were doubtful, I
went on to hint that perhaps in the future, if he governed
France quietly, wisely and modestly, confining himself to being
the first magistrate of the nation and not its suborner or its
master, it was possible that, when his mandate expired, he might
be re-elected despite Article 45 by almost unanimous agreement,
for the Monarchic parties would not see the limited prolongation
of his rule as the ruin of their hopes, and even the Republican
party might feel that a government such as his was the best

way of getting the country used to a Republic and ready to
acquire a taste for one. My tone in saying all this was sincere,
for I felt sincere about it. I did and still do think that my advice
was the best one could have given in the nation's interest, and
perhaps in his own. He gladly listened to me, without letting
me see the effect of my words on him: that was his habit.
Addressing words to him was like dropping stones down a well:
one heard the noise, but never knew what happened to them.[13]
In any case he seemed to like me better and better. It is true
that, as far as was compatible with the public good, I made
great efforts to please him. Should he by chance recommend
a capable and honest man for a diplomatic post, I showed
great alacrity in appointing him. Even when his protégé was not
so capable, if the post were unimportant, I generally gave it
to him. But more often it was jailbirds whom the President honoured with his recommendation, people who in time past, not
knowing where else to go, had plunged into his party, and to
whom he felt himself obliged. Then, too, he would attempt to
place in the main embassies what he called "people of my own,"
which generally meant intriguers and knaves. In these cases
I went to see him; I explained the regulations that stood in the
way of his wish, and the moral or political reasons that made
me unable to meet his desire. I sometimes even hinted that I
would rather resign than let what he wanted pass. As he saw
that no private concern influenced my refusals, and that I had
no systematic desire to oppose him, he yielded without bearing
me a grudge, or put the matter off.

I did not get off as cheaply with his friends. Their zest for
prey was unparalleled. They constantly assailed me with their
requests, with such impertinence and importunity that I often
wanted to have them thrown out of the window. But I forced

13 *The following passage has been marked for omission in the manuscript:*
However I think they were not entirely lost, for there were two distinct
men in him, as I soon discovered: the first was the former conspirator
and fatalistic dreamer who believed that he was called to be the master
of France and through her to dominate Europe; the other was the
Epicurean luxuriously making the most of his new prosperity and the
facile pleasures his present position offered, not caring to risk it in order
to climb higher. Each of those two personalities dominated him in turn,
but neither one for long enough to be grasped.

myself to restrain my feelings. On one occasion, however, when a real gallows bird was being arrogantly insistent, saying it was very odd that the Prince had not the power to reward those who had suffered for his cause, I did answer: "Sir, the best thing that the President of the Republic could do, would be to forget that he was once a pretender, and to remember that his duty is to look after the affairs of France, not yours."

The Roman expedition in which, as I will explain later, I firmly supported the President until his policy became exaggerated and unreasonable, finally put me in his good graces: once he gave me a great proof of this. Beaumont, during the short time at the end of 1848 when he was Ambassador in London, had made some very insulting remarks about Louis Napoleon, then a candidate for the Presidency, and they had annoyed him very much when he was told about them. Since I had been a minister, I had several times tried to get the President better disposed to Beaumont, but I should never have ventured to propose employing him, capable though he was and anxious though I was to do so. About September 1849, the post of Ambassador in Vienna became vacant. It was at that moment one of the most important diplomatic posts for us because of the crises in Italy and Hungary. The President of his own accord said to me, "I suggest that you give the Vienna embassy to M. de Beaumont. I have good cause to complain about him, but I know he is your best friend, and that is decisive."[14] I was delighted, no one was better suited for that post than Beaumont, and nothing would give me greater pleasure than offering it to him.[15]

All my colleagues did not take as much trouble as I did, without dereliction of my opinion or duties, to win the President's favour.

However Dufaure, unexpectedly, always behaved towards him just as he should; I believe he was half won over by the President's simplicity of manner. But Passy seemed to take pleasure in making himself disagreeable to him. I think that he felt he

[14] *Marginal note* (*Tocqueville*): I must leave this story about Beaumont in, as it proves the goodwill of which I speak and gives authentic evidence for my portrait; perhaps I ought to change it.
[15] Several lines about Beaumont have been crossed out. (Ed.)

had lowered himself by becoming the Minister of a man he considered an adventurer, and that he kept trying to reassert his standing by impertinence. He crossed him continually and unnecessarily, rejecting all his candidates, bullying his friends, and opposing his suggestions with ill-concealed disdain; so the President cordially detested him.

Falloux, who was, if you like, a Legitimist by birth, education, social connections and taste, fundamentally belonged only to the Church, as I have mentioned before. He did not expect the Legitimism he served to triumph, and he was only seeking a road through all our revolutions by which he could bring the Catholic religion back to power. His reason for staying on as a Minister was to be able to watch over the Church's interests, and he did so, as he told me on the first day with well-judged frankness, on the advice of his confessor. I am convinced that from the start Falloux had had some inkling of the way in which Louis Napoleon might be used to forward this design, and that, early on, he got used to the idea that the President might become the heir of the Republic and the master of France; his only thought was how to turn this inevitable event to the advantage of the clergy. He had offered his party's support, but without compromising himself.

From the time we took office to the prorogation of the Assembly on the 13th August, we never ceased to gain ground with the majority, in spite of their leaders. Every day they saw us wrestling with their enemies, and the unending fury of those enemies' attacks on us succeeded in advancing us gradually in their favour. On the other hand, all that time we made no progress with the President, who seemed to tolerate our presence at his councils rather than to let us into them.

Six weeks later exactly, the reverse was true. The deputies had come back from the provinces soured by the complaints of their friends, to whom we had refused to hand over control of local affairs, whereas the President of the Republic had come closer to us for reasons I shall explain later. One could say that we had advanced on one side in exact proportion to our setback on the other.

Thus supported on two badly joined props that were always

wobbling, the Cabinet leaned now to one side, now to the other and was continually in danger of falling between the two. It was the Roman business that brought about the fall.

Such was the state of affairs when parliamentary work recommenced on 1 October 1849, and when, for the second and last time, we dealt with the Roman affair.[16]

[16] After the assassination of his Prime Minister, Rossi, on 15 November 1848, Pius IX fled from Rome to take refuge in Gaeta, under the protection of the absolutist king of Naples. Rome was declared a republic in February 1849, and executive power was entrusted to a triumvirate of which Mazzini was the dominant member. The defeat of Piedmont by Austria at Novara on 23 March 1849 left Austrian forces free to march on Rome to reinstate the Pope. To prevent an Austrian occupation of Rome and the intervention of Spain and Naples, France sent an expeditionary force under General Oudinot, which landed at Civita Vecchia on 25 April 1849. The purpose of this expedition remains somewhat ambiguous, apart from the French Government's determination to keep Austrian forces out of Rome. It was not clear at the outset whether the French force was to assist the Roman Republic, or to crush it and restore the Pope to his throne. After the elections to the Legislative Assembly, which took place on the 13th May and resulted in a substantial Conservative majority, the French force became more decidedly hostile to the Roman Republic. The first attack on the city had been repulsed on the 30th April, and Oudinot made request to the government for reinforcements and siege equipment. At the same time Ferdinand de Lesseps was sent to negotiate a settlement with the Roman Republic. He requested Oudinot to cease hostilities, and an agreement was reached on the 31st May, at which time de Lesseps was recalled to France and disavowed. Oudinot began the siege of Rome on the 3rd June, and the city surrendered on the 1st July. A greater problem for the French Government was to extract some firm promises from the Pope to bring in liberal reforms on his reinstatement, and here it was less successful. Pius IX returned to Rome in April 1850 and continued to be as absolute a ruler as he had been previously, although he now required the support of a French garrison left in Rome to assure his position. For a suggestive account of the Roman affair see F. A. Simpson, *Louis Napoleon and the Recovery of France, 1848–1856*, London, 1923, p. 44 ff. See also The Cambridge Modern History, vol. IX, p. 121 ff. and M. Degros, Les "Souvenirs," Tocqueville et la question romaine in *Alexis de Tocqueville—Livre du Centenaire*, Paris, 1960. (Ed.)

CHAPTER FOUR

Foreign affairs

I did not want to interrupt my account of our domestic troubles by discussing the foreign embarrassments of which I bore the brunt. But now I will retrace my steps and deal with that aspect of my subject.

Once installed at the Foreign Office and able to see the state of our affairs, I was frightened at the number and importance of the problems to be faced. But what caused me more anxiety than anything else was myself.

By nature I am full of self-distrust. And that innate weakness had been made much worse by those nine rather wretched years spent in the Assemblies of the declining years of the Monarchy. The way I stood the test of the February Revolution had helped to raise me a little in my own estimation, but still it was with great hesitation that I accepted so important a responsibility at such a difficult time, and I felt very nervous on taking up my duties.

But I soon noticed several things that calmed me, even though they did not entirely reassure me. First I noticed that problems do not always increase in difficulty in proportion to their importance, as from a distance one tends to assume; indeed the opposite is more often the case. The complications of problems do not grow with their importance; often they look simpler when their consequences spread wider and are more menacing. Moreover, when a man's decisions will influence a whole nation's fate, he will always find plenty of people at hand to enlighten and help him, to take charge of the details, and also to encourage and defend him, all of which is not the case with anybody in a subordinate office dealing with matters of secondary importance. Finally, all one's powers are so stimulated by the consciousness of the importance of the task that, although it may be a little harder, the workman is at the top of his form.

I had felt perplexed, discouraged and anxious when faced by minor responsibilities. But I felt peculiarly tranquil and calm when faced by great ones. I can never work up a fictitious enthusiasm. But consciousness of the importance of what I was doing raised me and sustained me at that level. Previously the idea of a setback had seemed intolerable to me; now the prospect of a crashing fall from my high position in one of the greatest theatres of the world did not trouble me at all, which made me realize that there was much more of pride than of timidity in my constitution.[1] I soon noticed, too, that in politics as in so many other matters—perhaps in all—the vividness of our reactions depends not so much on the importance of a matter as on the frequency of its recurrence. A man who may have got worried and upset coping with one little matter that happened to come his way may find his balance when dealing with great affairs if they recur daily, for familiarity blunts their impact. I have mentioned how many enemies I used to make by steering clear of those who did not attract my attention by any good qualities, and how often my boredom was construed as arrogance. I was very much afraid of that reef in the great voyage I was going to undertake. But I soon noticed that, although with some people insolence may increase in precise proportion to advancement in the world, with me it was otherwise and I found it much easier to be affable and even cordial when raised above competition than when I was one of the crowd. The reason, of course, was that, being a minister, I did not have to go and search people out or fear that I would be coldly received, for men put themselves out to approach people in my sort of

[1] *Variant:* That my weakness was not timidity but pride
that my weakness was much less timidity than pride (and that I feared mediocrity more than downfall) *the second part of this variant was intended for omission.*

position, and they are simple-minded enough to attach great importance to their slightest words. Moreover, as a minister I was concerned with not only the ideas of fools but also with their interests, which always provide a ready-made subject for facile conversation.

Thus I found myself much less unsuited than I had feared to the task I had undertaken, and that discovery emboldened me, not only for the moment but for the rest of my life. If any one asks me what profit I derived from such an anxious, thwarted and short period in office, without time to finish anything I had begun, my answer is that I gained one great benefit, perhaps the greatest this world can give, namely confidence in myself.

In foreign as in domestic policy our greatest difficulties arose less from the nature of the affairs themselves than from the people with whom we had to conduct them. I was conscious of that from the start. Most of our diplomats were creatures of the Monarchy, who from the bottom of their hearts savagely detested the government they served, and, in the name of democratic, Republican France, encouraged the restoration of old aristocracies and secretly worked for the re-establishment of every absolute monarchy in Europe. Other diplomatic officials, brought out of the obscurity in which they should always have remained, by the February Revolution, gave underhanded support to those demagogic parties against which the French Government was struggling. But the main vice of most of them was timidity. Most of our envoys were afraid of becoming attached to any particular policy in the countries where they represented us, and they were even afraid to express to their own government opinions for which they might later be blamed. Accordingly, they carefully kept themselves hidden under a mass of trivial facts which filled out their reports (for in diplomacy you have to keep writing, even if you know nothing or do not wish to reveal what you know); they were at pains not to express any opinion about the events they recorded, still less to indicate what conclusions we ought to draw from them.

This self-chosen futility to which most of our envoys were reduced, although, truth to tell, in the case of most of them art had needed only to perfect nature in this respect, led me, when I realized how things stood, to employ new men at the main Courts.

I wished I would have got rid of the leaders of the majority too, but, as I could not do that, I resolved to live on good terms with them and did not despair of pleasing them, while remaining independent of their influence: a difficult undertaking, but one in which I succeeded, for of all the ministers I was the one who thwarted their policy most, and yet the only one who remained in their good graces. My secret, if I must reveal it, was to flatter their vanity while disregarding their advice.

Something I had observed in trivial matters seemed applicable to great ones: I had found that negotiating with men's vanity gives one the best bargain, for one often receives the most substantial advantages in return for very little of substance.[2] To take advantage of the vanity of others, it is, of course, essential to put one's own entirely aside and to think of nothing but the success of one's plans, and that always makes this procedure difficult. In the circumstances of that time, however, I practised it very successfully and reaped great profits. There were three men who, because of the rank they had previously held, thought they had a special right to direct our foreign policy: M. de Broglie, M. Molé and M. Thiers. I overwhelmed all three of them with deference; I often invited them to visit me and sometimes went to visit them in order to consult them and modestly ask for advice, which I hardly ever took,[3] but that did not prevent all these great men from displaying great satisfaction. It was more to their taste that I should ask for their advice without taking it than that I should take it without asking for it. Especially with M. Thiers this policy worked out

[2] *The following words have been marked for omission in the manuscript:* One will always get less good bargains from their ambition or their greed.
[3] *Marginal note (Tocqueville):* Bring some phrase in here to make it plain that I did not *systematically* reject their advice; that I did adopt some suggestions that I thought good but felt myself bound to reject most of them, as they seemed to have been prompted by party interests, or to be weak. For instance, M. Thiers, who had adopted such a madly risky policy in 1840, and thereafter, as his way was, seeing only one object at a time, was in favor of unlimited tolerance, said to me . . . (try and remember his very characteristic expression).

wonderfully. Rémusat, who, without personal pretensions to forward, sincerely wanted the Cabinet to survive and who had
had twenty five years in which to become familiar with M.
Thiers' weaknesses, once said to me: "The world does not understand M. Thiers; he has much more vanity than ambition; he
values respect more than obedience, and the appearance of
power more than its substance. Consult him a lot, and then do
as you please. He will care more about your deference than
about your actions."

I acted accordingly and with great success. In the two main
problems needing attention during my term of office, Piedmont
and Turkey, I did exactly the opposite of what M. Thiers desired, and nonetheless we stayed quite good friends to the end.

As for the President, it was foreign affairs especially that revealed how ill-prepared he was for the role thrust on him by
blind fate. I very soon realized that this man, whose vanity made
him long to manage everything, had not the sense to take the
slightest step to keep informed about anything. It was I who
suggested having a daily analysis of all the dispatches made and
shown to him. Before that he had relied on hearsay for any
knowledge of what went on in the world and knew only what
the Minister of Foreign Affairs thought fit to tell him. His mental
manoeuvres, therefore, always lacked a solid background of fact,
as one could easily see from the wild dreams that filled his mind.

Sometimes I took alarm at seeing how vast, fantastic, unscru-
pulous and confused his plans were. Admittedly, when I explained the true state of affairs, I easily got him to agree about
the difficulties in the way, for argument was not his strong suit.
He fell silent, but he did not yield. One of his fantasies was
an alliance with one of the two great powers of Germany to
help him redraw the map of Europe and wipe out the boundaries imposed on France after 1815. When he saw that I did
not think there was a chance of finding either of those two
powers inclined to accept an alliance of that sort and aid him
in such a scheme, he decided to sound out their ambassadors
in Paris himself. One day one of them came to me in great excitement to tell me that the President of the Republic had asked
him whether, in return for an equivalent, his Court would allow

France to gain possession of Savoy. On another occasion he took it into his head to send a private envoy, a man of his own as he called him, to come to a direct understanding with the rulers of Germany. He chose Persigny and asked me to provide him with credentials, which I did, knowing well that nothing would come of such a negotiation. I think that Persigny had a double mission: he was to facilitate usurpation at home and aggrandizement abroad. He went to Berlin first and then to Vienna; as I had anticipated, he was well received, fêted and sent on his way.

But that is enough about persons, let us now turn to policies.

When I came into office, Europe was, so to speak, on fire, although by then the blaze had been put out in certain countries.

Sicily had been conquered and subdued; the Neapolitans had returned to their obedience or even slavery; the Battle of Novara had been fought and lost; the victorious Austrians were negotiating with the son of Charles Albert, King of Piedmont after his father's abdication; beyond the frontiers of Lombardy, Austrian armies occupied part of the Papal States, Parma, Piacenza, and even Tuscany where they had come in uninvited and in spite of the fact that the Grand Duke had been restored by his own subjects, who were very ill-repaid later for their loyalty and zeal. But Venice still held out, and Rome, having repulsed our first attack, was calling all the demagogues in Italy to its aid and exciting the whole of Europe with its clamour. Never, perhaps, since February had Germany seemed more divided or disturbed. Although the fantasy of German unity had gone, the reality of the old Germanic organization had not yet reassumed its rank.[4] The National Assembly, which had until then been trying to create this unity, was reduced to a few members and had fled from Frankfurt; it was hawking around from place to place the spectacle of its impotence and ridiculous rages. But its fall did not restore order; on the contrary, it left a freer field for anarchy.

The moderate revolutionaries, one might call them the innocent ones, who believed that arguments and decrees could bring

[4] *Marginal note* (*Tocqueville*): The whole state of Germany ought to be explained earlier in connection with my visit to Frankfurt.

the peoples and princes of Germany to submit peacefully to a single government, had failed and withdrawn discouraged from the stage, leaving room for the violent revolutionaries, who had always maintained that Germany could be led to unity only by the complete destruction of all its former governments and the abolition of the old social order. Thus on all sides riots took the place of parliamentary debates. Political rivalries turned into class warfare; the natural hatreds and jealousies of the poor against the rich became socialist theories in many places, especially in the small States of Germany and in the great Rhine valley. Würt-temberg was disturbed; there had just been a terrible insurrection in Saxony, which had been suppressed only with help from Prussia; Westphalia, too, had been disturbed by insurrections; the Palatinate was in open rebellion, and the people of Baden had just driven out their Grand Duke and appointed a provisional government. Nonetheless, the final victory of the princes, which I had foreseen when travelling through Germany a month before, was no longer in doubt; these acts of violence actually precipitated it. The large monarchies had regained their capitals and control of their armies. Their rulers still had difficulties to overcome, but not dangers. Being, or shortly to become, masters in their own States, they could not fail to gain the mastery in the States of secondary importance. For such violent disturbance of public order had given them the desire, the chance and the right to intervene.

Prussia had already begun to do this; Prussian arms had suppressed the rebellion in Saxony; they were marching into the Palatinate of the Rhine, offered to intervene in Württemberg and were on the point of invading the Grand Duchy of Baden. In this way almost the whole of Germany was filled with their soldiers or their influence.

Austria had come through the terrible crisis threatening her existence, but she was still in great trouble. Her armies had been victorious in Italy, but defeated in Hungary. Despairing of getting the better of her subjects by herself, she had called on Russia for assistance, and the Tsar's manifesto of the 13th May had just announced to Europe that he would march against the Hungarians.

Until then the Emperor Nicholas had stayed calm in his undisputed might. He had seen the agitation of nations from afar, secure but not indifferent. He alone of all the powerful governments represented the old society and the ancient traditional principle of authority in Europe. He was not only the representative but considered himself the champion of it. His political theories, religious beliefs, ambition and conscience equally urged him to play his part. He had therefore turned the cause of authority in the world into a sort of second empire even vaster than the first, encouraging by his letters and rewarding by his decorations all those who, in whatsoever corner of Europe, won victories over anarchy, or even over liberty, as if they were his subjects and had helped to assure his own power. Accordingly he had just sent one of his decorations to the extreme south of Europe, to Filangieri, the conqueror of the Sicilians, and he had written him a signed letter expressing his satisfaction with his conduct as general. From the lofty superiority of his position the Emperor tranquilly considered the various incidents of the struggle convulsing Europe, judging matters freely and with a certain contempt not only for the follies of the revolutionaries whom he was pursuing, but also for the vices and mistakes of those parties and princes to whose help he was coming. He expressed himself simply on this matter as the occasion arose, without either eagerness to expound his thoughts or concern to hide them.

"The Tsar told me this morning," Lamoricière wrote in a secret dispatch of 11 August 1849, "'You think, General, that your dynastic parties would be capable of combining with the radicals to overthrow a dynasty they dislike in the hope of setting their candidate in its place; and I am sure that is so. Your Legitimist Party, in particular, would not hesitate to do that. I have long thought that it is the Legitimists who make the elder branch of the Bourbons impossible. That is one of the reasons why I have recognized the Republic; another reason is that I discern an element of common sense in your nation, which the Germans lack.'

"Later on the Emperor made this comment to me: 'My brother-in-law, the King of Prussia, with whom I had close ties of friendship, has taken no notice of my advice. A pronounced coolness in our political relations has had its effects even on our family relations.

"'Look at his behaviour: putting himself at the head of the madmen who dream of German unity! And now that he has broken with the Frankfurt Parliament, hasn't he just had to agree to fight himself, if necessary, against the troops of the Duchies of Schleswig and Holstein, troops that were recruited under his patronage! Can you imagine anything more discreditable? And at the moment, who knows where he is going with his project for a constitution?' He added: 'Don't think that because I intervene in Hungary, I wish to justify Austria's conduct in that matter. Austria has piled mistake on serious mistake and tremendous folly on follies; but, when all is said and done, she allowed the country to be invaded by subversive doctrines; government there had fallen into the hands of men serving the forces of disorder. That could not be tolerated.' Speaking of Italian affairs, he said, 'We Greeks have no taste for ecclesiastics performing secular duties at Rome; but it matters very little to us how those clerics arrange things among themselves, provided that something is fixed that holds, and that you establish the authorities there in such a way that they can maintain themselves.'"

When Lamoricière, who was wounded by the frivolous and slightly autocratic tone of these remarks, combined with a sort of rivalry as between one pope and another, felt it his duty to defend Catholic institutions: "All right, all right," said the Emperor bringing the conversation to an end. "Let France be as Catholic as she chooses; only let her keep clear of the theories and mad passions of the innovators."

Hard and austere in the exercise of his power, the Tsar was simple and almost bourgeois in his habits, keeping only the substance of power and letting the pomp and the fuss go. On the 17th July the French agent at Saint Petersburg wrote to me from Warsaw: "The Emperor has been here since the 12th; he arrived unexpectedly and without any escort in a post chaise (his own coach having broken down sixty leagues away), so as to be in time for the Empress' saint's day which has just been celebrated. He did the journey extraordinarily quickly in two days and a half and is going back tomorrow. People here are struck by the contrast between simplicity and power, seeing a sovereign who has launched a hundred and twenty thousand men on the battlefield travelling over the roads like a courier so as not to miss his wife's saint's day. Nothing could be more in keeping with the spirit of the Slavs, for family feeling is the mainspring of their civilization."

It would, of course, be a great mistake to suppose that the immense power of the Tsar was based on nothing but force: its firmest foundations lay in the wishes and ardent sympathies of the Russian people. For, whatever anyone says, the principle of the sovereignty of the people is at the base of all forms of government, and it hides under the least free of institutions. The Russian nobility had taken over the principles and, especially, the vices of Europe; but the Russian people had no contact with our West and the new spirit stirring it. The people saw the Emperor not only as the legitimate ruler but also as God's representative and almost as God himself.

In the Europe I have just described, France's situation was embarrassed and weak. The revolution had nowhere succeeded in establishing an orderly and stable freedom. Everywhere the former powers were in process of rising up again from the revolutionary ruins, not, it is true, quite the same as when they fell, but very similar. We could not help them strengthen their position or make their victory secure, because they were establishing regimes antipathetic to not merely the institutions created by the February Revolution but the very basis of our ideas, to all that is most permanent and invincible in our new mores. Moreover they distrusted us, and with reason. So we could not play the main role as restorers of order throughout Europe. In any case someone else was already cast for that part: it belonged as if by right to Russia, and only the supporting role would have been left for us. It was even more impossible to dream of putting France at the head of the innovators for two reasons: first, it was absolutely impossible to advise the present leaders and fancy that one was leading them, because of their exorbitance and infuriating lack of experience; secondly, we could not support them abroad without falling under their attack at home. Contact with their passions and their doctrines would quickly have set France on fire, and questions of revolution would have dominated all other matters.[5] We could not therefore combine with the peoples who accused us of inciting and then betraying them, or with the princes who blamed us for shaking their thrones. We were left with nothing but the sterile goodwill of the English; the isolation was the same as it had been before February, except that the Continent was more hostile and England more lukewarm. So it was necessary to carry on humbly from day to day as we had done, but even that was difficult. The French nation, which had once cut such a figure in the world and, in some respects, still did, kicked back against the necessity of the time, though seeing the need for it. Preponderance had gone, but pride remained: the nation feared to act but wished to raise its voice; it insisted that its government should act proudly, but would not allow it to take the risks of such a role.

It was a sorry plight to be a minister of Foreign Affairs in such a country at such a time.[6]

[5] *The following passage is marked for omission in the manuscript:* Moreover the wars of principle into which we would have been dragged by following this path would have forced us, in order to avoid conquest, to loose with our own hands the furies of revolution. Between those two extremes there was no room to attempt any great enterprise or form any great alliance.
[6] *There follows the long passage which Tocqueville wished to omit because, he writes,* ". . . this interrupts the movement":

After deep reflection about the matters I have just mentioned, I adopted two maxims of conduct, which were of great use to me during my brief term as Minister of Foreign Affairs, and which, I think, should be followed by anybody in charge of France's external relations in the age in which we live.

The first was unreservedly to break with the revolutionary party abroad: we were in no state to imitate Richelieu's act when he crushed the Protestants in France at the same time that he was helping them to rise in Germany. But equally I resolved not to let myself be carried on to a denial of the principles of our Revolution: liberty, equality and clemency. I would work for the restoration of order but without ever sharing the passionate feelings of former rulers whom it was in any case impossible to win over; thus France should, though fighting the revolution, not lose her proper and natural reputation among the nations as a liberal country. Of course, such an attitude could not reap great dividends in the short run, for licence had badly discredited the Republic, but it would at least

Never had France been the cynosure of more anxious attention than at the moment when the Cabinet was formed. The ease and completeness of our victory in Paris on the 13th June had repercussions throughout Europe. Some new rebellion in France had been generally anticipated. That was the one event on which the half-suppressed revolutionaries counted for their rehabilitation, and they redoubled their efforts in order to be able to take advantage of it. The half-victorious governments, fearing to be caught off guard by such a crisis, held their hands before striking their final blows. The 13th June was greeted with cries of grief or of joy from one end of Europe to the other. It tipped the balance at once and set armies moving towards the other side of the Rhine.

The Prussian Army, already in control of the Rhenish

---

serve a turn and make France respected, while biding time to make her feared.

A second maxim was never to attempt anything obviously beyond our powers; never to promise what we could not perform; not to encourage those we could not support, or threaten those we could not strike; in a word, not to aspire to the rank that was ours in other ages but that we could not maintain in the present state of the world, but yet to be proud of the high position that did remain to us, and, facing all risks, to hold that position, should it be disputed. Also, should the President or the Assembly trouble me, to resign at once. "Gentlemen," I said to the ambassadors on the first occasion when they came to see me, "I am no diplomat, and I will say my last word at the very start and after that change nothing. I know that France is in no state to dominate Europe and make her wishes prevail in distant lands. Therefore we shall not attempt that. You can count on us leaving you perfectly free in matters beyond our scope, for we shall not worry about making ourselves look important and pretend to be concurring in such things. But in bordering countries and on questions that affect her directly, France has the right to exercise not just great but preponderant influence. We will not meddle in what happens at the far end of Europe, in the Principalities, in Poland, or in Hungary. But I warn you that you cannot do anything in Belgium, Switzerland, or Piedmont without our advice and concurrence. There we shall not limit ourselves to negotiation but will, if need be, go to war, risking everything to keep our position. I am not trying to hide the fact that a foreign war would be very difficult and dangerous for us at this moment, for the whole social structure might break under the strain, sweeping away our fortunes and our lives. Nevertheless you must realize that, in the case I mentioned, we would even go to war. At least you can be quite certain that I should resign if the President or the Assembly were not ready to follow me so far."

I expressed myself in similar terms to our representatives at all the Courts.

Palatinate, marched into the Grand Duchy of Baden, scattered the rebels, and occupied the whole country except for Rastadt, which held out for a few weeks.[7]

[7] *Here follows another passage, put in a note by the Editor of the first edition, which Tocqueville would have omitted: "To cut out perhaps, at least when reading it aloud." (Tocqueville probably read several chapters of the Recollections to his wife. [Ed.])*

Nothing could have been more wretched than the behaviour of these revolutionaries. The soldiers, who at the beginning of the rebellion had driven out or killed their officers, turned tail before the Prussians. Their leaders did nothing but argue and insult each other instead of defending themselves and then fled to Switzerland after pillaging the public treasuries and holding their own countries up for ransom.

While the struggle lasted, we maintained a very strict control to prevent the rebels from receiving any help from France. The great numbers of them who crossed the Rhine were given asylum by us, but disarmed and interned. The victors, as one could readily have foreseen, immediately abused their victory. Many prisoners were put to death, all liberties were indefinitely suspended, and even the goverment, which had just been restored, was kept under strict supervision. I soon saw that France's representative in the Grand Duchy, far from trying to restrain these abuses, thoroughly approved of them. I at once wrote to him:

Sir,

I am informed that a number of military executions have taken place and that many more are announced. I cannot understand why these facts were not reported by you, or why, without having to wait for our instructions, you did not attempt to prevent them. We have helped, as far as was possible without joining in the struggle, to suppress the rebellion; that is an additional reason for desiring that the victory to which we contributed should not be soiled by acts of violence of which France disapproves, and which we judge to be both hateful and impolitic. There is another matter that causes me great concern, but that does not seem to be of equal importance to you. I refer to the political institutions of the Grand Duchy. Do not forget that the government of the Republic intended to help suppress anarchy in that country, but not to abolish liberty: we cannot in any way assist an anti-liberal restoration. The Constitutional Monarchy needed to maintain free States on France's borders. Even more does the Republic need to do so. Therefore the government asks all its agents loyally to conform to the necessities of our situation, and it categorically commands that each of them should do so. See the Grand Duke and make him understand clearly what France desires. We shall certainly never allow a Prussian province to be established on our border, or an absolute government to be put in the place of an independent constitutional one.

Shortly afterwards the executions ceased. The Grand Duke protested his attachment to constitutional forms and his resolution to maintain them. For the moment that was all that could be done [for he was only the nominal ruler. The Prussians were the real masters]. *The words between brackets are marked for omission in the manuscript.*

The revolutionaries in the Grand Duchy took refuge in Switzerland. Just then refugees were pouring into that country from Italy, France, and all the corners of Europe, for, Russia excepted, the whole of Europe had recently been, or still was, in a state of revolution. Soon the refugees amounted to ten or twelve thousand. That was an army ever ready to fall on the neighbouring States. Every Cabinet felt alarmed.

Austria and, worse, Prussia, both of whom had had occasion previously to complain of the Confederation, and also Russia, who was hardly concerned, spoke of an armed invasion of Swiss territory and of policing the country in the name of the threatened governments. That was something that we could not tolerate.

At first I tried to make the Swiss see reason: I urged them not to wait to be threatened, but, in accordance with their obligations under the law of nations, to drive out of their territory all the main leaders who were overtly threatening the tranquillity of neighbouring nations.

"If in this way you anticipate the requests that could fairly be made to you," I kept saying to the Swiss Representative in Paris, "you can rely on France to protect you against any unfair or exaggerated claims from the Courts. We would rather risk war than see you oppressed or humiliated by them. But if you do not first put yourselves in the right, then count on yourselves alone and defend yourselves alone against the whole of Europe."

This had little effect, for there is nothing to equal the pride and presumption of the Swiss. There is not one of those peasants but firmly believes that his country can defy all the princes and nations of the earth. I then took the matter up in a different way with better results. This was to advise all the foreign governments, who were only too willing to take the advice, not to grant any amnesty for a certain time to those of their subjects who had fled to Switzerland and to refuse them all, no matter what their degree of guilt, permission to return to their own country. For our part, we closed our frontiers to all who had taken refuge in Switzerland and wanted to go across France on their way to England or America, stopping the crowd of inoffensive refugees as well as their leaders. All outlets being thus closed, the Swiss were left encumbered by between ten and twelve thousand adventurers, the most turbulent and disorderly people in Europe. They had to be fed, lodged, and even paid to prevent them from plundering the country. For the Swiss, this cast a sudden light on the drawbacks of the right of asylum. They could easily have arranged to keep a few distinguished leaders indefinitely in spite of the danger to the neighbouring states, but they found a revolutionary army very uncomfortable. The most radical cantons were the first to raise a clamour to be freed as quickly as possible from these inconvenient and expensive guests. And as it was impossible to get foreign governments to open their frontiers to the crowd of harmless refugees able and willing to leave Switzerland unless they first turned out the leaders who would have liked to stay there, in the end they did expel those leaders. After they had nearly brought the whole of Europe down on them rather than drive these men from their territory, the Swiss ended by expelling them in order to avoid a temporary inconvenience and a moderate expense. There could be no better example of the nature of democracies, which generally have only very confused and mistaken ideas about foreign affairs[8] and invariably decide questions of foreign policy for reasons of internal convenience.

While these things were going on in Switzerland, there was a change in the general aspect of affairs in Germany. The peoples' struggle against their government had been followed by the rulers' quarrels among themselves. I followed this new phase of the revolution with close attention and in great perplexity.

The revolution in Germany, unlike that in the rest of Europe, was not due to one single cause: both the general spirit of the times and ideas of unity peculiar to Germany played their part in it. At the moment demagogy had been defeated, but the thought of German unity had not been eradicated; the

[8] *The following sentence is marked for omission in the manuscript:* Always unaware of the true state of the forces of their enemies, and even of their own.

needs, memories and passions that had inspired it survived. The King of Prussia undertook to take it over and make use of it. That prince, a man of parts but with little common sense, had been wavering between fear of the revolution and eagerness to profit from it. He struggled as much as he could, or dared, against the liberal and democratic spirit of the age, yet he favoured aspirations to German unity: it was a blundering game in which, had he gone as far as he longed to go, he would have risked crown and life. For, in order to break down the resistance that existing institutions and the interests of rulers must inevitably put up against the establishment of a central power, he would have had to call to his aid the revolutionary passions of the peoples; but Frederick William could not make use of those without himself being shortly destroyed by them.

So long as the Frankfurt Parliament retained its prestige and power, the King of Prussia treated it diplomatically, trying to contrive matters so that it should put him at the head of the new empire. When the Frankfurt Parliament lost its reputation and its power, the King changed his behaviour but not his aim. He tried to make himself the heir of that Assembly and to make the dream of German unity a reality in order to combat the revolution, although the same dream had been used by the democrats to shake every throne. With this object in view, he invited all the German princes to agree to the formation of a new confederation more close-knit than that of 1815, and to give the direction of it to him. In return he would undertake to re-establish them in their States and make them secure there. These princes, detesting Prussia but terrified of the revolution, by and large accepted the usurious terms offered. Austria, which would have been driven out of Germany by the success of such a scheme, protested, unable to do more yet. The two main monarchies of the south, Bavaria and Württemberg, followed the Austrian example, but all the north and centre of Germany joined the ephemeral confederation that came into being on 26 May 1849 and is known to history as the Union of the Three Kings.

Thus Prussia suddenly became predominant throughout a vast stretch of land from Memel to Basle, and for a moment twenty six or twenty seven million Germans marched under her orders. All this had come about shortly after my arrival in office.

I confess that some strange ideas crossed my mind as I contemplated this remarkable spectacle, and I thought that perhaps the President was not so mad in his foreign policy as at first he seemed to me to be. That union of the northern Courts, which for so long had weighed on us, was broken. Two of the great continental monarchies, Prussia and Austria, were quarrelling and almost at war. Had not the moment come for us to form one of those intimate and fruitful alliances that for sixty years we had done without, and perhaps to make good some of the damage done in 1815? France, by helping Frederick William in this undertaking, which would not be opposed by England, could divide Europe and bring on one of those great crises that necessitate the redrawing of frontiers.

The times seemed so well suited to ideas of this sort that the minds of several of the German princes, too, were filled with them. The more powerful among them dreamed of nothing but changes of frontier and increases of power at their neighbours' expense. The revolutionary sickness of the peoples seemed to have infected the governments.

"No confederation is possible with thirty eight states," the Prime Minister of Bavaria, M. von der Pfordten, told our Ambassador. "We must mediatize a great many of them. How, for instance, can one hope to re-establish order in a country like the Grand Duchy of Baden unless one divides it among sovereigns strong enough to enforce obedience? In such a case," he added, "the valley of the Neckar would naturally fall to us."[9]

For my part I soon dispelled from my mind all such thoughts, considering them mere fantasies.

I soon realized that Prussia neither could nor would give us anything considerable in return for our good offices; that her power over the other German States was very precarious and would prove ephemeral; that one should put no reliance on the

[9] *Note by Tocqueville:* Dispatch of 7 September 1849.

Prussian King who at the first obstacle would fail us by failing himself; and, above all, that such wide-ranging plans were not suited to the unstable state of our society in dangerous and troubled times, nor could they suitably be handled by one, like myself, to whom chance had tossed a short-lived power.

There was one more serious question I put to myself; I mention it here because one should constantly bear it in mind: is it to France's interest that the bonds of a German Confederation should be drawn tighter, or relaxed? In other words, should we desire Germany to become in some respects a single nation, or should it remain an ill-joined aggregate of disunited peoples and princes? It is an ancient tradition of our diplomacy that we must strive to keep Germany divided among a great number of independent powers; that, of course, was obvious when there was nothing on the farther side of Germany but Poland and a semi-barbarous Russia; but is that still so in our day? One's answer to the question must depend on how one answers this other query: how far is Russia a real threat to European independence now? I think that the West is in danger of falling sooner or later under the yoke, or at least under the direct and irresistible influence of the Tsars, and I think that it is in our prime interest to favour the union of all the German peoples in order to oppose that influence. The state of the world is new: we must change our old maxims and not be afraid to strengthen our neighbour so that he may one day be in a position to help us repulse the common enemy.

From his point of view the Emperor of Russia sees what an obstacle a united Germany would be to him. In one of his private letters Lamoricière told me that the Emperor had said to him one day with his usual frankness and arrogance: "If the unification of Germany, which you doubtless desire as little as I do, should come about, it will require a man capable of things that Napoleon himself could not do to manage it; if such a man should come to the fore and all that mass of armed men become a menace, it would be our business, yours and mine, to see to it."

But the time when I was considering these problems was

not the right time for solving them, or even for arguing about
them, for Germany was irresistibly turning back of her own
accord to her former Constitution and the ancient anarchy of
rival authorities. The Frankfurt Assembly's attempt at unity
had failed. And the King of Prussia's efforts were to have the
same fate.

It was nothing but fear of the revolution that had driven
the German princes into Frederick William's arms; as soon as,
thanks to the Prussians, the revolution, suppressed everywhere,
no longer made them afraid, the allies, whom one might almost
call the new subjects of Prussia, aspired to regain their independence. The King of Prussia's enterprise was of the unhappy
sort in which success itself makes ultimate triumph harder, and,
comparing great things to small, his position was a little like
our own, for, like us, he was fated to fail when he had re-
established order and because he had re-established it. The
princes who had adhered to what was called the Prussian
hegemony seized the first opportunity to renounce it. Austria
gave them that chance when, having vanquished the Hungarians,
she could reappear on the German stage with all her material
strength and the memories clustering around her name. That
was what happened in the course of September 1849. When the
King of Prussia found himself face to face with his powerful
rival, behind whom he could see Russia, his heart suddenly
failed him, and, as I had expected, he gradually drew back to
his former position. The German Constitution of 1815 resumed
its sway, and the Diet met again; and soon there were only
two visible remains in Germany of the great upheaval of 1848:
the small States were more dependent on the great monarchies;
and all that was left of feudal institutions had suffered an
irreparable blow: their abolition, achieved by the peoples, was
sanctioned by the princes. From one end of Germany to the
other, ground rents in perpetuity, baronial tithes, forced labour,
rights of transfer, hunting and justice, all of which constituted
a great part of the wealth of the nobles, remained abolished.[10]

[10] *Note by Tocqueville:* Private letter from Beaumont at Vienna on
10 October 1849.—M. Lefèbre's dispatch from Munich on 23 July 1849.

The kings were restored, but the aristocracies did not lift their heads again.[11]

Being early convinced that we should play no part in this internal German crisis, I simply strove to keep on good terms with all the various contending parties. I took special trouble to keep on friendly terms with Austria whose concurrence was, as I shall mention later, needed by us in the Roman business. I strove first to bring her long drawn-out negotiations with Piedmont to a satisfactory conclusion; I took special trouble about that matter, being convinced that until it was settled and a durable peace established in that part of the world Europe could not settle down but might at any moment be thrown back into the greatest dangers.

Piedmont had been negotiating with Austria to no purpose ever since the Battle of Novara. At first, Austria wanted to impose unacceptable conditions. Whereas Piedmont maintained pretensions no longer authorized by the state of her fortunes. The negotiations had just been reopened after several interruptions when I took office. We had several strong reasons for

[11] *Here follows the third passage that Tocqueville intended to omit:* "To be cut," *he wrote,* "or put in a note; this breaks the thread of the thought," *which the Editor of the first edition did put in a note:*

From the start I had foreseen that Austria and Prussia would soon return to their former sphere and both fall back under Russia's influence. I have a record of this foresight in the instructions I gave on the 24th July, a long time before the events I have just recorded, to one of our ambassadors who was passing through Germany. These instructions, in common with all my more important dispatches, were drawn up in my own hand. They read as follows:

I know that the disease that is attacking all the old societies of Europe is incurable; that when the symptoms change, the nature of the malady does not; and that all the old authorities more or less are threatened with modification or abolition. But it would not take much to convince me that the next event will be the reassertion of authority throughout Europe. It is not impossible that, under the pressure of a common need for defence and a common memory of recent events, Russia might have the desire and the power to bring about an understanding between northern and central Germany, bringing Austria and Prussia together; and that all this great upheaval might end in no more than a new alliance in principle between the three Monarchies at the expense of the less powerful governments and the liberty of citizens. Consider the position from this point of view and let me have your comments.

wishing peace to be established quickly in that quarter. Nothing in Europe could settle down permanently while that situation was in suspense. At any moment a general war might start from that corner of the continent. Besides, Piedmont was too close to us for us to allow her to lose the independence that kept her separate from Austria or to relinquish the new-found constitutional institutions that linked her to us. But a recourse to arms would risk both these things.

Accordingly, in the name of France, I eagerly interposed between the parties, addressing each in the language I thought most likely to convince it.

To Austria I pointed out the urgent need to use peace there to restore the general peace of Europe, and I went out of my way to demonstrate what was excessive in her demands.

To Piedmont I explained on what points I felt honour and interest would allow her to yield. I took especial pains to give the Piedmontese Government a clear and precise idea beforehand of what they could expect from us, so that they could not entertain or pretend to have entertained dangerous illusions.[12]

12 *In a note:* Dispatch of the 4th July to M. Boislecomte. *Marginal Note* (*Tocqueville*): To be put, I think, in a note.
Undoubtedly the conditions proposed by the Government of H.M. the Emperor of Austria are severe, but they are not a threat to the territorial integrity or the honour of Piedmont. They by no means deprive her of the power she ought to keep or of the healthy influence she should exercise over the politics of Europe in general and those of Italy in particular. The treaty she is asked to sign is certainly vexatious but not disastrous, and, after the fate of arms has been decided, it does not go beyond what was naturally to be feared.
France has done, and will continue to do, all she can to secure modifications to the draft; she will insist on the Austrian Government's making those changes she considers important, not in the interest of Piedmont alone but to facilitate a durable general peace; for this purpose she will make use of every possible diplomatic expedient, but she will not go beyond that. For, in view of the scale of the whole question and of the Piedmontese interests at stake, she does not think it opportune to do more. Such being her fixed and considered opinion, she does not hesitate to let it be known. To give the impression even by silence that extreme resolutions have been taken that have not been taken; to raise hopes one is not sure one will wish to realize; to urge others by words into action one does not feel bound to support by acts; in a word, to let others become involved without being involved oneself or, without knowing it, to get

I will not deal with the details of the conditions discussed, which are of no interest now; I need only say that finally the parties seemed on the point of agreement and a question of money was almost the only outstanding matter in dispute. This was the way things stood, and Austria had assured us through her Ambassador in Paris of her conciliatory disposition. I thought peace was already concluded when I heard that the Austrian Plenipotentiary had suddenly changed both attitude and language, having, on the 19th July, issued an ultimatum in very harsh and rigorous terms, leaving only four days for a reply. When those four days had expired, the armistice would be renounced and war would start again. Marshal Radetzky was already concentrating his army and making ready for a fresh campaign. After the pacific assurance we had received, the news came as a rude shock to me. Such excessive demands presented with such overbearing arrogance seemed to show that peace was not Austria's only aim and that she wished to threaten the independence, and perhaps the representative institutions of Piedmont, for, as long as liberty is to be seen in any corner of Italy, Austria feels ill at ease in all the rest.

I at once felt that on no account could we allow so close a neighbour to be oppressed, Austrian armies to occupy lands on our frontier, and political liberty to be destroyed in the one place where, since 1848, it had proved itself moderate. I also thought that Austria's behaviour towards ourselves indicated either an intention to deceive us or an attempt to discover how far our tolerance would stretch, to "sound us out" as one says.

I saw that this was one of those extreme cases that I had foreseen when I ought to risk not only my own tenure of office (and, of course, that was not much to risk) but also the fate

---

more involved than one realizes or desires: such behaviour, whether in a government or a private person, seems to me neither wise nor honest.

You may count on it, sir, that as long as I hold the post entrusted to me by the President, the Government of the Republic will not incur such a reproach; it will announce no intention that it is not ready to put into practice; it will make no promise that it is not resolved to keep; and it will feel it as much a point of honour to say in advance what it does not want to do, as promptly and vigorously to execute what it has said it will do.

Please read this dispatch to M. d'Azeglio.

of France. I went to the Cabinet meeting and explained the position.

The President and all my colleagues unanimously favoured action. Immediately, telegrams were sent ordering the army of Lyon to be concentrated at the foot of the Alps, and on my return home I personally (for the flaccid style of diplomacy was not suited to the circumstances) wrote the following letter[13]:

> If the Austrian Government persists in the demands outlined in your telegram of yesterday and if, overstepping the limits of diplomatic discussion, it renounces the armistice and sets out, as your telegram states, to dictate peace at Turin, Piedmont can be assured that we will not abandon her. The situation would not be the same as that after the Battle of Novara, when Piedmont of her own accord and against our advice took up arms and started the war again. In this case Austria would be taking the initiative without provocation; the nature of her demands and the violence with which they are pressed give us reason to believe that she is not concerned solely with peace, but that she is threatening the integrity of Piedmontese territory or at least the independence of the Sardinian Government.
>
> We will not allow such plans to succeed on our doorstep. If in such circumstances Piedmont is attacked, we will defend her.

I thought I ought also to summon the Austrian Representative to see me. He was a little man, very like a fox in both appearance and character. Convinced that, with such intentions in mind, the path of prudence was to show my anger, I took advantage of the fact that I could not yet be expected to be familiar with habits of diplomatic reserve to express our surprise and annoyance in such rude fashion that, as he told me afterwards, he had never been so badly received in his life before.

Before the telegram from which I have quoted reached Turin, the two powers had come to an agreement. The money question was settled, more or less on the terms we had earlier suggested.

The Austrian Government had wished only to bring the negotiations to a head by frightening the other side; it proved easy about settling the terms.

Prince Schwarzenberg sent me all sorts of explanations and excuses. Peace was finally signed on the 6th August. The terms were better than Piedmont could have hoped after so many

[13] *In a note:* Letter of the 25th July to M. Boislecomte.

mistakes and misfortunes, for they gave her more advantages than she had at first dared to ask.

This affair cast a strong light on English diplomacy and in particular that of Lord Palmerston who was then in charge. It is worth describing how it appeared. From the beginning of the negotiations England had consistently shown great animosity towards Austria, loftily advising the Piedmontese not to submit to the conditions the Austrians wanted to impose, which they had made very plain at Turin. My first concern, having just taken the before-mentioned resolutions, was to inform England about them and try to enlist her co-operation. Accordingly, I sent my dispatch to Drouyn de Lhuys, who was our Ambassador in London, requesting him to read it to Palmerston and try to find out that Minister's intentions.

"While I was informing Lord Palmerston of the resolutions you had taken and the instructions sent to M. Boislecomte," Drouyn de Lhuys answered me,[14] "he listened with every sign of lively approval. But when I said to him, 'You see my lord how far we are ready to go. Could you let me know how far you are ready to go yourselves?' Lord Palmerston at once replied, 'The British Government, whose interest in this matter is not as great as yours, will give the Piedmontese only diplomatic assistance and moral support.'"

Is that not characteristic?

England, protected from the revolutionary sickness by the wisdom of her laws and the strength of her ancient mores and protected from the anger of princes by her power and her isolation in our midst, likes to play the part of advocate of freedom and justice in the internal affairs of the Continent. She likes to censure and even insult the strong and to vindicate and encourage the weak. But for England it seems to be merely a matter of striking a good pose and discussing a reputable theory. If her protégés come to need her, she offers her moral support.

I must add, before changing the subject, that this procedure worked out very well for her. The Piedmontese remained convinced that England alone had defended them, whereas we

[14] *In a note:* Dispatches of the 25th and 26th July 1849.

had almost abandoned them. England remained extremely popular at Turin, while France was treated with great suspicion. For nations are like men in that they prefer a fuss made on their behalf to real services rendered.

We had hardly emerged from this awkward position before we found ourselves in a worse one. We had watched what was happening in Hungary with sorrow and apprehension, sympathizing with the misfortunes of that unlucky people. We did not, of course, like the Russian intervention, which for a time made Austria subordinate to the Tsar, allowing his hand to stretch farther and farther over the general affairs of Europe. But all this occurred beyond our reach, and we could do nothing.

"I need not tell you," I wrote in instructions to Lamoricière (24 July 1849), "with what acute and sorrowful interest we watch events in Hungary. Unhappily we can as yet play only a passive role in the matter. The letter and the spirit of the treaties offer us no right to intervene, and in any case our distance from the theatre of war would, in the present state of Europe and of our own affairs, impose a certain reserve. As we can neither speak nor act effectively, a sense of our own dignity ordains that we should not show a futile excitement or impotent goodwill. So our duty with regard to events in Hungary is limited to careful observation of what takes place and foresight about what may yet occur."[15]

It will be remembered that the Hungarians, overwhelmed by numbers, were defeated, or surrendered, and that their main leaders, together with a certain number of Polish generals who had joined their cause, crossed the Danube at the end of August, throwing themselves on the mercy of the Turks at Widdin. From there their two chief leaders, Dembinski and Kossuth, wrote to our Ambassador at Constantinople.[16] These letters were characteristic of the two men's habits and ways of thought. The soldier's was short and simple; that of the lawyer and orator was long and ornate. One of the phrases in it that I remember was "As a good Christian I have chosen the inexpressible sorrow of exile over the peace of death." Both ended by asking for French protection.

15 *Marginal note* (*Tocqueville*): Perhaps this should be in a note.
16 *In a note:* Letters of the 22nd and 24th August.

While the outlaws were imploring France for help, the Austrian and Russian Ambassadors appeared before the Divan and asked that they be handed over. Austria based this demand on the Treaty of Belgrade, which gave her no such right; the Russian claim was based on the Treaty of Kainardji (10 July 1774) whose meaning was, to say the least, very obscure. But basically the appeal was not to international law, but to the better known and more often used right of the stronger. Both their behaviour and their language made this plain. From the first day, the two Ambassadors made clear that it was a question of peace or war. Refusing argument, they required a yes-or-no answer and announced that in the event of a negative reply they would immediately break off diplomatic relations with Turkey.

The Turkish ministers answered these violent demands gently, saying that Turkey was a neutral country; that the law of nations forbade them to hand over outlaws who had taken refuge on their territory; and that the Austrians and Russians had often pleaded the same law when asked to hand over Moslem rebels who had sought refuge in Hungary, Transylvania or Bessarabia. They modestly suggested that what was right on the left bank of the Danube should be so on the right bank too. In conclusion they asserted that the demand made on them was contrary to their honour and their religion; that they would gladly agree to intern the refugees and even to put them in places where they could do no harm, but that they could not agree to hand them over to the executioner.

"The young Sultan," our Ambassador informed me, "answered the Austrian Envoy yesterday by declaring that, while he had nothing to say for the behaviour of the Hungarian rebels, he could not now regard them as anything but unlucky men seeking to avoid death, and that humanity forbade his handing them over. Reshid Pasha, the Grand Vizier," our Envoy continued, "said this to me on his behalf: 'If I lose power over this, I shall be proud of it,' and he added with deep conviction, 'According to our religion, any man who asks for mercy should obtain it.'" That was speaking like civilized people and Christians. The Ambassadors replied like Turks, saying that they must give up the fugitives, or suffer the consequences of a rupture that would probably lead to war.

The Moslem population, too, was moved, approving and supporting its government; the Mufti came to thank our ambassador for his aid to the cause of humanity and sound law.

From the beginning of the argument the Divan had addressed itself to the Ambassadors of France and England. It appealed to the public opinion of the two great countries they represented, asking their advice and calling for their aid in case the Northern Powers carried out their threats. The Ambassadors at once replied that in their opinion Austria and Russia were going beyond what was right, and they encouraged the Turkish Government in its resistance.

Meanwhile an aide-de-camp of the Tsar arrived at Constantinople. He brought a letter, which the Tsar had taken the trouble to write in his own hand, demanding the extradition of those Poles who had served during the war in Hungary or, even before that, against the Russian armies. This undignified procedure, out of all proportion to the desired aim (unless one supposes that aim to have been war) seems very strange until one realizes the special reasons that made the Tsar act thus. The following extract from a letter of Lamoricière's very wisely points out what those reasons were and shows how greatly public opinion is feared in that extremity of Europe where it seems to have neither organ nor power.

"The Hungarian war, as you know," he wrote to me,[17] "was embarked on to support the Austrians, who are hated as a people and whose government is not respected, and was very unpopular; it has brought no return and has cost 84,000,000 francs. The Russians hoped, at the cost of all the sacrifices of the campaign, to bring back Bem, Dembinski and the other Polish prisoners to Poland. There is real anger against those men, especially in the army. Soldiers and civilians lost their heads in their desire for this somewhat savage satisfaction to national pride. The Emperor in spite of his omnipotence is obliged to pay a lot of attention to the feelings of the masses on whose support he relies and who are the true basis of his power. For him it is not simply a question of personal dignity: the national feeling of the country and the army are at stake."

17 *In a note:* Dispatches of 11 and 25 October 1849.

There is no doubt that these were the considerations that led the Tsar to take the risky step I have just mentioned. Prince Radziwill presented his letter and obtained nothing. He departed at once, arrogantly refusing the further audience offered him in order to take his leave. And the Russian and Austrian Ambassadors officially announced that all diplomatic relations between their masters and the Divan had ceased.

In these critical circumstances the Divan behaved with a firmness combined with consummate prudence that would have done credit to the most experienced Cabinets in Europe. While the Sultan refused to agree to the requests, or rather the orders, of the two Emperors, he wrote to the Tsar to tell him that he did not wish to discuss the question of law, which involved the interpretation of the terms of treaties, but that he wished to appeal to his friendship and his sense of honour, asking him to approve the Turkish refusal to do something that would lose them the world's respect. He also again offered to put the refugees somewhere where they could do no harm. Abdul Mejid entrusted one of the ablest and wisest men in his Empire, Fuad Effendi, the duty of taking this letter to Saint Petersburg. A similar letter was written to Vienna, but that one was to be presented to the Austrian Emperor by the Turkish Envoy resident at his court, a nuance of behaviour that clearly showed the relative importance attached to the agreement of each of the two Emperors. News of this reached me towards the end of September. My first concern was to communicate it to England. At the same time I wrote a private letter[18] to our Ambassador in which I said:

> The behaviour of England, who is more concerned in this affair than we are and less exposed to danger if a conflict results, in this matter should have a great influence on our own. The English Cabinet must say clearly and categorically *just how far* it intends to go. I am far from forgetting the Piedmontese affair. If they want anything from us, they must dot their i's. Possibly then they will find us very determined; if not, not. It is also very important that you should ascertain the reaction to these events among Tories of every shade of opinion for, under a parliamentary government, which is of necessity unstable, the support of the party in power is not always a sufficient guarantee.

18 *In a note:* Private letter of 1 October 1849.

Serious though the situation was, the English ministers who had scattered for the parliamentary holidays took rather a long time to reassemble, for in that country, the only one in which an aristocracy still rules, most of the ministers are also great landowners and, as a rule, great noblemen. At that moment they were taking a rest on their estates from the fatigue and boredom of affairs; and they were not in a hurry to leave. In the interval the whole of the English press regardless of party took fire.[19] They raged against the two Emperors and inflamed public opinion in favour of Turkey. With this encouragement the English Government, too, took a stand. It declared that it was not merely a question of the Sultan but of the influence of England in the world.[20] Accordingly it decided:

1. To make representations to Austria and to Russia. 2. That the English Mediterranean squadron should proceed to the Dardanelles to give confidence to the Sultan and, if necessary, to defend Constantinople.

We were invited to do the same and act in concert. The signal to sail was sent to the English fleet that very evening.

The news of these decisive resolutions threw me into great perplexity. I had no hesitation in approving the generous conduct of our Ambassador and backing up the Sultan,[21] but when it came to adopting a belligerent attitude I doubted whether it was prudent to take that line as yet. The English invited us to behave like them, but our position was not at all like theirs. By an armed defence of Turkey, England risked her fleet, but we, our existence. In this extremity the English ministers could count on Parliament and the nation to support them, but we were almost certain to be abandoned by the Assembly and even by the nation if matters went as far as war. At this moment, troubles and dangers at home made men unconscious of all else. Moreover I was convinced that in this case threats, far from forwarding our plans, would work against them. If Russia —for it was Russia alone that counted, Austria being in my view

[19] See K. Martin, *The Triumph of Lord Palmerston. A study of Public Opinion in England before the Crimean War*, London, 1924. (Ed.)
[20] *In a note:* Private letter of 2 October 1849 from Drouyn de Lhuys.
[21] *In a note:* Private letters of 5 and 9 October 1849 to Lamoricière and Beaumont.

no more than a satellite—did by chance desire to open the question of the division of the East by invading Turkey, which was something I could scarcely believe, sending our fleet would not stop that crisis; if, as seemed more likely, it was only a question of revenge against the Poles, it would make things worse, for the Tsar's pride as well as his resentment would become involved, and it would be harder for him to retreat. This was the frame of mind in which I went to the Cabinet meeting. There I at once found that the President had made up his mind and even, as he told us, committed himself. Lord Normanby, the English Ambassador, had inspired this decision. He was a diplomat in the eighteenth-century style and had got well established in Louis Napoleon's good graces by spending his time, and making his wife spend hers too, in the company of Miss Howard, the President's mistress, or, to be more correct, his favourite, for he always had many mistresses at once. Most of my colleagues thought as he did that we should unhesitatingly join in the common action proposed by the English and send our fleet, too, to the Dardanelles.

Unable to persuade them to postpone a decision I regarded as premature, I requested that, before it was executed, Falloux, who had gone for a short rest in the country on account of his health, should at least be consulted. Lanjuinais went to see him, explained the matter, and returned to tell us that Falloux without hesitation had advised sending the fleet. The order was sent out at once. But Falloux had spoken without consulting his friends, the leaders of the majority, and even without careful consideration of the results of such an act; he had yielded to an ill-considered impulse, as sometimes happened with him, for nature had formed him thoughtless and rash, before education and habit had made him calculating to the verge of duplicity. Probably, after talking to Lanjuinais, he received advice, or himself had reflections contrary to the view he had expressed. Accordingly he wrote me a very long and involved letter[22] in which he made out that he had not understood Lanjuinais (which was impossible, Lanjuinais being the plainest and most straightforward of men in word and deed) and anyway there

[22] *In a note:* Letter of 11 October 1849 from Falloux.

was no room for equivocation in the matter. He changed his opinion and tried to cover his responsibility. I at once answered with this letter:

> Dear Colleague, The Cabinet's decision has been taken, and now there is nothing to do but await events; in such a matter, the responsibility of the Cabinet is in any case indivisible. There is no such thing as individual responsibility. I was not in favour of the measure, but now that it is taken I am ready to defend it against all comers.[23]

But though I could teach Falloux a lesson, I was nevertheless anxious and embarrassed by the part I was called upon to play. I hardly bothered at all about what was going to happen in Vienna. But what was the Tsar going to do, now that he had committed himself so rashly and apparently so irrevocably in dealing with the Sultan, and now that his pride had been put to so severe a test by our threats? Luckily, I had at that time at Saint Petersburg and Vienna two able intermediaries to whom I could speak without reserve.

"Handle the business very gently," I requested them.[24] "Be careful not to enlist our adversaries' self-esteem against us. Avoid too great or obvious intimacy with the English Ambassadors whose government is detested at the Courts where you are, while, of course, keeping good relations with those Ambassadors. To gain your point, take a friendly tone and do not try to frighten them. Explain our true situation: we do not want war; we hate it; we fear it; but we cannot act dishonourably. We cannot advise the Porte, which asks our advice, to do a cowardly thing; and when it has shown courage in a way approved by us and is in danger we cannot refuse requested aid. So some way must be found out of the difficulty. Is Kossuth's skin worth a general war? Is it in the Powers' interest that the Eastern question should be opened at this moment and in this way? Can one not find some device to save everybody's face? After all, what is wanted? Do they want only to have a few poor devils handed over to them? That is certainly not worth such serious quarrels. But if that is only a pretext, if fundamentally they want to lay their hands on the Ottoman Empire,

[23] In a note: Letter of 12 October 1849 to Falloux.
[24] In a note: Private letters of 5 and 9 October 1849 to Lamoricière and Beaumont.

then they are certainly asking for a general war, for, ultra-pacific though we be, we should never let Constantinople fall without drawing our sword."

The matter had reached a happy conclusion before these instructions arrived in Saint Petersburg. Lamoricière had, without seeing them, acted in conformity with them. His prudence and restraint in this matter astonished those who did not know him but were no surprise to me. I knew his temper was impetuous, but he was trained in the school of Arab diplomacy, which was the wisest of all, being circumspect and subtle to the point of artifice.

Lamoricière, as soon as rumours of the quarrel reached him directly from Russian sources, promptly made it very plain, although expressing himself as a friend, that he disapproved of what had taken place at Constantinople; but he was careful to make no official and, above all, no threatening representations. While acting in concert with the English Ambassador, he sedulously avoided compromising himself by taking any joint steps with him. And when Fuad Effendi arrived with Abdul Mejid's message, he sent him a secret message saying that he would not go to see him for fear of compromising the success of the negotiation, but that Turkey could count on France.

He was admirably assisted by that Envoy of the Grand Seignior, who concealed under his Turkish skin a very quick and adaptable intelligence. Although the Sultan had requested the support of France and England, Fuad on his arrival in Petersburg would not even visit the representatives of those two powers. He refused to see anybody before he had spoken to the Tsar, on whose unfettered will, so he said, he depended for the success of his mission.

It must have been bitter for the Tsar to see how little success his threats had had and what an unexpected turn things had taken, but he managed to restrain himself. Fundamentally he did not want to open the Eastern question, although a little time before he had let fall the remark, "The Ottoman Empire is dead, all that remains is to arrange for the funeral."

It was a hard thing to go to war to force the Sultan to give up refugees and violate the law of nations. The savage passions of his own people would have been on his side, but public opinion throughout the civilized world would have been against him. He was already aware of what had gone on in France and England. He decided to give way before anybody had time to threaten him. So the great Emperor retreated, to the profound astonishment of his own subjects and even of foreigners. He received Fuad and withdrew the request he had made to the Sultan. Austria hastened to follow his example. When Lord Palmerston's note arrived in Saint Petersburg, everything was over. The best plan would have been to say no more. But whereas we were concerned only for the success of the negotiation, the English Cabinet was also interested in getting the credit for it, for it had to satisfy the excitement in the country. Accordingly, the day after the Emperor's decision became known, Lord Bloomfield, the English Ambassador, called on Count Nesselrode, who received him very coldly,[25] and read him the note in which Lord Palmerston requested in polite but peremptory language that the Sultan should not be forced to give up the refugees. The Russian replied that he could not conceive of the aim or object of this request; that the matter he apparently wanted to discuss had been settled, and that in any case it had nothing to do with England. Lord Bloomfield asked how matters stood. Count Nesselrode haughtily refused to give him any information, "Because," he said, "to do so would be to admit England's right to interfere in a matter that was no concern of hers." The Ambassador insisted on at least leaving a copy of the note in Count Nesselrode's hands. The latter at first refused but in the end accepted it with a bad grace and dismissed his visitor, saying carelessly that he would reply to the note, but it was terribly long and it would be a great bore to do so. "France," the Chancellor added, "has already made the same points, but she expressed them sooner and better."

Just as we learned of the end of this dangerous quarrel, the Cabinet, which had thus seen a happy ending to the two external problems that menaced the peace of the world, the Piedmontese and Hungarian wars, was itself about to fall.

[25] *In a note:* Letter of the 19th October from Lamoricière.

APPENDICES

I

G. de Beaumont's account of the 24th February

Today (24 October 1850) I had a conversation with Beaumont which is worth recording. This is what he said:

At seven o'clock in the morning of the 24th February, Jules Lasteyrie and another man (I have forgotten the name Beaumont mentioned) came to fetch me and take me to M. Thiers' house where Barrot, Duvergier and several others were expected to be.

Tocqueville: – Do you know what passed that night between Thiers and the King?

Beaumont: – I was told by Thiers (and this is confirmed by Duvergier who at once made a note of what Thiers told him) that he had been summoned at about one o'clock and found the King undecided; that he had told him from the very start that he could enter the government only with Barrot and Duvergier; that the King, after raising several objections, appeared to have yielded; that he asked Thiers to come back in the morning; but that, while showing him out, the King had said that they were neither of them committed. (Plainly the King was reserving the right to try out another combination before the morning.)

This is the moment, Beaumont continued, to record an odd story: do you know what Bugeaud was doing on that fateful night, right in the Tuileries where he had just been given supreme command? This is how it was: Bugeaud's ambition and hope was to become Minister of War when Thiers came into office. Things were turning out in such a way that he clearly saw the impossibility of that; but he was concerned to see that his influence at least was predominant in that Ministry even if he was not the Minister. So towards morning on the night of the 24th February in the palace, Bugeaud in his own hand wrote a four-page letter to Thiers, the substance of which was as follows: I understand the difficulties that make it impossible for you to make me your Minister of War, but I have always been fond of you, and I am sure that one day we shall be in the government together; but, of course, I understand the present impediments and yield to them; but I do ask you at least to appoint M. Magne, who has my confidence, as Under-secretary at the Ministry of War.

Beaumont, returning to his main theme, continued: when I got to the Place Saint Georges, Thiers and his friends had already left for the Tuileries. I hurried thither and arrived at the same time as they. Already the look of things in Paris was disturbing, but the King received us in his usual way, as garrulous as ever and with the manners you know. Before seeing him (at least I think that is the moment when Beaumont said this occurred), we were talking business among ourselves. I strenuously pressed for the dismissal of Bugeaud: "If we are going to use force," said I, "against the popular movement, then Bugeaud's name and boldness are needed; but if we wish to attempt conciliation and suspend hostilities[1] . . . Bugeaud's name makes no sense." The others supported me; Thiers yielded with hesitation and reluctance. The plan you know about was adopted: Bugeaud nominally retained the supreme command, and Lamoricière was put at the head of the National Guard. Thiers and Barrot went into the King's study, and I do not know what occurred there. Everywhere orders had been given for the troops to cease fire and withdraw to the palace, leaving the field clear for the National Guard. With Rémusat I hastily drafted a proclamation announcing these orders and explaining them to the people. At about nine o'clock it was

[1] *Marginal note* (*Tocqueville*): This shows clearly, apart from what Beaumont positively asserts later on, to what an extent the new Cabinet had accepted surrender as its role.

agreed that Thiers and Barrot should make an appeal to the people in person. Thiers was stopped on the staircase and, with difficulty I must admit, made to retrace his steps. Barrot went out alone and I followed him. (Here Beaumont's story is exactly the same as Barrot's.) Barrot was wonderful throughout the expedition, said Beaumont. I had trouble making him go back, although, once we had got to the barricade at the Porte Saint Denis, it was impossible to go on. Our return made matters worse: as we forced a passage through, we brought in our wake a mob more hostile than that we passed through in coming; on reaching the Place Vendôme, Barrot became afraid that, with the crowd that followed him, he might all unintentionally take the Tuileries by storm; he slipped away and got back to his home. I went back to the palace. The situation struck me as very serious but far from desperate, so I was astonished to see the inroads of chaos into all men's minds since I had left and the frightful confusion already prevailing in the Tuileries. I could not quite grasp what had happened, or what news had been received to turn everything topsy-turvy in this way. As I was dying of hunger and fatigue, I went up to the table and hastily took some food. Ten times within the three or four minutes it took me to eat it, one of the King's aides-de-camp or one of the royal family came to look for me, said something muddled and went off without properly understanding my answer. I hurried to join Thiers, Rémusat, Duvergier and one or two others supposed to form the new Cabinet. We went together into the King's study: it is the only Cabinet meeting I have ever attended. Thiers spoke, launching out into a homily about the duties of a King and the father of a family. "That is to say, you advise me to abdicate," said the King, not much affected by the touching part of the speech and coming straight to the point. Thiers agreed, giving his reasons. Duvergier very warmly supported him. I, who had had no warning, showed my astonishment and cried out that all was not yet lost. Thiers seemed very annoyed at my interruption, and I could not help thinking that from the start Thiers' and Duvergier's secret aim had been to get rid of the King on whom they could never rely and rule in the name of the Duke of Nemours or the

Duchess of Orleans after they had forced the King to abdicate.[2] The latter, who up to a certain moment had struck me as very firm, appeared towards the end to give himself completely up for lost. There is a gap here in my memory of Beaumont's story, which I must fill in later after another talk with him. I will move on to the scene of the abdication, which followed shortly.

Meanwhile events and reports of them grew worse and panic spread. Thiers said that he was no longer a possibility, which perhaps was true, and Barrot scarcely one. He disappeared then, or at least I did not see him again during the final moments, which was very wrong of him, for even if he declined office, he should not have abandoned the royal family at such a critical moment but stayed on as their royal adviser, although no longer their minister. I was present at the final scene of the abdication: the Duke of Montpensier begged his father to write and urged him on so that the King stopped and said, "But really I cannot write any faster." The Queen was desperate but heroic. Knowing that I had opposed the abdication in the Council, she took my hands and told me that we must not allow such an act of cowardice to be consummated; that we must defend ourselves; that she would die in front of the King before anyone could reach her. Nonetheless the abdication was signed, and the Duke of Nemours asked me to run and tell Marshal Gérard, who was at the far end of the Carousel, that I had seen the King sign, so that he could announce officially that the King had abdicated. I ran there and I came back, for all the rooms were empty. I went from room to room without meeting anybody. I went down into the garden, and there I met Barrot who, coming from the Ministry of the Interior, was bent on the same futile search as I. The King had escaped by the main avenue; apparently the Duchess of Orleans

[2] Rémusat, who says in his memoirs (vol. IV, p. 220) that only Thiers, Duvergier and himself were present at this part of the meeting with the King and his two sons, gives a different account. According to him, Louis-Philippe misunderstood a comment Duvergier made, thinking that the latter was in favour of his abdication. Duvergier protested against this idea, an idea that, says Rémusat, surprised them all. Rémusat is at pains to insist on this interpretation because he was sure that the facts would become distorted. (Ed.)

went by the underground passage to the waterside. No necessity forced them to leave the palace, which was then perfectly safe and was not invaded until an hour after it had been abandoned. Barrot was absolutely determined to rescue the Duchess. He had horses hurriedly got ready for her, the young prince, and ourselves, wanting us to throw ourselves all together into the midst of the people; it was the only chance left, but a very feeble one. Unable to rejoin the Duchess, we went on towards the Ministry of the Interior. You met us on the way, and you know the rest.

II

Conversation with Barrot (10 December 1850) – His version of the events of the 24th February

I think that M. Molé did not refuse office until after the firing had started in the Boulevard. Thiers told me that he was summoned at one o'clock in the morning and that he suggested me to the King as the man needed; that the King first objected and then yielded, and that finally he put off our meeting with him until nine o'clock in the morning.

At five o'clock Thiers came to my house to wake me; we talked; he returned home, and I did not join him there until eight o'clock. I found him peacefully shaving. It was a great pity that the King and M. Thiers thus wasted the time that slipped by between one and eight in the morning. His shaving finished, we went to the palace. Already the people were deeply stirred; barricades were being erected; and there had already been shots fired on the Tuileries from the neighbouring houses. Nevertheless we found the King very calm and behaving in his usual manner. He addressed the sort of conventional phrases you would expect to me. At that time Bugeaud was still commander-in-chief. I strongly urged Thiers not to accept responsibility under the colour of that name, or at least to correct the balance by giving the command of the National Guard to Lamoricière who was present. Thiers agreed to this, as did the King and Bugeaud himself. I then suggested to the King that he should dissolve the Chamber of Deputies. "Never! Never!" he said, and he grew angry and left us, shutting the door in our faces, Thiers' and mine. It was evident that he had agreed to take us only to save the first moment and that, as soon as he had compromised us with the people, he was counting on throwing us out with the help of Parliament. Therefore, at any ordinary time, I would have withdrawn at once, but the seriousness of the situation made me stay, and I suggested that I should address the people, telling them in person that the new Cabinet had taken office and calming them down. As there was no chance for us to have a poster printed and stuck up in time, I regarded myself as a sandwich man. I must give Thiers credit for wanting to go with me and confess that it was I who, fearing the ill effect of his presence, refused him. So I went out. I came unarmed up to each barricade. Rifles were lowered, the barricades opened, and people shouted: "Long live reform! Long live Barrot!" We proceeded in this manner as far as the Porte Saint Denis where we found a two-tier barricade manned by men who gave no sign of approving my speech and who did not look as if they would let us pass. I therefore was forced to retrace my steps. On my return I found the people more excited than when I went out; nevertheless I did not hear a single seditious shout or anything that augured an immediate revolution. The only serious remark I heard came from Étienne Arago. He came up to me and said: "If the King does not abdicate, we shall have a revolution before eight o'clock this evening." I thus reached the Place Vendôme. Thousands of men were following me, shouting; "To the Tuileries! To the Tuileries!" I asked myself what I ought to do. To have gone to the Tuileries followed by this crowd would have made me absolute master of the situation, but by means of an act that might have appeared revolutionary and violent. If I had known what was going on in those same Tuileries at that moment, I would not have hesitated; but as yet I had no anxiety. The people did not seem to me to have yet taken any decisive attitude. I knew that all the troops were withdrawing to the palace and that the government and the generals were there. Consequently I had no inkling of the panic that shortly afterwards allowed the crowd to invade the palace. I turned right and went home to rest a moment. I had not eaten yet and was worn out. A few minutes later Malleville sent me a message from the Ministry of the Interior saying that it was urgent that I come and sign telegrams to the Departments. I went there in my carriage, cheered by the people. Thence I went to present myself at the palace. I was still unaware of all that had been going on. When I got to the quay opposite the gardens, I saw a regiment of dragoons going back to barracks. The colonel told me: "The King has abdicated. All the troops are withdrawing." I started running. When I got to the wicket-gate I had great difficulty getting through into the courtyard as all the troops were pouring impetuously out by every exit. In the end I did get to the courtyard and found it already almost empty. The Duke of Nemours was there. I pressed him to tell me where the Duchess of Orleans could be found. He said he did not know but that he thought she was at that moment in the pavilion down by the river. I ran thither; they told me the Duchess was not there. I broke the door open and rushed into the rooms, which were indeed empty. I departed from the Tuileries, instructing Havin, whom I left there, not to go to the Chamber with the Duchess, should she be found, since nothing could be done with the Assembly. My plan had been, if I found the Duchess and her son, to mount them on horseback and to plunge with them myself into the midst of the people; I had even had horses prepared. But, not finding that princess, I went back to the Ministry of the Interior. I fell in with you on my way thither, and you know what happened at the Ministry. There I received a message to hurry to the Chamber; as soon as I got there the leaders of the extreme left surrounded me and carried me off almost by force to the nearest office; there they implored me to propose to the Assembly the nomination of a provisional government of which I was to be a member. I sent them packing and went back into the Chamber. You know the rest.

III

Incidents of 24 February 1848
Efforts on the part of M. Dufaure and his friends to
prevent the February Revolution – Responsibility of
M. Thiers for rendering these efforts futile

Today (19 October 1850), Rivet recalled and confirmed to me the details of an incident well worth remembering.

The week before the one in which the Monarchy fell, certain Conservative deputies were troubled by anxieties that did not trouble the government or their colleagues. They thought it would be better to overthrow the government, provided it could be done without violence, rather than run the risk of the banquets. One of them, M. Sallandrouze, approached M. Billault and made this suggestion to him: the banquet was due to take place on Tuesday the 22nd; on the day of the 21st M. Dufaure and his friends should introduce a motion drafted by Sallandrouze and the others for whom he spoke, a list of whose names, forty in all, he provided. They would vote for the motion on condition that, in return, the opposition would give up the banquet and restrain the people.

On Sunday the 20th February, we met at Rivet's house to discuss this proposition. As far as I can remember, those present were Dufaure, Billault, Lanjuinais, Corcelle, Ferdinand Barrot, Talabot, Rivet and I.

Billault explained Sallandrouze's proposition to us; we accepted it at once and drafted the required motion. I made the draft, which, with modifications, was accepted by my friends.

I forget its exact terms, but although they were moderate, its adoption would have necessitated the resignation of the Cabinet.

It remained for us to fulfil the condition required by the Conservatives, that is to say, the cancellation of the banquet. Since we had stood apart from that agitation, it was not our part to cancel it. It was agreed that one of us should set off at once to find Duvergier de Hauranne and Barrot and suggest that they take the necessary action. Rivet was chosen to negotiate this, and we arranged to meet again in the evening to learn what success he had had.

And he came that evening to give us an account of what had happened. This was the story.

Barrot had eagerly seized the proffered opening; he effusively grasped Rivet's hands and declared himself ready to do all that was required of him in the sense indicated; to have a chance of escaping responsibility for the banquet seemed to take a great weight off his mind. But he added that he was not engaged in this enterprise alone and that he must come to an understanding with his friends, without whom he would do nothing. How well we knew that!

Rivet went to Duvergier's house and found that he was at the Conservatoire of Music but was expected home before dinner. Rivet waited, and Duvergier came. Rivet informed him of the Conservatives' proposition and our motion. Duvergier received this information somewhat contemptuously; they had gone too far, he said, to retreat; the Conservatives were too late in mending their ways. He and his friends could not undertake to ask the people to drop the proposed demonstration without losing their own popularity and perhaps all their influence over the masses. "However," he added, "that is only my immediate personal reaction. But I am going to dine with Thiers, and I will send you a note this evening informing you of our final decision."

That note arrived while we were assembled; it stated briefly that Thiers shared the opinion voiced by Duvergier before dinner and that the suggestion should be dropped. We broke up at once. The die had been cast.

I have no doubt that the most important although unstated

motive influencing Thiers' and Duvergier's refusal was that if the government fell quietly from the combined action of some of the Conservatives and ourselves, on the occasion of a motion proposed by us, power would fall into our hands and not pass on to those who had taken such trouble to attain it by contriving all the complicated machinery of the banquets.

DUFAURE'S BEHAVIOUR ON 24 FEBRUARY 1848

Rivet told me today (19 October 1850) that he had never talked to Dufaure about what happened to him on the 24th February, but that in conversations with his family and his intimates he had gathered the following:

At about a quarter past six on the 23rd February, M. Molé, after concerting with M. de Montalivet, sent to ask Dufaure to come to see him. On his way to M. Molé's, Dufaure looked in on Rivet and asked him to wait for him to come back, for he meant to return thither on leaving M. Molé. Dufaure did not come back, and Rivet did not see him again until some time after. But he thinks it correct to say that Dufaure had rather a long conversation at M. Molé's and then went away, declaring that he did not wish to join the new Cabinet and that in his opinion the circumstances called for the men who had brought it about, that is to say, Thiers and Barrot.

He went home, seriously alarmed at the aspect of Paris, to find his mother-in-law and wife even more alarmed; at five o'clock on the morning of the 24th he escorted them to Vanves. He himself returned; I remember seeing him at eight or nine o'clock, and I do not remember his mentioning his morning journey. I had come to his house with Lanjuinais and Corcelle; we soon separated, agreeing to meet again at midday at the Chamber of Deputies. Dufaure did not come; apparently he did set out for there and actually reached the palace of the Assembly, which was probably invaded at just that moment. What is certain is that he went on and joined his family at Vanves.

IV

Notes for the Recollections covering the period from June 1848 to June 1849   *(April 1851)*

Notes for the part that should stretch from the days of June down to my entry into office.

Cavaignac in power. Character sketch of him.[1] Debate about the Constitution. My two speeches[2]; both successful. I find it easier to speak in this huge Assembly, which, though inexperienced, is more impressionable and more sincerely concerned with the larger interests of the country, dealing with immense questions at a most critical time, than I ever found it in our former Chambers where the parties were constantly fighting petty wars with ambushes and points turning on nuances of meaning. Tone of the debates. Broad tendencies in the Assembly (look at the debates again, or at least at the substantial extracts from them printed with the annotated edition of the Code). My vote in favour of two Chambers, which seems to separate me from my principal friends. Almost unanimous vote on the Constitution. Cavaignac, who at first wished to have only "Republicans of yesterday" in his government, realizes the impossibility of running things with them alone and so is obliged to ask some of the survivors from former Parliaments to join his Cab-

[1] *Marginal note (Tocqueville)*: Time following the June days down to my entry into office, the 11th May. Reread the yearbooks covering this period.

[2] *Marginal note (Tocqueville)*: The second speech was one of importance; state of public opinion urging me thereto; reasons that made me speak as I did.

inet. Negotiations to get Dufaure to join.[3] He wants two friends with him. He put forward Vivien's name for Public Works, and mine for Education. Corcelle was the go-between. Cavaignac wanted Dufaure alone. He gave way about Vivien, but pressed, or rather supported, by Marie and . . . ,[4] who said that they would resign if I came in, he stood out against me. Dufaure gives me up, and Vivien tells me that he will take office without me, but that he has made it a condition that I should be entrusted with the negotiations about the Italian affairs that had been started with England and Austria.[5] My disappointment. I accept with hesitation; I could find no serious intention in these negotiations, and they did not come to anything.

My votes on the Constitution, where I took a different line from my friends; Dufaure's recent jilting of me and the resentment I was supposed to feel make M. Thiers think that the moment has come to get hold of me and put me into line; indirect approach through Rémusat; M. Th(iers') opinion of me, according to him, "a superior mind." I accept such praise with great demonstrations of gratitude; I agree to come back to M. Th(iers') house, where I had not been since the days of the *Commerce*[6] and to maintain contact with him, I remain deter-

[3] *Marginal note (Tocqueville)*: Dufaure, more than any other, was the man indicated, although he had been more moderate than some before the Republic and had refused to take part in the banquets. He had not been compromised during the last administration under the Monarchy and had sincerely supported the Republic. Democratic fibre. He had become the "man of the Constitution" and indeed, with Vivien, its *rapporteur*. (The rapporteur is a member of a French parliamentary committee entrusted with the examination of parliamentary business. It is his function to report the findings of the committee to the whole chamber. [Ed.])
[4] Name left blank in the manuscript. (Ed.)
[5] Cavaignac had appointed Tocqueville in October 1848 to represent France at a conference to be held in Brussels. At this conference the mediation of France and Great Britain in the affairs of Piedmont and Austria was to be discussed, but it was never held. Tocqueville resigned his mission after Louis Napoleon Bonaparte's election. (Ed.)
[6] In 1844, Tocqueville was asked by the owners of this newspaper if he would exercise some influence over its policy. Tocqueville accepted, seeing an opportunity not only to put forward the ideas for which he stood in the opposition groups, but also to prevent Thiers, who already had control of several newspapers, from obtaining what Tocqueville termed a press monopoly. *Le Commerce* ceased publication in March 1848. See Tocqueville, *Oeuvres Complètes* (ed. J. P. Mayer), vol. VI, 1, p. 75, Paris, 1954. (Ed.)

mined, however, not to let good relations develop into any sort of tie. This *rapprochement* enabled me to see M. Th(iers) more intimately and in a clearer light than at any previous time. My full opinion of him; he deserves a proper portrait; the mistakes of the public in many respects concerning him, and my own misunderstandings; perhaps not better, but different from the man I had imagined.

The reactionary movement triggered off by the days of June continues to gain momentum in the nation; all the elections demonstrate this, and there are a thousand other signs. Even the government, while regarding this movement with apprehension, is in some degree carried along by it. The monarchical parties regain hope and unite. On the other hand, many Republicans who have been with us so far begin to withdraw towards the Mountain. Even during Cavaignac's administration this movement was increasingly noticeable, and it became general as the nation's support was withdrawn, especially after Cavaignac's fall from power.

Without wishing to be carried away by the monarchical parties, I have no hesitation in voting with them on all measures designed to re-establish order and discipline in society and to strike down the revolutionary and Socialist party.

Louis Napoleon's candidature. Here again one sees the stamp of the February Revolution; the people *properly so-called* is the main actor; events seem to create themselves without any outstanding figure or even the upper or middle classes appearing to do anything. Suddenness of the candidature and its success. The significance of this. From the first blow I consider Louis Napoleon's election certain and Cavaignac defeated. I tell Desessarts that. My conversation with him during the aftermath of the June days: we are steering towards a state less free than the Monarchy. Nevertheless I decide to support Cavaignac; my motives; Louis Napoleon struck me as the *worst* of ends for the Republic, and I did not want to be implicated therein; I thought that, having accepted a public duty from Cavaignac, it would be undignified to pass over to his rival. I therefore remained firm in support of him in spite of the shouts and threats of my constituents, but I did not throw myself into the fore in a cause

I thought lost in advance. Opposite view taken by Cavaignac's main friends; the ministers' illusions teach me a lesson I shall never forget; Lamoricière's mathematical calculations; the prefects' reports to Dufaure, Cavaignac triumphing over his opponents in the Assembly, crushing them as he defends himself; Dufaure reviling Louis Napoleon with his cold irony. As public opinion increasingly favours Louis Napoleon, he carries the parliamentary leaders with him; how Barrot was won over; motives of vanity and ambition, which estranged Molé and Thiers from Cavaignac and propelled them into the opposite camp. Thiers, a strong opponent to begin with, becomes a strong supporter. The Legitimists go on hesitating right to the end; most of them in the end let themselves be swept along in the maelstrom; it is emphatically society's tail that wags its head. Only the middle classes, generally speaking, continue to support Cavaignac; the majority of the Parisian National Guard is for him; evening demonstration in the rue de Varennes; account of the 10th December; attitude of Cavaignac and his ministers. The surrender of power: the most important parliamentary session I have ever witnessed and certainly one of the most important in history. Enthusiasm for the newly elected President; first impression, seeing him for the most part from a distance; my profound sadness; I think I can see my country's freedom vanishing under an illegitimate and absurd monarchy. Perhaps in that first moment he could have overthrown the Republic. Indeed his special friends were urging him to do that: Persigny's letter. I resign as plenipotentiary; although I had no reason to be enthusiastic about Cavaignac, I thought it more dignified to withdraw from affairs with him. I fall ill; I remain very much out of touch with what is going on in the Assembly in the first months of 1849. At the end of April I go for a trip along the Rhine in hope of recovering my health. Before this, my conversation with Barrot on the eve of the Roman expedition; my comments. My travels in Germany; my stay at Frankfurt during the last moments of the German National Assembly; the pedagogic and the revolutionary aspects of that Assembly. I remain firmly convinced of two things, and I write to all my friends about them. (1). Germany suffers from a revolutionary disease, which may be temporarily arrested but which cannot be cured; and this disease is in the process of destroying the old society beyond recall. (2). The immediate phase of the disease is bringing a complete triumph of the princes and military power. At Frankfurt I learn of the check to the Roman expedition, the last convulsions of the Assembly, and finally the general election (itself the result of the two former events), which cause me surprise and anxiety. Although absent and silent, I come out first in the list for La Manche. I hurry back to France; I find the moderate party in an extraordinary state of stupefaction after its exaggerated confidence of success; people felt lost because the success achieved was less complete than what they had expected; they were at sea; terror, a passion more powerful than hate or even vanity, forced the leaders of parliamentary parties to clamour loudly for Dufaure and his friends to join Barrot's administration; I found the ministerial crisis already started.

In writing about my German trip, make a full description of the state of Germany at the time.

To help in this: (1). The notes in the little notebook, including among other things the table made for me analyzing opinion by districts. (2). Ask Corcelles and Beaumont to let me have the letters I wrote to them at that time, if they still possess them.[7]

Finish the chapter with news from France, quoting part of Rivet's letter, probably the bit that describes the *dinner party*.[8]

[7] *Marginal note (Tocqueville)*: For the time between Dufaure's taking office under Cavaignac and the elections of the 10th December, reread Beaumont's letters covering that period.
[8] *Marginal note (Tocqueville)*: "Immediately after reading this letter, I set out."
On 21 May 1849, Rivet wrote a letter to Tocqueville pressing him to return. After an exceedingly sombre account of the political situation in France immediately after the elections to the Legislative Assembly, he continued:
"At the point things have now reached, those who are stricken down by fear only hide their heads, declaring society lost; whereas those whom the situation drives towards violence dream of a thousand mad exploits, for which, luckily, they would need a compact and energetic army. Finally, there are a very few people who think that it is still possible to save the state and bring the country back from its momentary straying by advancing candidly within the spirit and the letter of the Constitution. Of all those

Perhaps move back to there a few lines of the first chapter of my account of my term of office.

---

whom I have met holding this view, none is more stalwart and courageous than Dufaure. His success in Paris has taught him the true measure of his powers, and I must say that, far from simply finding satisfaction for his vanity therein, he feels under an obligation to use them in his country's service. I was really very touched two days ago by the firmness and resolution of his attitude. With power clearly coming his way, he shows neither false modesty nor vain eagerness. We made eight around our table, where your absence was strongly felt. Of those eight there were two, not counting myself, who had been kicked out by the elections, Freslon and Lanjuinais; one, General Bedeau, was newly elected. Our conversation was serious, as indeed was the situation that brought us together, but one satisfactory result sprang from it, namely that the men called on to play a part, animated by Dufaure's constancy and resolution, all understood that they had an important duty to perform. I reckon that, between now and the time the next Assembly is to meet, there will not have been any riot putting everything in jeopardy; to me it seems proved that a new administration formed under such energetic and patriotic inspiration is the only government that could calm men's minds, allow some hopes for the future, and baffle the anarchists' plans." (Tocqueville Archives.)

V

Various notes for the still unwritten parts of my Recollections
(April 1851 on my way back home)

May 1849

My journey to Germany and stay in Frankfurt towards the end
of the Diet, when many members had already withdrawn.

My impression: a country profoundly affected by the spirit of
revolution; the old society mortally struck down; in the immediate future, triumph of the princes.

I hear news of the elections and the unexpected successes of
the Reds. I return with all speed. The new Assembly should
open on the 28th or 29th May. Aspect of the country: exaggerated fright supervening on exaggerated confidence. Two ideas
in all minds: a crisis close and inevitable, need for an administration calling the moderate Republicans to power to deal
with the crisis and leaving the revolutionary party properly so-
called isolated. All eyes turned towards Du(faure) and his
friends as the ministers needed.

Repeated attempts of B(arrot) to get us to join the government with him: we are only moderately keen on accepting
power, myself especially. I have never seen the future more
clearly: an internal crisis to be faced; responsibility for the Roman business to be accepted; no solid support to be expected
either from the President or from the party leaders; to be taken
up by both President and party leaders to see them through
a difficult pass, with the secret intention of getting rid of us as
soon as the danger is over; our very victory would certainly

lead to our fall. Useless and in the way, once we had established order.

In brief, in power we would stand for the idea of a moderate, reasonable Republic, a thing almost nobody desired, some wanting more, some less and some something other.

I see all that. However, basically I do want to take office; a mixture of ambition and the desire to save the country from the crisis.

FORMATION OF THE CABINET

Difficulties of all sorts. I am one of them (as at the time D(ufaure) took office under Cavaignac). The President wanted at all costs to hold on to Falloux (the latter had gained his confidence and really was necessary to bring in the Legitimists without whom no progress could be made, a point I did not sufficiently appreciate at the time). Now, there was agreement that . . .[1]

. . . impossible to take over responsibility at a more critical moment.

The order to attack Rome had been given two days before in spite of the Constituent Assembly's vote. News of this began to penetrate; revolutionary agitation in Paris; meeting of the new Assembly in the old hall of deputies; *warlike* and *unconstitutional* attitude immediately adopted by the Mountain, mad from its recent unexpected success in the elections and finding the Roman business a good text for revolution; impeachment of the ministers demanded; my cruel embarrassment: I did not want to take responsibility for the *past* of the Roman expedition. (I had announced that to Barrot before I took office.) But nonetheless, I did not want to give it up. Exaggerations, false reports and an attack on the Chair by Ledru gave me a pretext to take the initiative and vigorously attack the latter; the majority supported me enthusiastically, so that my popularity was established from that day; and, the occasional cloud apart, I remained to the end the member of the Cabinet who got on best with the majority.

[1] There is a page of the manuscript missing here. (Ed.)

The streets monopolized our attention: clearly some attempt at revolution was being prepared; reports from the departments; reports from the police; their exaggerations. This revealed to me how governments are pushed away from the truth, and how, all things considered, it is safer to base one's judgement on a general appreciation of the situation than on knowledge of petty, and maybe false or exaggerated, details. Although the police made the situation out as infinitely more dangerous than I judged it, I stuck firmly to my view the whole time, and I was right. However, inevitably, I felt ill at ease.

Events of the 13th June.[2] Characteristics thereof: one year before, army without H.Q.: this time, H.Q. without army. Thiers' fright; fear of insurrection and of cholera; stretched out in an armchair in the President of the Assembly's house, rubbing his stomach and ill-temperedly demanding that Paris be put under a state of siege, a measure not yet requested by the government; impatience of the Assembly on the same count. I go to look for Duf(aure) in the Ministry of the Interior and ask him to come and make the request. At three o'clock he comes into the Assembly. Paris is put under a state of siege; the riot is dispersed; some of the leaders arrested. It was only from the 13th June that we really began to pay attention to our position and the business in hand.

My observations about myself and my aptitude for my new task.[3] I find myself better suited to succeed in great matters than in small; less worried by great responsibilities than by trivial ones. In some way the grandeur of the situation and events sustained me. I gradually regained a confidence in myself of which I had begun to despair.[4] I also discovered that the difficulty of affairs does not increase in proportion to their importance and that they are not so awkward to manage as would appear from the distance. I could well apply a famous

[2] *Marginal note* (*Tocqueville*): Calm and resolute attitude of the President during these days.
[3] *Marginal note* (*Tocqueville*): My views about the line I should take with the President, the party leaders, and the Assembly, and about Europe and its affairs.
[4] *Marginal note* (*Tocqueville*): Why is this? Go into the matter. Curious psychological study.

line of poetry to myself and say: "He shines in the highest rank, but is eclipsed in the second."[5]

French internal affairs: state in which I found them; state of Europe; all the former powers rising amid the ruins; nowhere has the February Revolution succeeded in establishing a freedom that is reasonable and stable; the revolutionaries everywhere mad; practically nothing changed in France's political situation; no part for her to play; the old powers distrust her and in any case profess principles antipathetic to our new spirit and new institutions, not to mention the fact that Russia, not ourselves, must play the leading role in defending these principles. The party opposed to these old powers is extravagantly revolutionary and impossible to patronise, first because there is no hope of leading it and getting it to be reasonable; secondly, because its passions and excesses would in no time throw France herself into disorder.

Looking at things from another angle, one finds it equally impossible for France to undertake any great matter abroad: any external effort would almost certainly lead to collapse at home. The government's only immediate support would come from the demagogic party; besides, the balance of power had changed unfavourably to French interests. In brief, the sad sight and sad plight of a Minister of Foreign Affairs having to manage the business of a nation that imagines it has an influence it can no longer exercise; a nation that is proud without being strong, and one that always wants its government to talk very loud, but would be sorely displeased if that government led it into a situation where it had to draw its sword.[6]

I had caught a glimpse of all that in the distance; now I see it in detail. This leads me to think that we attacked the foreign policy of Louis-P(hilippe)'s government too much (although that government really did lack both shame and patriotic feeling, but its difficulties really were great, too).

[5] *Marginal note (Tocqueville)*: I also find that it is very much easier for me to be kind, friendly and attentive when I am without a rival than it was when I was one of the crowd.

[6] *Marginal note (Tocqueville)*: Always wants to give orders and no longer wants to wage war; wants to be both arrogant and pacific.

I saw that there was nothing to be attempted on a great scale; one must wait on events, seeking to preserve the reputation of a liberal and moderate power; not to fuss; to keep on as good terms as possible with England, which, all things considered, was the only sympathetic power; to stay firm without haughtiness; no boasting; to say what is due to France, ask for it, and, if others will not grant it, rather risk all for all, or resign, than let the country be humiliated by my fault.

Amid these difficulties of a general nature, there were particular complications arising from the Roman business.[7] Internal difficulties connected with that affair; I decide for a time to give that business precedence over all other matters.

Whatever embarrassments I may have had from Europe, those springing up on the home front were much worse.

As we sincerely desired to demolish the demagogic party and reinvigorate the law and government, we ought to have been able to establish a good understanding with the majority for a reasonably long time (I say "for a time" because basically the majority wanted more than that; they wanted places of power and a real return to the Monarchy), but what made our position dangerous from the first minute and as soon as the 13th June was passed was the detestable vanity of the party leaders who did not want to undertake the government and would not put up with anybody governing them. Now they plainly saw that we could be their friends but that we should never be their agents. That started a small war, silent but incessant[8]; a permanent intrigue; the President's constant effort to dominate the government. In the matter of overthrowing the Republic, the party leaders agreed with the President; it was the Legitimists that prevented it.

It was not possible to satisfy them completely, but Dufaure exasperated them by his rough, cold manners.[9]

[7] *Marginal note (Tocqueville)*: My way of addressing Courts and ambassadors; I am appreciated for it; the plain simple language, without elaborate phrases, of a man determined to get the *moderate* things he requests.
[8] *Marginal note (Tocqueville)*: Personality of Changarnier.
[9] *Marginal note (Tocqueville)*: Examples of his manners; interview with Castellane; his *chef de cabinet*; overriding fear of seeming to be governed; gives nothing to his friends; often allows himself to be led by subordinates.

I take an altogether different line and find it thoroughly successful. I let them have a bit of apparent influence to satisfy their vanity, while keeping the real power to myself. In small matters and in personal ones, I go as far as I can to please them.

I make a special point of asking their advice and listening with great attention to it, frequenting their houses and inviting them to mine. It is odd how I keep their goodwill while not doing what they want in great matters. Thiers is the best example: I do the opposite of what he wishes in the Piedmont affair and in that of the Hungarian refugees, and partly too in the Roman business, but we stay good friends.

Embarrassments and difficulties within the Cabinet. All the members homogeneous, except Falloux; there is real confidence, sympathy and mutual esteem between the rest (more, so those who were ministers in earlier governments tell me, than there was in any other cabinet); Falloux is an extraneous element. What manner of man was Falloux? Mainly a representative of the Church rather than of any political party. I noticed the traces of old quarrels, before I came on the scene, between him and Barrot; but it was the natural antipathy between Dufaure and Falloux that nearly broke up the Cabinet at once; relations between these two[10]; difficulties in getting them to live together; I was the only person who could help in this, being liked and esteemed by Dufaure and cut from the same wood as Falloux; my efforts.

Finally, the greatest of all our difficulties, the President. My opinion concerning him: much inferior to what his partisans would have liked, but much superior to the opinion of him held by his enemies and even some of those who had had him appointed thinking they could dominate him and be rid of him at a given moment. From the beginning I took the line that one must find some *regular* future career for him to prevent him from looking for an irregular one; for it was no use dreaming that he would be President for a time and nothing more; I try to get this idea accepted by my friends in the Administration. I talk to the President in the same manner: "I will not help you to overthrow the Republic," I kept telling him, "but will gladly help you to

10 *Marginal note* (*Tocqueville*): Trouble over the prefect at Angers.

APPENDICES

win a great permanent place within it." My way of behaving soon put me on good terms with him, better than any of the others except Falloux. But I had to stand up to him about appointments, for he was constantly suggesting deplorable candidates; but I gave good reasons for objecting and sincerely tried to please him when that was possible.[11]

His entourage: "Knaves and rascals" in Changarnier's phrase, always very hostile to the Cabinet, and always in treacherous communication with the leaders of the majority; basically their great grievance is that that we would not let them lay their hands on all the offices.

The President's old friends and his friends-for-the-election. Dufaure's stiffness in dealing with him; Passy's bad manners and teasing rudeness.

COURSE OF EVENTS

Internal: growing storm against us within the majority on account of Dufaure's stubbornness and retaining in office men unwelcome to the majority; impossible to satisfy that majority, but means to make it less hostile by secondary concessions and concessions in matters of *form*.[12]

FOREIGN AFFAIRS

Deal with all the matters listed in the margin[13] after rereading the documents, and end up with the Roman business. That business was the reason for the creation and the fall of the Cabinet. Tell the story from beginning to end, recounting it right up to our resignation, with a little epilogue to describe what happened after we had been thrown out; that we did not show

[11] *Marginal note (Tocqueville)*: The President is a "gentleman," which makes a great bond between him and me. The tactful way in which he suggested bringing Beaumont back into public life; my joy at being able to do that; why?
[12] *Marginal note (Tocqueville)*: Higher up I think.
[13] *Marginal note (Tocqueville)*: The affairs of Switzerland, Piedmont, Hungary and Rome.
Make the whole story of the Roman business into the final chapter.

enough energy: everything was surrendered, not only at Rome but throughout Italy.

If, instead of this long exposition at the beginning, I could introduce some ideas in the course of the narration, that would be better, being more natural and interesting, for instance, the quarrels between Dufaure and Falloux.[14]

[14] *Marginal note (Tocqueville)*: Separate stories to place somewhere or other—my relations with Lord Normanby—Lamoricière's mission to Russia —violation of the secrecy of the post; uselessness of that wretched expedient; secret agents; the President's counterpart betrayed in turn.

VI

*My conversation with the President of the Republic on
15 May 1851*
(I was seeing him for the first time after my return from
Italy.)

On the 15th May I received a note from the A.D.C. on duty saying that the President would like to see me the next day at
one o'clock. I kept the appointment. After the usual greetings,
the President abruptly asked me what I thought of things:

Myself: – Will you allow me to talk candidly?

The President: – Certainly.

Myself: – Well then, I find the situation has got much worse,
worse for everybody, for France and for you.

We beat around the bush for a few moments. Then I made
my mind up and said:

"We must come to closer grips with these questions. Since you
asked me, this is how I see your position. There are three ways
in which you might overstep the Constitution: you could do it
with the help of the Assembly, or of the people, or using your
own powers, that is to say, those at the disposal of the executive.
On the last possibility, I am convinced that, if you tried it, you
would not only throw the country into the midst of a great
crisis, but you would throw yourself into an adventure in which
you would probably go under.

As to overstepping the Constitution with the Assembly's support, there have been moments when that was practicable, but
I think that at this moment you should give up such a hope and

not suppose that the majority, which would go as far as to say that the Constitution ought to be revised, would follow you in violating that Constitution in your own interest. All those who tell you that you could achieve that aim by changing your ministers and taking others are wrong." (I thought that was true and good to say in order to show him that the object of my talk was not to ask for office.)

He made a sign of agreement.

"There remains the third alternative: to overstep the Constitution with the people's support. That is to say, to get re-elected in spite of the Constitution, the people undertaking to carry through the *coup-d'état* themselves. That is the least violent and the least illegal of all solutions. I think it is still possible. But by acting differently from you . . ."[1]

"(1). . . . Your internal administration is vexatious, provocative and high-handed, being employed to favour certain ambitions and certain local grudges. All these vices will be further increased under Faucher's control. Such a way of ruling not only continually alienates friends, it drives those of pinkish tendencies into the arms of the Reds and menaces us with the prospect of a revolutionary election.

"(2). Your government seems too dependent on the clergy, throwing itself into the arms of ultra-Catholics and priests. That is dangerous not only for you, but also for religion, and again it is calculated to drive the undecided towards the Reds."

The conversation again changed subject and we talked of the law of the 31st May.[2]

"I regard that law," said I, "as a great misfortune, almost as a crime. It has deprived us of the only moral force society possesses today, that is to say, the moral power of universal suffrage,

---

[1] A page of the manuscript is missing here. (Ed.)

[2] The basic provisions of the electoral law passed by the Legislative Assembly on 31 May 1850, were these: 1) Each citizen had to satisfy the authorities that he had been resident in his commune for a minimum of three years; 2) No individual found guilty of crimes or of political offences had the right to vote. Thus, the law, whilst appearing to maintain the principle of universal manhood franchise, had in fact the consequence of disenfranchising nearly three million electors, mainly from the urban working classes. See P. Campbell, *French Electoral Systems and Elections since 1789*, p. 66, second edition, London, 1965. (Ed.)

without ridding us of the dangers of that voting system. We are left to face a multitude, but an unauthorized multitude."

The President seemed as hostile to the law of the 31st May as I was.

"However," he said, "one cannot but agree that this law has had some excellent effects. But I am not like Faucher and Baroche who regard it as a sacred cow. It must be changed, but shortly before the election. Do you suppose that, having once been elected by six million votes, I would like an electoral system that would give me only four million?"

After three quarters of an hour of talk we separated. Far from being annoyed at the slightly crude way in which I had spoken to him, he thanked me and effusively asked me to come and see him from time to time.

Nothing is harder than to dive into his mind through the immobile surface of his face; after a conversation with him, one can never take away more than *impressions*.

My impressions are:

1. He has *almost* (not completely) given up the idea of obtaining his objective through the Assembly.

2. He is far from renouncing the possibility of a *coup d'état* on his own account.

3. He is very ready to envisage the possibility of a popular *coup d'état* by his re-election and considers that one of the best conclusions, but without wishing to adopt any part of the procedure I suggested. Finally, his intention to break the law of the 31st May is decided, but he wants to do it at the last moment, as a sort of appeal to the people and a blow against the Assembly.

VII

Revision of the Constitution – Conversation with Berryer when I invited him to my house on 21 June 1851 – We were both members of the Committee for the revision of the Constitution

I broached the matter thus: "Between you and me, let us forget about appearances. You are waging not a revisionist but an electoral campaign."

He replied: "That is true. You have understood the matter correctly."

"All right," I said to him. "We will soon see whether you were right. What I must tell you at once is that I cannot join in a manoeuvre whose only object is, at the coming elections, to save one part of the moderate party and neglect several other sections of it, in particular the section to which I belong. Either give moderate Republicans an honest reason for voting for revision by making that revision republican in character, or expect us to do our best to dismantle your batteries."

He agreed, but pleaded the difficulties that arose from the passions and prejudices of his party. For some time we discussed what was to be done, and at last we came, at the bottom of everything, to the very policy he was pursuing.

This is what I said to him on that subject, and I want especially to keep a record of it.

I said to him: "Berryer, you are dragging us all off into a plight for which you, please note, alone will bear the responsibility. It might still have been possible to put up a fight if the

Legitimists had joined those who are eager to oppose the President. You have dragged your party, somewhat against its will, in the opposite direction. Since then all resistance has been impossible; we cannot stay alone with the Mountain; because you have yielded, we must yield, but what will be the result? I see what you are thinking; it is perfectly clear: you believe that circumstances make the President's ascendancy irresistible and do not think it possible to withstand the surge of public opinion in his favour. Unable to force your way against the stream, you throw yourselves into it, taking the risk that you will thereby increase the violence of the current, but hoping that that current will land you and your friends and other sections of the party of order who are out of sympathy with the President, in the next Assembly. You think that it is only there that you can find solid ground from which to oppose him; and by doing his business now, you think you will be able to keep a nucleus of men in the next Assembly who are capable of holding him in check. To struggle against the stream that at this moment is carrying him along would make you unpopular and ineligible and would be handing the party over to the Socialists and the Bonapartists, neither of whom you wish to have triumph. Very well! There are plausible aspects to that plan, but there is one main mistake in it, viz: I could understand you if the election were due to take place and you would gather the fruit of your manoeuvre at once, as after the December election. But we have almost a year before the next election. You will not succeed in holding them before next spring, if then. Between now and then do you think that the Bonapartist movement, which you have encouraged and precipitated, will halt? Do you not see that, after having required revision of the Constitution, public opinion, prompted by every agent of the executive and led on by our own feebleness, is going to ask for first one thing and then another, until finally we are led overtly to favour the illegal re-election of the President and to play his game purely and simply? Can you go as far as that? Will your party want it, if you do? No. Therefore you will inevitably reach a point where you will have to stop, hold your ground and resist the combined efforts of the nation and the executive power; that is to say, you will both become unpopular and lose the support or at least the electoral neutrality of the government, which you want. You will have enslaved yourselves and immensely strengthened the forces opposed to you, and that is all. I predict this: either you will go on forever into the President's Caudine Forks,[1] or you will lose, just as you go to pick it, all the fruit of your manoeuvre and will be left with nothing, before your own conscience and the nation, but the responsibility for helping to raise up the power that perhaps, in spite of the man's mediocrity, through the extraordinary pressure of circumstances, may prove to be the heir to the revolution and our master."

Berryer seemed tongue-tied, and, as the time had come for us to part, we parted.

[1] The Battle of the Caudine Forks occurred during the second Samnite war in 321 B.C.—and was a complete disaster for the Roman army, which was cut to pieces after falling into a trap from which it was unable to extricate itself. It is for this reason that the name of the battle has passed into common parlance as a synonym for a trap from which there is no escape. (Ed.)

VIII

SPEECH BY M. DE TOCQUEVILLE
on the Roman expedition delivered in the Legislative
National Assembly on 18 October 1849

M. DE TOCQUEVILLE, Minister of Foreign Affairs:

Gentlemen, the government thought that before opening this debate it might be of advantage for the discussion and agreeable to the Assembly that they should inform it of the progress and purpose of the negotiations that are to be the subject of the debate. This, gentlemen, is the task I am here to fulfil. I do not intend to discuss the matter, discussion will come later. All I intend to do for the moment is to state the facts, and the only credit to which I mean to lay claim is that my exposition will be made with the utmost candour and absolute accuracy. Moreover, after every one of my statements I shall ask the Assembly's leave to read to them the relevant documents. To tell the truth, gentlemen, the history of these negotiations should begin only with the taking of Rome.

Believe me, I have no intention of going into the past history of the debates that took place before that date. I would merely observe that when I reflect as to what was the desire of all—I repeat all—those who voted for the Rome expedition, I think I am justified in stating that they all desired the restoration of Pius IX.

ON THE LEFT: No! No!

ON THE RIGHT: You, you voted against it.

M. BERTHOLON: M. de Lamoricière protested against it. (Objections on the right)

M. LATRADE: And M. Jules Favre, the Rapporteur.

M. HEECKEREN: M. Jules Favre did not vote on the findings of his own report. He abstained.
(Excited comments)

THE PRESIDENT: Do you wish this to be a debate or a wrangle? Which do you want, one or the other?

(Applause on the right, protests on the left)

Here are the names of the members who have given notice of their intention to speak for and against the findings of the Commission.
Against: MM. MATHIEU (la Drôme) Victor HUGO, Emmanuel ARAGO, SAVATIER-LAROCHE, MAUGUIN, Émile BARRAULT, JOLY, Edgar QUINET, Francisque BOUVET, CAVAIGNAC.

M. LATRADE: Does this answer the question? (Noise on the left)

THE PRESIDENT: And now here are the names of the speakers for the findings: MM. THIRIOT DE LA ROSIÈRE, de MONTALEMBERT, d'OLIVIER, FABVIER, de MONTIGNY, de la MOSKOWA.
All speakers on both sides will use parliamentary language and will refrain from noisy interruptions against which I protest from the outset.
(Hear! Hear!)

THE MINISTER OF FOREIGN AFFAIRS: Gentlemen, I would observe for the benefit of those who interrupt me before I have been able even to finish my sentence or to make my idea clear that I am not speaking of those who have voted for this expedition (renewed interruptions from the left) and I say that in the beginning if not all—then almost all, if you like—of those . . .

VOICE ON THE LEFT: You know nothing about it.

MANY VOICES ON THE RIGHT AND IN THE CENTRE: Do not interrupt. Order! Order!

THE PRESIDENT, turning to the left: We must at least know whether you mean to permit us to have a free discussion in this Assembly.

VOICE ON THE RIGHT: Call to order!

GENERAL TARTAS: We call for the strict application of the orders.

THE PRESIDENT: I do not know who the interrupters are. I hear them but do not see them. Continue, Minister.

THE MINISTER OF FOREIGN AFFAIRS: What I say, even at the risk of being interrupted a third time, is that nearly all if not all those who voted for the Rome expedition might have differed as to the conditions under which Pius IX was to be re-established, but that all were in favour of this restoration.

This is what I say.

On the other hand I assert that on all sides it was recognized that this restoration must be both liberal and lenient. This was the view expressed by the government and by the various speakers, and not a voice was raised against it. It was said not only here but was repeated officially beyond the mountains, and there also nobody protested.

I am justified, therefore, in saying that according to France's original views and wishes our Rome expedition was to end in the restoration of Pius IX, but this restoration was to be liberal and lenient.

Well, gentlemen, this is the point of view that has governed my own and the whole government's negotiations and actions.

No sooner had Rome been taken than we encouraged— we exercised no pressure—we encouraged to the best of our ability the restoration of Pius IX. We did this all the more readily since we were then convinced—a conviction that has since been confirmed—that the restoration of Pius IX was in accordance with the wishes of the vast majority of the inhabitants of the Roman States, although it might present different aspects according to the principles held.

(Noise and protest on the left, applause on the right)

SEVERAL MEMBERS ON THE LEFT: How do you know? Ask them!

M. DUFAURE, MINISTER OF THE INTERIOR: It is indisputable.

M. CHARLES ABBATUCCI: Except for the Roman citizens here.
(Laughter)

THE MINISTER OF FOREIGN AFFAIRS: That was our conviction and
this conviction was further strengthened by subsequent
events. As I said before, I am not arguing, I am merely
giving an account of the actions of the French Government.
They will be discussed and judged later. It is no use
interrupting me now, you will have plenty of time to speak
later on.

Once Pius IX was re-established, what was our attitude
towards him?

Some reproached us with having attempted to coerce the
Pope, others accused us of the contrary. I may state here
and now, most categorically, that never has it entered the
French Government's mind to use the force in its hands
to coerce the Holy Father. (Hear! Hear!)

We would never have dreamt of doing so for two reasons:
firstly, because here we were dealing not only with a Prince
but with a Sovereign Pontiff, and that Pontiff is the head
of the Catholic religion, and a government that represents
a nation that is essentially Catholic could not contemplate
using violence against a Prince who is at the same time
the Supreme Head of that religion. (Hear! Hear!) Our
second reason, if we need give a reason for such actions,
was that the Pontifical Power is a power immaterial, in-
compressible, intangible (noise on the left, approval on the
right and in the centre) which at all times has worn
down the greatest material powers on earth and against
which they will never prevail. (Dissent and approval as
before.) The only means by which this Catholic government
could—I will not say coerce, Heaven forbid that I should
use such a term—the Pontifical Power, but exercise over it a
legitimate and powerful influence, would be to require of
it things that are fair, wise and equitable, in conformity

with the interests of the Catholic peoples, of the populations under its sway and in accordance with reason, good sense and justice; to demand these things on behalf of all enlightened Catholics in the world, to demand them respectfully, but straightforwardly and publicly before the whole world. (Hear! Hear!)

This we did, and this we are doing to this day.

What was it then that we asked for? I will state plainly at the outset that in our negotiations with the Pope we did not press for the grant of institutions that might immediately establish great political liberty. We refrained from doing so because recent history and our own experiences had taught us that in the state in which the Roman people are at present, faced as they are with a moderate liberal party disorganized and terrified, an anarchical party full of folly and fury, and an inert mass, it would have been unwise to ask the Holy Father too insistently to restore the institutions that had already led to his overthrow. Therefore we did not press, I say again, for institutions conferring great political liberty. What we did ask for were institutions that would immediately ensure the welfare and civil liberty of the Roman States and at the same time prepare them for political liberty as well within a reasonable time. That is what we asked for.

Now, gentlemen, in order to leave these generalities and to come to particulars, I cannot do better than read to you the dispatches that bear out what I have had the honour to explain to you.

The dispatch, or rather the note, that I propose to read to the Assembly is by MM. de Corcelle and de Rayneval. It is dated the 19th August and addressed to Cardinal Antonelli. The first part of this note is only a repetition of one of my dispatches of the 4th August. The second part is the work, more particularly, of M. de Corcelle. Although very seriously ill he nevertheless in his ardent patriotism and zeal found the necessary strength to write, as it were, with a dying hand the lines I am about to read to you. (Ironical laughter on some of the benches of the left)

A VOICE FROM THE RIGHT: Very good, gentlemen, we know you respect nothing.

THE MINISTER OF FOREIGN AFFAIRS: The note concludes with the following words:

"The Government of the Republic submits to the Holy Father the following demands which they consider it their right and their duty to persist in advancing . . ." (You see that these demands had been presented before.)

"1). that several of the general principles set forth in Article 1 of the Statute of 17 March 1848, be formally recognized, in particular those that guarantee personal liberty, sanction the public debt and safeguard the inviolability of private property.

"These are conservative principles common to all civilized societies whatever political form they may adopt.

"2). that a new organization of the Courts of Law should afford real legal safeguards to the citizens.

"3). that civil laws be promulgated similar to those governing the status of persons and property in Upper Italy and the Kingdom of Naples, laws taken from our own Code of Civil Law.

"4). that elected communal and provincial assemblies be set up.

"5). that the public administration be secularized.

"6). His Holiness intends to re-establish the Council of State, which he had set up in 1847 to advise in legislative and financial questions. The Government of the Republic would prefer that the members of this Assembly should be elected by the local bodies and not selected from a list drawn up by those bodies. They consider it desirable and important that this Assembly should retain a deliberative vote in matters of taxation. Besides, it would be very easy to devise a new form borrowed from certain foreign laws, which would place spiritual sovereignty quite out of reach of the assaults of some persons, without, however, meaning to suggest that such sovereignty could be endangered by these concessions.

"These, then, are the demands that the Government of the Republic has for a long time instructed its representatives to submit to His Holiness. The Government of the Republic noted with profound regret and deep concern that according to the declarations of the Cardinal Pro-Secretary of State at the last Conference the Pontifical Government's intentions are not exactly in conformity with the French Cabinet's ideas. Since His Holiness has been good enough to defer his final decision until France had made her ideas perfectly clear the undersigned thought that the time had come to comply with the orders they had received should the contingency arise. They, therefore, repeat and formally lay down the demands of France. They do not abandon the hope that these demands will be accepted by Pius IX in his generosity and they take the liberty of urging these demands upon the Pontifical Government with the profoundest respect but with the insistence that France's consistent concern for the greatness and prosperity of the Church must justify. In conclusion, the undersigned would draw His Eminence's attention to considerations of a more general and a more lofty order. They will not remind His Eminence how anxious is France, in particular, in view of her faith and public morals, that the Church should not abandon the liberal attitude which in 1848 won for it the approbation of the whole world a short time before that great and salutary revolution that reconciled the faith with the spirit of the new institutions. Nor will they remind him to what extent the general trend at that time differed from what it has become since. In political discussions as well as in the vagaries of literature there was nothing but hatred and reaction against the faith.

"Pius IX appeared and at his first words the war against the faith subsided as by a miracle. How great was the joy of the French clergy who felt that this happy pacification restored them to their proper place in the minds of the peoples. And how great was the enthusiasm with which the hopes held out by the Holy See were greeted not only by

Catholics but by the very people who up to then had been their bitter opponents.

"There can be no question that religion then won one of its greatest triumphs. (Cheers and dissenting shouts)

"It must be admitted that the reforms introduced by Pius IX gave rise to deplorable incidents, but the strength born of the reforms and the hopes which had aroused such ardent and generous response nevertheless constituted a providential support for the Church as a whole.

"Is France doomed again to witness a complete reversal in the policies of the Council of the Holy See, bringing in its train as complete a reversal in the moral tendencies of the peoples? Such a renewed reaction against religion would become a serious danger. Would this danger remain confined to France alone, would it not arise also among all Catholic nations where free discussion is possible? Would Italy remain immune from the infection?

"The undersigned have no doubt that His Eminence's enlightened mind will duly weigh these lofty considerations and that His Holiness will not fail to realise their full import." (Cheers from a few benches)

THE MINISTER OF FOREIGN AFFAIRS: The demands contained in the document I have just read have not been expanded, they have merely been further defined and detailed in a subsequent dispatch, which I will not read to the Assembly, but which I shall hand to the *Moniteur*.

Gentlemen, you have heard the nature of the demands presented by the French Government to the Holy See. We have urged them from the first day and have continued to do so to the very end. I was bound to acquaint you with them before referring to a document that, although it is not a diplomatic note, nevertheless made a deep impression, natural and legitimate enough considering its importance and its author. I am speaking of the letter written by the President of the Republic to one of his aides-de-camp. (Show of keen attention)

I have only a few words to say.

We have been asked outside this Assembly and within the Commission it appointed whether the policy laid down in the President's letter was ours, whether it was the policy we had put forward and supported and for which we assumed responsibility. We replied—and I am very glad of this opportunity to give the reply publicly here—that this policy was exactly the same as that followed in our dispatches. (Murmurs of approval on several benches) The Assembly has just had an opportunity to judge for itself.

When all is said and done, what does the note of MM. de Corcelle and de Rayneval contain that is not to be found in substance in the letter of the President of the Republic? What are the demands contained in the letter that we have not already put forward as you have just heard? The letter of the President of the Republic may be regarded as a summary—a summary in familiar terms if you like—of our policy, but it is a faithful rendering of this policy. He interprets it in a generous and lofty spirit. We never have and never will disclaim it.

(Sensation. Murmurs of approval and dissent)

M. PASCAL DUPRAT: Are you against the findings of the Committee then?

THE MINISTER OF FOREIGN AFFAIRS: Gentlemen, now that you are acquainted with the contents of our principal diplomatic documents I must say a word regarding the *Motu Proprio*[1] which concludes the series. (Hear! Hear!) I will not conceal from you—indeed, how could I in view of the documents I have just read to you?—that the *Motu Proprio* has not fully realized our expectations.

A MEMBER ON THE LEFT: And yet you accept it!

THE MINISTER OF FOREIGN AFFAIRS: One thing, however, must be said which is not known here—this *Motu Proprio*, which

[1] Cf. F. A. Simpson, *op. cit.*, p. 81 sqq. See also *History of Modern France: 1815–1913*, vol. I, 1815–1852 by Émile Bourgeois, Cambridge, 1919. Pius IX issued the *Motu Proprio* on 12 September 1849, in which he promised reforms without specifying any in particular. (Ed.)

does not fully and immediately fulfil all the wishes of our diplomacy, has aroused the most profound misgivings and lively opposition among the party of the old régime in Rome. This party saw in it—or affected to see in it—the first steps in the Holy Father's descent down the slope of liberalism which brought him to the brink of the abyss—yes, yes, to the abyss. This is what we must bear in mind. On the other hand it is only fair to say that the Pope's *Motu Proprio* provides for the majority of the most essential reforms we asked for, and that those that are not explicitly provided for are contained in it in the germ, as it were, in the hopes that it holds out.

VOICE ON THE LEFT: Come! Come!

ON THE RIGHT: Hear! Hear!

M. BELIN: This is really charming.

THE MINISTER OF FOREIGN AFFAIRS: What surprises me, gentlemen, is the disbelief with which my words are received.

I ask leave of the Assembly to enter for one moment into the debate. I had no intention of doing so, but your scepticism leaves me no choice.

What were our demands? We asked for civil reforms, judicial reforms; the *Motu Proprio* promises them. (Ironical laughter on the left) You may doubt His Holiness' word, but you cannot deny that he has promised these reforms. (Renewed interruptions from the left)

I was saying that these gentlemen (indicating the left) may doubt the Holy Father's word, that is their affair—for my part, I do not doubt it—but they cannot deny that the *Motu Proprio* gives a definite undertaking in that sense. (Renewed noise on the left) I resume then and I say: we have demanded reforms of civil and criminal law; they have been promised. We demanded municipal and provincial liberties; they have not only been promised, but actually granted on the most liberal scale. (Outcry on the left)

M. ODILON BARROT, President of the Council: Yes, yes, and perhaps on a larger scale than you will get!

THE MINISTER OF FOREIGN AFFAIRS: We demanded the Consulta; it has been granted. I am therefore fully entitled to say that several of France's demands have been immediately and fully complied with by the *Motu Proprio* and that the fulfilment of the others has been announced and promised. (Dissentient murmurs on the left) As soon as the French Government had learned the contents of *Motu Proprio,* with mixed feelings of regret and approval they sent the following dispatch to their Minister in Rome.

"30 September 1849

"Gentlemen,

"The Government have taken note of His Holiness' manifesto of the 12th of this month. They feel bound to inform you of their views on this document and of the conclusion it suggests to them.

"The manifesto confirms the institution of the Council of Ministers established by Pius IX; it sets up a Council of State; it institutes a deliberative chamber under the name of Consulta, the direct result of elections, which will discuss all financial questions, examine the budget and advise on the levying, basic rate and collection of taxes. It grants or maintains far-reaching communal and provincial liberties.

"In conclusion it announces the coming reform of civil law, of judicial institutions and the rules of criminal justice.

"The institutions promised by the manifesto seemed to us lacking in some respects; you have informed us that you have already entered reservations in this connection. I fully approve of your action; at the same time we recognize that these institutions would to a large extent meet the demands put forward by France and would introduce very notable and desirable innovations in the administration of the Papal States if, as he is in duty bound to, Pius IX sees that they are properly carried out. Your chief duty, gentlemen, will be to expedite to the best of your ability by disinterested and urgent advice the prompt and effective realization of the principle of liberal institutions adopted in the manifesto. . . . I ask the Assembly's leave to pause for a moment for I can hardly speak . . .

THE MINISTER OF FOREIGN AFFAIRS after a few minutes' rest resumes as follows:

Gentlemen, I have little to add. I have spoken of the institutions, I must now say a few words regarding the principles.

In regard to the principles, we thought it right to speak in more forceful and more pressing terms than in regard to the institutions themselves. In this case, indeed, our object was not to coerce the Sovereign Pontiff to grant institutions that might seem unwise to him or repugnant to his conscience, but to be saved ourselves from seeing acts committed under our very eyes and our own hands, as it were, which would be contrary to our principles and offend French generosity. (Hear! Hear!)

Immediately after our entry into Rome we realized that we had a duty as well as rights. Our duty was to complete the rout of, or rather to master the demagogic faction we had already defeated . . . (Violent interruptions from the left, cheers on the right)

A VOICE ON THE LEFT: Republican!

THE MINISTER OF FOREIGN AFFAIRS: . . . the demagogic faction we had already defeated, and to confer upon the country we were occupying a real and lasting peace. We immediately applied ourselves to this task, as will be apparent from a brief dispatch I ask your leave to read to you. It was written before we took Rome, on the 26th June: it is couched in very few words but it is clear and precise: "I repeat, once we are in Rome, this town must first of all be occupied administratively and militarily. Everybody must be disarmed; all dangerous aliens must be deported or arrested, then a Roman municipality must be set up and efforts must be made to gather together and to form a moderate liberal party." (Laughter and ironical remarks on the left)

What we had been enjoined to do, thank God, was done. Aliens who were a disturbing element were expelled, those who resisted were arrested, and thus real peace was restored in the town and the States we were occupying.

A VOICE ON THE LEFT: What about the Roman Constituent Assembly? You expelled its members!

THE MINISTER OF FOREIGN AFFAIRS: We were not content with this measure to facilitate the removal of the dangerous men of whom I have just spoken. (Laughter and whispering on the left) We took steps to have them deported to France or elsewhere. We offered them admittance to our territory as an exceptional measure, and they were received there. We even went so far as to give them assistance while taking the necessary precautions. We had recourse to these measures in order, as I said just now, to master the demagogic party we had defeated.

VARIOUS VOICES ON THE EXTREME LEFT: Republican! You can be strong enough against the weak.

THE MINISTER OF FOREIGN AFFAIRS: While we were taking these steps, confident that we were discharging a duty, we were conscious that we had a right as well. That right was, as I said just now, to prevent acts of violence from being committed under our eyes and almost through our own hands against certain persons. Nevertheless, I am bound to admit that several of the men whom we were thus protecting were not particularly deserving of our goodwill. Many of them were among those who, having overthrown liberty at home, did not allow us to restore it. (Ironical laughter on the left)

Several of them had fought against us with the utmost violence and often unfairly: many of them after their defeat pursued us with insults, calumnies and contumely. Their friends scattered throughout Europe even now continue to attack our nation and its army. (Interruption from the left)

A MEMBER ON THE LEFT: It is only you they are attacking.

THE MINISTER OF FOREIGN AFFAIRS: Why did we want to shield and save them? For a reason everybody will understand. Because France could not surrender those she had defeated even though they were unworthy of her clemency.

ON THE LEFT: You must not insult them.

M. ANTOINE THOURET: What have you done with the Constituent Assembly?

THE PRESIDENT: I wish the *Moniteur* to place these interruptions and their character on record.

THE MINISTER OF FOREIGN AFFAIRS: Those who are interrupting me would doubtless think it more patriotic to applaud the insults scattered throughout the vile pamphlets to which I have referred.

A VOICE FROM THE LEFT: They are directed against you, not against the army.

THE PRESIDENT: M. Pierre LEROUX and M. Pascal DUPRAT. I request you by name to be silent. You will have an opportunity to speak if you wish to, but do not interrupt.

VOICE ON THE RIGHT: Recall them to order.

THE MINISTER OF FOREIGN AFFAIRS: They would no doubt think it even more patriotic to go and hiss our flag and our soldiers in some theatre or other.

ON THE LEFT: It is not the flag that is being hissed, it's the policy, the Ministry.

THE MINISTER OF FOREIGN AFFAIRS: Not only did we ask that the acts to which I have referred should not be committed, but as His Holiness was not in Rome and his intentions might be misinterpreted, we took steps to prevent them. It is in this sense that this dispatch, sent on the 19th August last to the General commanding our armies, must be understood: "So long as we remain in Rome we cannot allow political violence to be committed under the very shadow of our flag."

There can be no question that we had the right to prevent them and we are determined to prevent them. Violence perpetrated against persons is one of the things which must not be permitted at any price.

(Hear! Hear!)

Subsequently, when the Commission of Cardinals introduced limitations to the amnesty granted by the Holy Father, we considered that we should immediately submit the following observations.

"Paris, the 30th September.

"The Minister of Foreign Affairs to the Counsellor in Rome.

"The Government have taken note with pained surprise of the notice relating to the amnesty which the Commission of Cardinals saw fit to publish on the 18th of this month.

"Had the Commission refused to apply the amnesty promised by the Holy Father to certain men who were particularly dangerous to public order, we should have understood and approved. We did, however, expect that such persons would be few and would be mentioned by name and in advance so as not to cause the others unnecessary apprehensions as to their fate. We were far from expecting that such numerous and ill-defined categories would be excluded from this act of clemency and prudence.

"I shall be glad if you will be so good as to represent to the Government of the Holy Father that an amnesty of this nature cannot fail to cause keen apprehension, continued unrest, profound resentment and great dangers, and that it could not lead to the appeasement of the public temper and a voluntary return to law and order.

"In the interest of the Pontifical Power and the welfare of the Church, entreat it to reconsider this measure and to modify radically its principle and effect.

"The Holy Father who, as he himself so truly says, is

inclined to mercy by virtue of his pontifical office, did not wish his benevolent intentions to be so inadequately carried out. When he announced an amnesty of this kind, he had no intention of making a vain promise. We appeal against his government's decision to him personally. Represent to His Holiness, with the filial respect we owe him but also with the firmness that is our duty and our right, that France could not agree to be associated either directly or indirectly with the severe measures such numerous exceptions foreshadow. France considers that they are diametrically opposed to one of the principal aims that the Catholic Powers had set themselves, namely the conciliation of the parties and the true pacification of the country."
(Hear! Hear!)

These, gentlemen, are the demands we have respectfully laid before the Holy Father. (Ironical laughter on the left)

THE PRESIDENT: You do not want anything to be respected, do you?

M. HEECKEREN: They cannot even bear us to be polite.

THE MINISTER OF FOREIGN AFFAIRS: I hope that our requests will be granted. I cherish this hope because I have faith in the word and the character of Pius IX, because in heeding our appeal he will be carrying out his great design—referred to by M. de Corcelle—to reconcile liberty with religion and to continue to play the lofty part he has so gloriously begun (Ironical laughter on the left), this great part which has aroused so much enthusiasm and won him such noble support when at his first steps the whole of Europe acclaimed his efforts and on all sides, on this very tribune, eloquent voices called out to him: "Courage, Holy Father, courage." (Shouts on the left)

A MEMBER: That is M. Thiers.

MANY VOICES: Yes! Yes! Hear! Hear!

THE MINISTER OF FOREIGN AFFAIRS: I believe, therefore, that our plea will be heard. Some of the limitations introduced in the amnesty have already been removed or modified in a sense that is extremely favourable to those to whom it applies. In any case, so far as it is possible to tell at present, this Roman revolution which began with violence and murder . . . (Commotion on the left, shouts of: "No, no, that is a libel"; on the right: "Yes, yes, quite true. Hear! Hear!")

THE MINISTER OF FOREIGN AFFAIRS: . . . which began with violence and murder. (Renewed clamour and interpolations on the left)

M. TESTELIN: You lie! (Oh! Oh!)

MANY VOICES: Order! Order! (Continued commotion)

THE PRESIDENT: M. Testelin (Renewed shouts of Order! Order!) Wait, Gentlemen, please—(Turning to the extreme left) M. Testelin, I have heard many interruptions from this side, but they were simultaneous and I was waiting for the moment when I should be able to recognize an individual voice saying things that deserved censure. The word you have used is an insult, and I call you to order.

M. TESTELIN: I submit.

(On the right and in the centre: Order! Order!)

THE PRESIDENT: Instead of submitting, you go on. For the second time I call you to order, the fact to be entered in the verbatim record.

ON THE RIGHT: Hear! Hear! Censure!

(On the left excited shouts and turbulence)

M. PASCAL DUPRAT rises and addresses the President, but in the midst of the uproar it is impossible to hear what he says. Several members of the extreme left appear for a moment on the point of leaving the Chamber.

THE PRESIDENT: M. Duprat, you are not called upon to speak.

Please sit down and be silent. (M. Pascal Duprat sits down and calm is restored)

THE MINISTER OF FOREIGN AFFAIRS: I have the most profound contempt for such insults, and I repeat that one thing is certain up to the present and that is that this revolution which began with violence and bloodshed . . . (Renewed shouts on the left: It is not true)

MANY VOICES: It is true. Hear! Hear!

THE MINISTER OF FOREIGN AFFAIRS: . . . which continued in the midst of violence and folly, has up to the present cost no man his liberty, his goods or his life for political reasons. That is the truth. When I remember—without wishing to allude to any particular incident—the more or less tragic events to which the restoration of former powers has given rise in recent times in Italy and elsewhere in Europe, when I think of all this I feel justified in declaring here and now that those whom we have defeated should thank Heaven

(Outcry on the left. On the right: Why obviously!) . . . I say that those we have defeated must thank Heaven that it was the arm of France that struck them and not that of another. (Lively applause on the right and in the centre)

Gentlemen, I have said all I had to say. I have explained in the midst of interruptions that were, to say the least, uncalled for and certainly improper, the ideas and actions of French diplomacy. France and the Assembly will be the judges.

ON THE LEFT: Yes! Yes!

ON THE RIGHT: Hear! Hear!

(Lively applause from many sides)

Apart from the books mentioned in the text and in the Introduction, the following studies may be of use to the reader.

*Actes du congrès historique du centenaire de la révolution de
1848*, Paris, 1948.

Arnaud, R., *La deuxième république et le second empire*, Paris,
1929.

Aron, R., *La Révolution introuvable. Réflexions sur les Évène-
ments de Mai*, Paris, 1968. (See pp. 161 ff.)

Bastid, P., *Doctrines et institutions politiques de la seconde
république*, Paris, 1945.

Bastid, P., *Les Institutions politiques de la monarchie parlementaire française: 1814–1848*, Paris, 1954.

Bastid, P., *Le Gouvernement d'Assemblée*, Paris, 1956.

Bernstein, S., "Marx in Paris: 1848", *Science and Society*, New
York, 1939.

Bertaut, J., *1848 et la seconde république*, Paris, 1937.

Buenzod, J., *La formation de la pensée de Gobineau et l'Essai
sur l'inégalité des races humaines*, Paris, 1967.

Burckhardt, C. J., *Bildnisse*, Frankfurt, 1958.

Burckhardt, J., *Historische Fragmente*, Stuttgart, 1957.

Cassou, J., *Quarante-Huit*, Paris, 1939.

Cochin, D., *Louis-Philippe*, Paris, 1918.

Cohen, J., *La Préparation de la Constitution de 1848 (Pouvoirs
législatif et exécutif)*, Paris, 1935.

Curtis, E. Newtown, *The French Assembly of 1848 and American Constitutional Doctrines*, New York, 1918.

Dansette, A., *Louis Napoléon à la Conquête du Pouvoir*, Paris,
1961.

Dautry, J., *Histoire de la révolution de 1848 en France*, Paris, 1948.

Deslandres, M., *Histoire constitutionnelle de la France de 1789 à 1870*, vol. II, Paris, 1932.

Droz, J., *Les Révolutions allemandes de 1848*, Paris, 1957.

Duveau, G., *1848*, in the series *Idées*, Paris, 1965.

Duverger, M., *Constitutions et Documents politiques*, Paris, 1966.

Fraenkel, E., *Die repräsentative und plebiscitäre Komponente im demokratischen Verfassungsstaat, in Deutschland und die westlichen Demokratien*, Stuttgart, 1964. (pp. 71–109; fundamental)

Franz, E. G., *Das Amerikabild der deutschen Revolution von 1848–49*, Heidelberg, 1958.

Gargan, E. T., *Alexis de Tocqueville: The Critical Years 1848–1851*, Washington, 1955.

Genet, L., Vidalenc, J., *L'Époque Contemporaine I: Restaurations et révolutions (1851–1871)*, Paris, 1953.

Gesztesi, J., *La Révolution de 1848 vue par les témoins*, Paris, 1948.

Girard, L., *La IIme République*, Paris, 1968.

Hobsbawm, E. J., *The Age of Revolution. Europe 1789–1848*, London, 1962.

Jouvenel, B. de, *L'Explosion estudiantine*, in *Analyse et Prévision*, VI, 3, Paris, 1968.

Leroy, M., (ed.) *Les Précurseurs français du Socialisme. De Condorcet à Proudhon*, Paris, 1948.

Mayer, J. P., *Alexis de Tocqueville. A Biographical Study in Political Science*, New York, 1960.

Mayer, J. P., *Political Thought in France: From the Revolution to the Fifth Republic*, third revised and enlarged edition, London, 1961.

Mayer, J. P., *Alexis de Tocqueville und Karl Marx: Affinitäten und Gegensätze*, in *Zeitschrift für Politik*, Jahrgang 13 (Neue Folge), Heft I, 1966.

McKay, D. C., *The National Workshops: A Study in the French Revolution of 1848*, Cambridge, Mass., 1933.

Namier, L. B., *1848: The Revolution of the Intellectuals*, London, 1944.

Ponteil, F., *Les Classes bourgeoises et l'avènement de la démocratie*, Paris, 1968.

Ponteil, F., *Les Institutions de la France de 1814–1870*, Paris, 1966.

Quentin-Bauchart, P., *La Crise sociale de 1848. Les origines de la révolution de février*, Paris, 1920.

Robertson, P., *Revolutions of 1848*, Princeton, 1952.

Sée, H., *Évolution et révolutions*, Paris, 1929.

Spring, E., *Tocqueville's Stellung zur Februarrevolution*, in *Schweizer Beiträge zur Allgemeinen Geschichte*, Band 12, 1954.

Stadelmann, R., *Soziale und Politische Geschichte der Revolution von 1848*, reprint: Darmstadt, 1962.

Stadler, P., *Geschichtsschreibung und historisches Denken in Frankreich: 1789–1871*, Zürich, 1958.

Stern, A., *Geschichte Europas von 1848 bis 1871*, vols. VI and VII, Stuttgart, 1911 and 1916.

Talmon, J. L., *Political Messianism. The Romantic Phase*, New York, 1960.

Talmon, J. L., *Romanticism and Revolt: Europe 1815–1848*, London, 1967.

Thompson, J. M., *Louis Napoleon and the Second Empire*, Oxford, 1956.

Tocqueville, A. de, *Democracy in America*, ed. J. P. Mayer, New York, 1969.

Tocqueville, A. de, *The Old Régime and the French [sic] Revolution*, New York, 1955.

Tudesq, A.-J., *Les Grands Notables en France (1840–1849)*, 2 vols., Paris, 1964.

Tudesq, A.-J., *L'Élection présidentielle de Louis-Napoléon Bonaparte 10 décembre 1848*, Paris, 1965.

Tudesq, A.-J., *Les Conseillers Généraux en France au temps de Guizot, 1840–1848*, Paris, 1967.

Valentin, V., *Geschichte der deutschen Revolution: 1848–1849*, 2 vols., Berlin, 1930.

Vigier, Ph., *La Monarchie de Juillet*, Paris, 1962.

Vigier, Ph., *La Seconde République*, Paris, 1967.

Vigier, Ph., *La Seconde République dans la Région Alpine*, 2 vols., Paris, 1963.

Woodward, E. L., *French Revolutions*, Oxford, 1934.

his fear of insurrection, 284
the influence of his *History of the Revolution*, 74
Tocqueville, Charles Alexis Henri Maurice Clérel de (1805–59), his purpose in writing these memoirs, 3 f.
his relations with Louis-Philippe, 7 f.
his estimate of the state of France in January 1848, 11 ff.
his picture of the state of the Chamber of Deputies towards the end of the July Monarchy, 9 f., 11 f.
his speech in the Chamber of Deputies, January 27th, 1848, 13 ff.
remarks on his speech by Dufaure and others, 16
his position on the affair of the banquets, 18 ff.
his estimate of Duchâtel, Minister of the Interior, 22 ff.
his thoughts on the policy of the Radical Party, 23 f.
his knowledge of how the affair of the banquets turned into a rebellion, 27 f.
in the Chamber of Deputies on February 22nd and 23rd, 1848, when the gloom of the Revolution began to gather, 29 ff.
private conversation with Dufaure, 33
private conversation with Beaumont, 34
private conversation with Lanjuinais, 34
hears of the firing in the streets on February 24th, 1848, 37
sees preparations for barricades, 37 f.
meets a defeated party of National Guards on the boulevards, and hears shouts of "Reform", 40
reflections which this occasions, 41
goes to Chamber of Deputies on February 24th, 1848, 41
recognises Bedeau on his way, 41 f.

his estimate of the character of Bedeau and of his situation on that day, 42 f.
appearance presented to him by the Chamber of Deputies, 45
sees the Duchess of Orleans, the Duke of Nemours and the Count of Paris in the Chamber of Deputies, 47 f.
tries to get Lamartine to speak, 50
his interest in the Duchess and her son, 53 f.
leaves the Chamber and meets Oudinot and Andryane, 56
contradicts an assertion of Marshal Bugeaud, 56
converses with Talabot about the movements of Thiers, 57
reflects on the nature and structure of history, 61 f.
his argument with Ampère, 67 f.
walks about Paris in the afternoon, 70 ff.
reflections on what he sees, 70 ff.
keeps in retirement for some days, 77
further reflections on the Revolution, 77 ff.
his own individual feeling and intentions, 80 ff.
resolves to seek re-election, 85
visits the department of La Manche, 86
makes Valognes his headquarters, 88
his circular to his electors, 88 f.
meets the electors at Valognes, 90 f.
addresses workmen at Cherbourg, 91 ff.
goes to Saint-Lô to the General Council, 93
his reflections on a visit to Tocqueville, 94
returns to Paris and hears of his election, 96
his view of the state of politics and of Paris, 96 ff.
account of the meeting of the National Assembly, 99 f.